HILL OF SQUANDERED VALOUR

HILL OF SQUANDERED VALOUR

The Battle for Spion Kop, 1900

BY RON LOCK

CASEMATE
Newbury & Philadelphia

Published in Great Britain and the United States of America in 2011 by
CASEMATE PUBLISHERS
17 Cheap Street, Newbury RG14 5DD
and
908 Darby Road, Havertown, PA 19083

ISBN 978-1-61200-007-7
Digital Edition: ISBN 978-1-61200-018-3

Cataloging-in-publication data is available from the British Library
and the Library of Congress.

10 9 8 7 6 5 4 3 2 1

Printed and bound in Malta.

For a complete list of Casemate titles please contact:

CASEMATE PUBLISHERS (UK)
Telephone (01635) 231091, Fax (01635) 41619
E-mail: casemate-uk@casematepublishing.co.uk

CASEMATE PUBLISHERS (US)
Telephone (610) 853-9131, Fax (610) 853-9146
E-mail: casemate@casematepublishing.com

CONTENTS

Acknowledgments 7

Introduction 9

CHAPTER 1   Reassessing The Foe   13

CHAPTER 2   15,000 Horsemen Descend   29

CHAPTER 3   The Armoured Train   45

CHAPTER 4   Colenso   51

CHAPTER 5   Inside Ladysmith—Ready To Sally Forth   81

CHAPTER 6   Churchill Returns   89

CHAPTER 7   The Generals Converge   93

CHAPTER 8   Inside Ladysmith—The Fight For The Platrand   113

CHAPTER 9   Potgieter's Drift   131

CHAPTER 10   Inside Ladysmith—Death's Waiting Room   147

CHAPTER 11   Trichard's Drift   151

CHAPTER 12   Spion Kop   165

CHAPTER 13   Ladysmith Relieved   209

Epilogue 215

Bibliography 221

Endnotes 225

Index 233

··

ACKNOWLEDGMENTS

I am in debt to many people for the help and support they have provided to make the writing of this book possible. In gathering material over a period of 15 years, the most important acquisition, for which I must thank Arthur Konigkramer, the Chairman of AMAFA kwaZulu-Natal, has been the *Spion Kop Despatches*. At first glance this is a rather mundane document, but read deeper and it becomes apparent that the intention of most senior officers, in penning their reports, was to acquit themselves of blame and heap upon others the onus of defeat.

I am grateful to Fred Herbert, John Smallwood, Alan Slater and other 'old soldiers', all long departed, whose combined military service encompassed many theatres of war. It was they who, back in the 1970s, formed *BONS* (Battlefields of Natal Society), and first introduced me to Spion Kop and many other battle sites throughout the beautiful province of kwaZulu-Natal.

Major Paul Naish (Rtd) has not only been a constant support but on the many times we have walked the summit of Spion Kop together, his enquiring mind, sharpened by a lifetime in military intelligence, would invariably pose a new facet of the battle to explore. He also kindly gave me access to his collection of Anglo-Boer War literature.

Once again, I must thank Elizabeth Bodill who typed the manuscript and its numerous revisions more times than either of us care to remember. The drudgery, however, was brightened to our delight in the occasional howler emerging from the text.

My thanks also to Nicki von der Heyde of *Campaign Trails* who, despite her busy schedule, found time to scrutinize the draft. Her knowledge of the Anglo-Boer War and a degree in English Literature made her comments and suggestions particularly valuable.

In the UK my thanks are due to Colonel I. H. McCausland, of the Royal Green Jackets Museum, for details of the King's Royal Rifles involvement in the battle; the Fusilier Museum for details of the Lancashire Brigade's ordeal on Spion Kop; and the National Army Museum for its assistance. Thanks also to Philip Peplow, who kindly made literature available from his library, and to Anita Baker, my editor, whose meticulous eye brought a number of oversights to my attention and whose suggestions were much appreciated.

In South Africa I have to thank Msasa Books, Hillcrest; Adams and Company, Durban; ABC Books, Umhlanga Rocks; and Christison Rare Books, Port Elizabeth, for finding books long out of print and, better still, inexpensive reprints. I must also express my thanks to Johan du Plessis for his patience and skill in enhancing the illustrations and placing them on disc; Chris Smallwood in making available his rare copy of Gibson's *The Story of the Imperial Light Horse*; the Campbell Collections, formerly the Killie Campbell Library; Elizabeth Spiret of the Ladysmith Siege Museum; and finally my dear wife Brenda for her enduring support and patience as the author's clutter of 'raw materials' once again engulfed the house.

INTRODUCTION

In 1899 Britain, the ruler of the greatest empire on earth, was set to crush the insignificant Boer republics of the Transvaal and the Orange Free State. Her cause was expansion of Empire and accumulation of wealth laced with a desire for vengeance, an emotion that had been stewing within the nation and her army for over 18 years. As will be seen, the Boer republics desired no more than to govern themselves and to get on with their pastoral way of life without foreign interference. It was their misfortune that below the ground upon which their cattle grazed and their crops grew, there lay concealed gold and diamonds in quantities hitherto unknown.

During the preceding 100 years Britain had fought many wars in Africa from the Cape in the south to Egypt in the north and from Ashanti land in the west to Abyssinia in the east. It was Britain's fortune to eventually win her wars, albeit after an initial bloody set back. However, there had been one conflict, usually referred to as 'the First Boer War', that had seen some of Britain's crack troops in humiliating headlong flight before a throng of armed farmers. The subsequent terms of peace following this ignominious defeat, lamely negotiated by Brigadier-General Sir Evelyn Wood VC, were equally humiliating. Now 18 years later, the Boers, who were master horsemen and amongst the hardiest stock in the world, had come to regard themselves as a white race of Africa. Furthermore, they were prepared to take on the might of Britain once again. During the years since they had first defeated Queen Victoria's soldiers many things had changed, especially the weaponry that the western nations were churning out for sale to approved customers. The Boers, despite their reluctance to engage in war, had, with their new found wealth of gold, not been slow in availing themselves of a formidable arsenal, mainly acquired from Germany.

The Boer commandos were armed with a great variety of rifles, often individually owned by the burghers themselves. They included the German Mauser—'We put our trust in God and the Mauser'—likely the most popular, but other makes included the Lee-Metford (British), mainly captured during the Jameson raid and other later battles; the Martini-Henri, originally the British Army's standard issue, but now manufactured in Belgium; and half a dozen lesser known makes of different calibre. It will be noted that when the number of casualties inflicted by the Boers are quoted, those wounded seem to be excessively high in proportion to those actually killed. The reason for this was the shape and size of the Mauser bullet and the very high muzzle velocity: if it did not hit bone or a vital organ, it would likely penetrate and exit the victim without inflicting lasting damage. The Mauser, as with the Lee-Metford, was magazine-fed, whereas the Martini-Henri was a single-shot breech-loader but, nevertheless, capable of firing 12 rounds a minute and preferred by the older generation for its stopping power. Handguns would have been an individual choice and expense. Bayonets, except for those carried by the state artillery men, were not favoured or used by the Republic.

On the other side, the British had the standard issue Lee-Metford rifle which was, with bayonet fixed, a formidable weapon. British officers were issued with a standard .45 revolver but many purchased their own handguns and, during the early days of the war, still carried swords. Lancer regiments were equipped with a fearsome bamboo-shafted lance, topped with a pointed steel triangular head capable of inflicting appalling wounds. They also carried a curved sabre in a steel scabbard and a standard issue revolver. Dragoon and Hussar regiments were similarly equipped apart from the lance.

Undeterred by the Boer arsenal, Britain deliberately set in motion events that would eventually lead to war, its politicos and generals being supremely confident that the Boers would capitulate or suffer a quick defeat.

The war began in October 1899 and within two months Britain had lost six out of eight major engagements with the enemy; had suffered almost 7,000 casualties; 17,000 troops had been besieged in three major towns; two generals had been killed; and the general officer commanding had been demoted and replaced. Worse still at Ladysmith in Natal, the most strategic of the three beleaguered towns, the troops and inhabitants were close to starvation. Now a second attempt at relieving the besieged town—the first having been a spectacular failure—had been initiated. However it too, after a week of heavy fighting, was about to flounder. The generals conferred and, blind to the task to which they were about to commit their troops for there had been no reconnaissance and there were no maps, it was decided that a flat topped massif, 1,500 feet in height and held by the enemy, should be attacked at night. The name of the objective was Spion Kop.

The following pages describe the events and the clash of personalities that led to one of the most notorious blunders in British military history. The Boers, however, saw the hand of God in their miraculous triumph.

The Battle of Spion Kop was also infamous as an introduction to the holocaust that modern weaponry could inflict: a brief glimpse into the future that would see the carnage of Flanders and Gallipoli. However, perhaps more than anything, the battle revealed the valour that was squandered by Boer and Britain alike.

....

CHAPTER ONE

REASSESSING THE FOE

When Lieutenant-General Sir Redvers Buller stepped ashore in Cape Town on 30 October 1899 and was apprised of the military situation, one could hardly have blamed him had he resigned as Commander-in-Chief Southern Africa and reboarded the RMS *Dunnotar Castle*, the ship that had brought him from Southampton.

With his staff and a number of subordinate generals, he had left England to almost hysterical acclaim and expectation at a time when Britain and Boer forces were yet to engage with each other. Were they to do so, it would be the fourth time in a little more than half a century that Britain had embarked on a war with this insignificant nation.

Having spent 19 days at sea, Buller and his staff, devoid of communication with the outside world (there was no telegraph transmission aboard ship), could only guess at what might be happening in southern Africa. The general feeling had been one of great optimism: how could a Boer army of untrained, ragtag farmers stand against British regulars, the best soldiers in the world? However, the British had, to their chagrin and dismay, thought that before and now, once again the Boers had out - manoeuvred and out-generalled them. Two days after Buller had set sail the Boers, much more mobile on their tough ponies than the cumbersome, foot-slogging British infantry, had besieged the strategic centres of diamond-rich Kimberley in the northern Cape and, adjacent to the Bechuanaland Protectorate, Mafeking a further 150 miles north. In Natal the news was even worse.

As early as May 1899, Britain had had a brigade of imperial troops stationed in northern Natal. Under the command of Major-General Sir William Penn Symons, they had been mainly deployed between the coal fields in the Dundee area and the garrison town of Ladysmith. Penn Symons was an energetic and experienced officer who, at the age of 56, had seen plenty of active service—much of it in South Africa. A great deal of time had been spent reconnoitring northern Natal and Penn Symons was confident he and his troops could dispatch any Boer army that might confront them.

When, in the autumn of 1899, it appeared that there would be war with the South African Republic and, possibly, the Orange Free State, Britain, in anticipation of increasing her military strength in Natal, dispatched Lieutenant-General Sir George White VC to act as Commander-in-Chief Southern Africa. White was one of Britain's most distinguished soldiers, having succeeded Lord Roberts in 1893 as Commander-in-Chief, India. He had fought through the Indian Mutiny and later as a young major had won the Victoria Cross whilst fighting with the Gordon Highlanders in Afghanistan. Now in Natal he did not share the confidence of Penn Symons, believing that his force of approximately 13,000 men, mostly infantry, would be vastly outnumbered by a Boer army consisting of entirely mounted men who would be able to get behind a Dundee vanguard and cut it off from its Ladysmith base. On 10 October, White sought a meeting with the Governor of Natal, Sir Walter Hely-Hutchison, and proposed that the entire British force fall back to Ladysmith. Hely-Hutchison was appalled at the suggestion, believing it would be taken as a sign of weakness that might well cause an uprising of the Zulu population, whose warriors were estimated to number 75,000, in favour of the Boers. It might also cause an insurrection of the Afrikaner populations in the Cape and in Natal.

White, out of his depth when confronted with the intricacies of local matters, decided not to disturb the distribution of Penn Symons' troops. A few days later, out of swirling mist and pouring rain and without warning or detection, the Boers struck. Weeks earlier they had begun to assemble at Sandspruit, a small railway station 50 miles from the Natal border and slightly further than that from Dundee. Ageing 68-year-old Commandant-General Piet Joubert was in command and was accompanied, as always when on campaign, by his wife to whom he had been married for 48 years. Soon there were 15,000 burghers gathered around the station, each man with a horse—most with two—

all armed and equipped for immediate departure.[1]

On 10 October, President Kruger's birthday, a mass parade was held and the Commandant-General addressed the men, telling them of an ultimatum that would expire on the morrow, which demanded that all British troops along the Transvaal border be instantly withdrawn; that all troops that had arrived in South Africa after 1 June 1899 be withdrawn; and that troops on the high seas be diverted elsewhere. Should Britain fail to comply with the terms of the ultimatum a state of war would exist between the two countries. His speech was received with emotional acclaim, the men standing in their stirrups, waving hats and bandoliers, a mass of 'shaggy men on shaggy horses'[2]. Two days later the jubilant army moved off and split into two columns, all the easier to negotiate the passes through the mountains to Dundee.

Northern Natal, sometimes in the month of October, can be a miserable place. Rain and mist obscuring the hills are as reminiscent of Scotland as the names of its towns. October of 1899 was no different and the 'saddle commandos'—the commandos riding and sleeping rough without tents and with all their supplies for five days in their saddle bags—were soaked to the skin and remained that way. By the time the columns neared the border the burghers were suffering from exhaustion and exposure. Nevertheless, the weather had concealed their approach. Commandant Daniel Erasmus commanded one column and Commandant Lukas Meyer the other. Erasmus was to place artillery on Impati Hill and Meyer was to do likewise on Talana Hill, both positions dominating Dundee and the British camp situated between the town and the nearby hamlet of Glencoe. In the gloom and mist, Erasmus, a cantankerous man, lost his way and seemed reluctant to get back on course.[3]

Nevertheless, on the morning of 20 October 1899, Penn Symons and his army were taken completely by surprise: no patrol, picquet or spy had detected the mass of horsemen approaching Dundee. In the stirring camp, breakfast was on the go and tea was on the boil.[4] When the mist cleared on Talana Hill, the silhouettes of Boers were revealed standing to their guns, which had been manhandled, undetected, into position during the night.

As the bugles sounded the alarm, the first Boer shell landed in front of Penn Symons' tent but, fortunately, due to the rain soaked ground, failed to explode. Confusion reigned, but not for long. The Royal Field Artillery came into action quickly, shelling the Boer positions and forcing their guns to withdraw while the British infantry prepared to make a frontal assault on Talana Hill, which overshadowed the town. They were met by an equally determined Boer force and, for a while, there was stale-mate as a hail of Lee-Metford and Mauser bullets lacerated the intervening space of no-man's land and the dead and wounded piled up.

Impatiently, Penn Symons called for his charger and sallied forth, urging his men forward. Conspicuous though as a mounted general could be in the midst of what amounted to trench warfare, it was not enough for Penn Symons and he insisted that he be accompanied by a mounted orderly flying a general officers' pennant from a lance head.[5] Moments later, mortally wounded in the stomach, Penn Symons, still astride his horse, was led from the field to die in agony later while the infantry took shelter in a gum tree plantation. As the rifle fire ripped furiously through the soft trunks, it released an aroma of eucalyptus, a redolence that those there would remember for the rest of their lives and, if smelt, would immediately transport them back to the horrors of the battlefield.

One might pause to ask who these people were who called themselves Boers, who, with no standing army, apart from their *Staatsartillerie*, could twist the mighty lion's tail? One could arguably say they were, in fact, a new race with a new language: in the mid-17th century the Dutch, having established a sea route to the Indies, set up a victualling station at the Cape, manning it with Dutch settlers. Over the years French, Germans, Malays and other races found their way into this society to leave their mark on its evolving language, Afrikaans, of which the Boers (meaning 'farmers') were fiercely proud.

In 1806 the British had taken occupation of the Cape and English was declared the official language. This was just one of what became legendary acts of injustice, as the Boer saw them, such as the impoverishment caused to the Boers by the abolition of slavery in 1834 and the British govern-ment's refusal to pay compensation elsewhere other than London, 6,000 miles and two months' journey away. Earlier still, in 1812, an annual circuit court travelled the Cape Colony, its rule being imposed by British officers leading black troops. Its purpose was to hear complaints brought by black servants against their Boer masters. In 1815 a number of Boers rose in open rebellion against this system and one of them was shot by the British for resisting arrest. Finally, the revolt was quelled. However, five of the rebels were publicly hanged.[6] In addition, the Cape Frontier of that time had become an increasingly dangerous place in which to live, with the administration seemingly incapable of giving even a semblance of protection to its white citizens whom it taxed and on whom it continually made demands.[7] By 1836 thousands of farmers, including many of British descent, were prepared to sell their properties, or even abandon them, in order to *trek* and seek a new existence, free of British rule, in the vast hinterland to the north. Such was the discontent that thousands of wagons departed to travel thousands of miles into the interior, to cross barriers of mighty mountains, deserts and wide rivers; and to do battle with some of the fiercest warrior tribes in Africa. However, they went with an ominous caution from Sir Charles Napier, the Governor of the Cape:

> I hereby warn all British-born subjects [the Boers] and particularly those who, after the 18th day of January 1806, have been born within the Colony [Cape Colony] of parents who at the time of their birth, by reason of their permanent residence in this Colony, or otherwise, owe allegiance to, and are subjects of the Crown, that they cannot, by their removal from this Colony [Cape] to any place whatsoever, divest of themselves of the allegiance which they owe by reason of their birth to the British Crown.[8]

Within a year or so, the Boers engaged in one of the most significant battles in South African history, the Battle of Blood River, and established the Republic of Natalia, a nation of fewer than 5,000 souls all told. The jewel of this wild frontier state was the great natural harbour called, at the time, Port Natal, later to become Durban. Britain had been interested in its acquisition five years earlier but had walked away leaving the Boers to hoist their Republican flag. Then, in 1842, with its naval interests in mind, Britain had second thoughts and despatched a contingent of 263 imperial troops on a 200-mile march to reclaim the Boer possession and to bring the would-be Republicans under British authority. However, the imperial troops were besieged and it took a Royal Navy warship and other reinforcements to vanquish the enemy. Those Boers who could, inspanned their wagons and set out once again for the vast interior of Africa, determined to forge another republic and to assert their independence. However, they would look back over their shoulders towards the 'Promised Land' of Natal and, 60 years later, would avow that Natal was rightfully theirs, the land that they had won by conquest from the Zulu. One newly married, 18-year-old man would certainly remember; his name was Paul Kruger.

Then, in 1848, Sir Harry Smith, a famous fighting general who had served under Wellington, met in battle with an equally renowned Boer general, Andries Pretorius, the victor of Blood River. Some months earlier, Sir Harry, in his capacity as Governor of the Cape, had arbitrarily declared a huge area of Africa between the Vaal and Orange Rivers to be British territory, naming it the Orange River Sovereignty, and by so doing fore- stalling yet again the establishment of a Boer Republic. Furthermore, Sir Harry contended, all the Boers within the Sovereignty owed allegiance to the Queen. The Boer response was not unexpected; Pretorius, leading 1,000 men, advanced on Bloemfontein, evicted the British Military Resi- dent, dispersed the garrison and advanced southwards towards the Cape. Sir Harry was quick to react. Crossing the Orange River with 1,200 troops, he engaged the Boers at a farm called *Boomplaats*. After a four- hour battle the Boers took flight and Sir Harry marched on to Bloem- fontein where he declared Pretorius and his followers to be rebels and put a price on their heads.

However, there was wilderness aplenty in Africa at that time and those Boers still clutching to what had become a sacred mission for independ- ence, *trekked* once more, this time across the Vaal River. Sir Harry coun- tered this move simply by declaring that Britain had dominion over more land: the whole of Africa south of 25° latitude, which included all the Boer settlements in what was to become the Transvaal.

Then, almost miraculously it must have seemed to the Boers, Britain tired of chasing unwilling subjects up and down Africa and suddenly rescinded the proclamation outlawing Pretorius and his followers. The Orange River Sovereignty, by Royal Proclamation, became the Orange Free State and at the same time approval was given for the establishment, by the Boers, of the South African Republic (The Transvaal). Furthermore, Britain assured the fledgling Boer republics that there would be no encroachment of their territories, nor would there be any interference in their affairs. However, at the time, gold in massive quantities, the like of which the world had never seen, had yet to be discovered beneath the often baking hot, sterile landscape of the Transvaal. For the next quarter of a century the Boers pursued their pastoral lives, ever guided in all their actions by the Bible, revelling (if one can apply such a joyous word to their dour lives) in isolation and non-interference, arguing amongst themselves and fighting local tribesmen.

As a self-governing nation, the infrastructure of the Transvaal was virtually non-existent. The national coffers were empty, its civil servants remained unpaid, and it was not giving much of a showing in its frequent clashes with the native tribes living within its self-proclaimed borders. In fact, Britain feared the Transvaal was so letting down the prestige of the white man in its inability to subdue these tribes that the situation could well lead to a native insurrection throughout southern Africa—or at least, that is what Britain claimed.[9]

Although gold, in any great quantity, had yet to be discovered in the Transvaal, there were plenty of miners panning in the streams to the north-east of the territory. However, gold aside, after 25 years the British were again in an expansionist mood. What they wanted was the confederation of all the territories in southern Africa and Zululand. The Transvaal and the Orange Free State, one way or another, would have to comply. Lord Carnavon, the Colonial Secretary, and his man at the Cape, Sir Bartle Frere, decided to tackle the Transvaal first, no doubt believing, quite rightly, that it would be an easier nut to crack than the Zulu Kingdom.

With little ado, Sir Bartle appointed the recently knighted Sir Theophilus Shepstone, who until recently had been Secretary of Native Affairs in Natal, as his representative. With an escort of 25 Natal Mounted Police, Shepstone set out in a horse and carriage on the 300-mile journey to Pretoria; he had stowed amongst his kit a Union Jack that was to be raised over the Boer capital at the moment of annexation. It was one of the most audacious enterprises in the history of southern Africa; and Shepstone got away with it.

There were promises of aid, security and all the other benefits of living under the rule of bountiful Britannia. Finally, the Boer president, Thomas Burgers, succumbed to Shepstone's wooing words. The flag of the South African Republic was lowered and the Union Jack was raised by the hand of Shepstone's then poorly paid clerk, H. Rider Haggard,[10] and in marched the British infantry.

However, Shepstone's regime and his juggling of finances fared no better than had the Boer administration—and his punitive expedition of 1878, commanded by Colonel Hugh Rowlands VC, against the dissident baPedi tribe, was also a dismal failure.

Meanwhile, Britain, leap-frogging events, attacked the Zulu Kingdom and initially suffered humiliating disaster and defeat. If anything, both British and Boer regarded the Zulu as the common enemy of the white man. However, with the exception of 40 horsemen, the Boers made no offer of assistance when, for a few weeks, it seemed likely that the Zulu Army would rampage through a defenceless Natal. The Boers had decided to sit on the fence and see who came out on top, and, as it happened, it was the British—but only just. The margin was fine enough to inspire the

Boers to reclaim their independence: a desire burning deeply in the heart of every back-veldt Boer for they, unlike their ex-president, Thomas Burgers, and the Transvaal civil servants, had never given their consent to the annexation. Little did they understand or care that their nation was insolvent to the extent that it could not pay the postmaster's salary; and they cared even less that they had no national army to defend the *volk* (the people). The *volk* could look after themselves. After three years of insufferable occupation, burdened with regulations and taxes, they were ready to rise up and rid themselves of the detested British.

The British, however, had just conquered Zululand and Shepstone was replaced with the victorious Sir Garnet Wolseley (Britain's 'Only General') as Her Majesty's High Commissioner to the Transvaal. There were both hotheads and moderates amongst the Boers: the former were all for immediate insurrection whilst the latter, who included such fighting men as Paul Kruger and Piet Joubert, were still hoping for a negotiated independence. However, Wolseley, riding hard for Pretoria with 1,400 British infantry, 400 colonial horsemen and 6,000 Swazi warriors in his wake, left little cause for hope as he declared at every opportunity along the way: '. . . As long as the sun shines, the Transvaal will remain British territory.'[11]

Wolseley's first objective was the conquest of the warlike baPedi who had on several occasions defeated the Boers and, two years earlier, the British expedition under Rowlands. Wolseley, full of confidence, predicted the exact time he would partake of a cup of tea in the vanquished baPedi fortress: his prediction was correct to within an hour. This spectacular victory made little impression on the truculent Boers for on the same day as Wolseley paraded his victorious troops, and the vanquished baPedi chief in Pretoria, thousands of armed and mounted Boers gathered on an outlaying farm—despite the warning that they would be committing treason—to protest at the occupation of their country. Nevertheless, nothing transpired and Wolseley, by then sick of Africa, managed to wangle his return to England and, on arrival, assured the British government that the Transvaal was 'supremely quiet'[12]. So quiet in fact that the man left in charge as Governor of the Transvaal, Sir Owen Lanyon, consented to a drastic reduction of British troops in the territory. Indeed, not one cavalry trooper was left in a country full of hostile horsemen whilst the prevailing British attitude towards the Boers continued to be one of contempt and disdain. Wolseley, before he left, had commented:

I believe the Transvaal Boer to be a coward pure and simple, who will swagger and talk big while he knows he can do so with impunity . . . I regard them as the lowest in the scale of white men. [13]

And Colonel Philip Anstruther of the 94th Foot had boasted:

The Boers will turn tail at the first beat of the big drum. [14]

However, Lieutenant-General Lord Chelmsford, who had commanded the recent war against the Zulus, had a more realistic idea of the Boers, having written to the Duke of Cambridge the previous year saying:

. . . There is no further news from Pretoria regarding the action of the Boers, and I am inclined to think that they are in no way inclined to bring matters to extremities . . . but I am afraid they are too stupid and obstinate to be brought over by reasoning. The Transvaal must be a trouble, expense and anxiety to us for many a year to come and it is a thousand pities that we ever annexed it.[15]

The Boers had had enough and, in December of 1880, 4,000 of them, armed and mounted, met at a farm called *Paardekraal*. They elected leaders, formed commandos, laid siege to various scattered towns and garrisons, demanded the restoration of full domestic independence—though consenting to Britain controlling foreign policy—and gave Lanyon 24 hours to surrender.[16]

Suddenly, almost by magic it must have seemed to Lanyon, what had been a second rate nation of farmers transformed itself into an army of tough and formidable mounted men, each with his own rifle and a full bandolier slung across his chest.

This sudden change of the Boers' warlike ability caused Lanyon in Pretoria to call for reinforcements. The first of these were 260 men of the 94th Regiment, led by Colonel Anstruther, followed by a mile-long baggage train. They included the regimental band of 14 musicians who were playing a popular tune as the column, marching at ease, headed towards its camping ground, a pleasant spot on the side of a small stream called *Bronkhorstspruit*—which translated into the delightful name of 'The Watercress Stream'. Suddenly the column was confronted by a mounted Boer with a white flag tied to the muzzle of his rifle. He delivered a message, written in English, that informed the colonel that the Transvaal was now a republic and, should the soldiers cross the stream, it would be regarded as an act of war. Anstruther replied that he had orders to proceed to Pretoria and that was where he was going. The Boer courier swung away and Anstruther ordered his men to extend in skirmishing order. As they did so, the Boers, at 200 yards, opened fire. The war had started.[17]

It has been dubbed the 'First Boer War' by many historians, but, arguably, it was the third, taking into account the conflicts of 1842 and 1848. There was now no going back and the British column, taken completely by surprise and unable to get at its ammunition supply, quickly became a scene of carnage. All the officers were killed with the exception of Anstruther who lay mortally wounded. There were over 100 British dead and wounded whereas the Boers had lost but two. When the news reached Lanyon, he put Pretoria under martial law and telegraphed the governor of Natal, Major-General Sir George Pomeroy Colley, urging him to come to the assistance of the beleaguered city. Colley was regarded as one of Britain's most brilliant soldiers, an opinion that was endorsed by Sir Garnet Wolseley. He was also one of the few who had never expressed contempt for the Boers. However, like all British officers in South Africa, he had excessive confidence in the prowess of his men and he too believed that the Boers would not stand against his disciplined infantry.

However, Colley himself was inexperienced in actual combat, never having commanded troops in action. Throughout southern Africa he had fewer than 2,000 men upon whom demands were made in several trouble spots along Natal's border with Pondoland and Basutoland. Also, as a wary eye had to be kept on recently conquered Zululand, there were few troops to spare to suppress rebellion in the Transvaal. Nevertheless, Colley banded together a scratch force of imperial and volunteer troops, including 120 sailors from HMS *Bodicea* which happened to be in Durban harbour, and it was not long before he received telegraphic news from London that reinforcements were on their way from around the Empire. However, impulsively, Colley decided not to await their arrival but to advance at once on the Transvaal.[18]

By the time his little army arrived at the frontier town of Newcastle, 280 miles north-west of Durban, it numbered fewer than 1,200 men. Still Colley remained full of confidence and put great store by the six canons that comprised his artillery although two of the guns, which were pulled by mules, had been dubbed with the dubious nickname of the 'Royal Ass Artillery'! On 23 January, Colley held a review and addressed his men

with stirring words. The army then advanced towards the Transvaal border a few miles distant. The way lay towards steeply rising ground that
was dominated to the west by a fortress-like mountain named Majuba—
the Hill of Doves. The eastern slopes of the mountain gradually ran into
other hills over a saddle called Laings Nek, through which a path led into
the Transvaal. Beyond the Nek, already barring the way, was the Boer
Army. The solemn burghers sung hymns, smoked their pipes, and waited.

Colley despatched an ultimatum that went unanswered and after five
days he could wait no longer. The British attacked uphill towards the Boer
positions after bombarding them to the brink of submission, or so Colley's
officers believed. Astride their chargers, with waving swords, they led the
58th Regiment of Foot, with bayonets fixed and colours flying, up the
steep and rugged hill towards the concealed marksmen.

It was a brave sight. It would be the last time that a British regiment
carried its colours into battle, for it was a virtual sentence of death for the
men who carried them: they were the first to be downed, prestigious
targets for a score of eager marksmen.

As the line of redcoats neared the crest, the Boers, almost unaffected
by the artillery bombardment and concealed in the long grass of summer,
lay prone, each with a British soldier comfortably viewed between the fore
and back sites of their rifles. The officers and standard bearers were the
first to fall; then, as though the best prizes had been taken, the Boers
sought quantity, slaughtering the gallant 58th, the 'Steelbacks' as the
regiment had been nicknamed in bygone days out of its contempt for the
lash. Yet the 58th pressed on and almost took the bayonet into the Boer
lines before one of its few surviving officers had the sense to order the
'retire'. Colley's cavalry, if a hodgepodge of inexperienced riders on
untrained mounts could be described as such, had fared worst. The site
of their 'charge' was marked by the corpses of men and horses.

It was a military disaster for the British and Colley's efforts to subdue
the Transvaal Boers were quickly followed by two more disasters, the
battles of Ingogo and Majuba, the latter being one of Britain's most
humiliating defeats. Ingogo was fought days after Laings Nek, well before
reinforcements arrived from around the Empire. However, by mid-
February, troops by the thousands were disembarking in Durban. Accompanying the reinforcements was Brigadier-General Sir Evelyn Wood VC,
one of Britain's most distinguished fighting soldiers and undoubtedly an
admired hero of the recent Anglo-Zulu War. The British Government
hoped that he would assume command but, being junior to Colley in rank,

Wood would have to serve as his subordinate; Colley promised Wood the honour of leading a column into the Transvaal.

The reinforcements that now started on the long road to Newcastle included the most famous of Britain's regiments, many fresh from recent successes in India and Afghanistan. There were two full regiments of cavalry, hussars and dragoons, five regiments of infantry including the illustrious Gordon Highlanders, replacement drafts for the 58th, artillery, and a naval contingent. The Boer cause and its chances of victory now seemed hopeless. Wood appeared in Newcastle ahead of the reinforcements and Colley agreed that there would be no advance into the Transvaal until the new regiments arrived. With that assurance Wood sped back to chase them along.

The Boers, well aware of the new arrivals, began to fear what was in store. Peace negotiations recommenced and a proposal from the British Government was despatched by Colley to Paul Kruger on 21 February, giving the Boer leader 48 hours in which to reply. However, Kruger was not around and the message did not reach him until seven days later. His reply accepting the British proposal did not reach Laings Nek for a further week by which time it was too late. Colley, aware that his career was at stake, was at pains to do something that might add a little lustre to his record.

During the days of waiting he had observed that the Boers had moved some of the forward picquets nearer to his camp. He also observed that the Boer picquet which occupied the summit of Majuba during the day was withdrawn every evening. Furthermore, the northern summit directly overlooked and commanded the Boer *laager*. Colley resolved to take Majuba that very night and, taking 650 men from the 4,000 now under his command, he discarded his boots for tennis shoes and led the way in a nightmare climb of 2,000 feet, to reach the summit before daylight.

It was a triumph. As dawn broke the men and their General surveyed the Boers below. With artillery, which they did not have for the moment, but which they could well bring up, the enemy camp was at their mercy and could be devastated. Both officers and men began to shout and shake their fists in bravado. A few even fired their rifles, a practice which Colley quickly stopped. For a moment there was panic in the Boer camp, but then Commandant-General Piet Joubert, taking no heed of his wife's stricture not to fight on a Sunday but taking inspiration from the Bible, started to gather up men for a counter-attack. Soon the plain was dotted with galloping horsemen as they raced towards the mountain where, leaving their ponies out of sight, they began the slow ascent. Using the cover of dead ground, rocks and bush with consummate skill, they fired at the enemy silhouetted above. One of the first to fall was Colley's second-in-command, Commodore Romilly RN, who was mortally wounded.

It took the Boers over six hours to reach the top, and Colley, despite increasing casualties and the agitated warnings of his officers along the crest, continued to believe his position to be impregnable. He was actually having a nap when the first of the Boers came over the rim, firing point blank into the crowded troops. Colley refused an officer's request for a bayonet charge and, alas, British marksmanship was no match for that of the Boers who were mainly half-concealed in safety below the shelter of the crest.

There was utter confusion amongst the soldiers and sailors and some began to run back down the hill the way that they had come. Despite the efforts of brave men who tried to stem the rout, there was soon an avalanche of panicking troops bolting down the mountain. The ignominy of Britain's finest soldiers fleeing in dismay before a riffraff army of farmers would be for the British almost impossible to comprehend as British soldiers were not supposed to flee: they fixed bayonets and died like British soldiers do. Worse still, an illustrated magazine, whose war artist had accompanied Colley's column, published pictures for Britain's enemies to gloat over, of kilted Highlanders and bearded sailors in headlong flight.[19] Colley decided to face the enemy rather than the future and walked towards the Boers inviting death which quickly came. One officer later wrote: 'His death was a most fortunate thing for him, and, as someone said, for the Natal Field Force too.' In all, killed, wounded and captured, the British had lost over 200 men on Majuba. Boer losses were two killed and several wounded.

With the death of Colley, Wood hurried back to take over as Governor and Commander-in-Chief. Concentrating on the political situation, he was supported by Colonel Redvers Buller who supervised military affairs.

In Britain, political parties variously demanded a negotiated peace or, conversely, military retribution. To cover both possibilities, the government instructed Wood to open negotiations on the spot while General Sir Frederick Roberts VC, one of Britain's most renowned soldiers, was despatched by sea with an additional army to take vengeance in the event of political failure.

To the disgust of the troops and the scattered garrisons that had withstood siege, privation and numerous casualties, Wood's negotiations met with a somewhat one-sided success in favour of the Boers. To the dismay of her loyal subjects and to the dishonour and humiliation of her troops, it became clear that Britain was about to abandon the Transvaal. In one regiment alone over 300 men applied for discharge; in Pretoria Britons burnt the Union Jack; and when Roberts arrived in Cape Town, to his consternation and fury, he and his army were ordered to stay aboard ship and immediately return to London. Negotiations dragged on for over three years but, eventually, the Transvaal was restored to the Boers with only a vague stipulation that they acknowledge the Queen's suzerainty over their republic, a suzerainty that was ill-defined and which would be a source of mischief in years to come.

The Boers gave thanks to God and returned to their farms and Boer pursuits. However, unbeknown to them, below the surface of their arid land, there was another enemy: vast quantities of gold. It took time for this fabulous wealth to be revealed and those who did the digging, in ever increasing numbers, were the *uitlanders*, the foreign miners, most of whom were British, and they were to give the new republic more trouble than Britain's soldiers ever had. How true was to be the prophecy of Commandant-General Piet Joubert when he said: 'This gold will cause our country to be soaked in blood.'

At about the time of the battle on Majuba, only a fraction of the world's gold output came from the Transvaal; by 1887 it had increased significantly to one percent; then, within a further five years to 20 percent, and by 1898 it had outstripped the gold production of the whole of United States and reached an amazing 30 percent of the world's output. To paraphrase 'Othello', Britain had thrown away a prize richer than all her empire—or, at least, so the relinquishing of its rule over the Transvaal must have seemed to the politicians of the day. To make matters seem worse, it was British know-how that was extracting all this wealth, thus enabling President Kruger and his *Volk* to purchase the most sophisticated weapons that were available from Germany and France. Worse still, the *uitlander* miners and businessmen were being treated as second rate citizens by the arrogant and overbearing Boers, or so it was alleged. It was claimed that they were burdened with discriminatory taxes and not treated with the great respect that Britons were usually accorded throughout the world. The *uitlanders* wanted the vote and a say in the political affairs of the Transvaal as their skills contributed so much towards its wealth. However, there were too many of them, for they outnumbered the native Boer population; and, as Kruger so plainly put it: 'If I give them the vote,

I give them my country'. He was not going to do that.

In the meantime Britain, competing in the scramble for Africa, had acquired vast tracts of land, ten times the size of the Transvaal. To the west, Bechuanaland, and to the north, Rhodesia, the latter ruled by that commercial colossus Cecil Rhodes and his chartered British South Africa Company. It was an organisation that financed private armies with which to control its territories: the Bechuanaland Mounted Police and, later, the British South Africa Police.

In 1895, Rhodes, possibly with the connivance of the British Government as some believe, instigated a situation whereby the oppressed *uitlanders* would rise up and revolt. To give backbone to their rebellion, Rhodes' right-hand man, Dr Leander Starr Jameson, led a raid into the Transvaal of 500 mounted men, many drawn from the chartered company's police, with artillery and Maxim machine guns. The events which followed became known as the Jameson Raid which collapsed into a complete fiasco. The oppressed *uitlanders* did not rise up and Jameson and his followers, deep inside the Transvaal, were surrounded and forced to ignominious surrender by Commandant Joubert.

The Jameson affair fuelled the simmering feelings between the two governments, and did nothing to blunt Britain's desire to get the Republic back into the Imperial fold. Britain aired the vague terms of its suzerainty and elaborated on the grievances of its oppressed subjects as the Republic remained intransigent, and so the two nations sped towards armed conflict. President Steyn of the Orange Free State, doing his utmost to prevent war, hosted a peace conference between Sir Alfred Milner, the British High Commissioner, and President Kruger. However, after three days of wrangling, negotiations collapsed and a state of war came into being.

CHAPTER TWO

. . . .

15,000 HORSEMEN DESCEND

When General Penn Symons was carried from the field mortally wounded, command at Dundee devolved upon Brigadier-General James Yule who wisely decided to delay another frontal attack on the steep, boulder-strewn, 600-foot high face of Talana Hill, preferring instead to pound the Boer positions before committing his infantry. Furthermore, all was not well amongst the Boer command on the heights above. Ammunition for General Meyer's guns was running low and despite continual heliographed messages to General S. P. Erasmus for support, Erasmus had not fired a shot all day. By noon, Meyer had decided that without cooperation, his position would become untenable, and he began to move his commando and guns away from the crest, down the rear and off Talana Hill.

As the Boer artillery fire diminished, Yule ordered the King's Royal Rifles and the Dublin Fusiliers, with the Irish Fusiliers in support, to take Talana. However, the Boer riflemen were far from beaten. Soon the slopes of the hill were strewn with khaki clad bodies whilst the men of the Indian Stretcher Bearer Corps, which accompanied the column, bravely moved amongst the casualties carrying them downhill to the town.[20]

However, despite the casualties and with the Boer rearguard undercover amongst the rocks, the infantry pressed on, step by step, slowly taking possession of the hill. Finally, Talana was theirs, but even as they gave a yell of triumph, the British artillery, unaware of the renewed assault, suddenly brought its guns to bear on Talana's slopes, inflicting carnage on both friend and foe. In an effort to silence the guns, a brave signaller rose to his feet, exposing himself to the flying shrapnel and, legs and arms flailing, raced down the rocky slope in an effort to stop the bombardment.

The pause in the British attack gave the Boers respite to withdraw unmolested. They were neither followed by artillery, as the colonel commanding the British guns was most probably fearful of firing at the wrong target again, nor were they pursued by Yule's cavalry, the 18th Hussars. Said cavalry, who having been ordered earlier in the day to scout forward and 'act as the situation demanded', now found themselves surrounded by the lately arrived men of Erasmus' commandos. Deneys Reitz, a young burgher, later recalled the action that followed:

> How this handful of men came to be right in the rear of the whole Boer Army I never heard, but they were on a desperate errand, for between them and their main body lay nearly 15,000 horsemen, and now that the fog was lifting, their chance of regaining their base unobserved was gone. Already Boer marksmen were appearing out of the mist, firing from the saddle as they came, and shepherding the soldiers still further from their own people . . . we mounted our horses and rode down the mountainside as fast as we could go. Arrived at the foot, we raced across the veldt in the wake of the English troops, guided by the sound of dropping rifle-shots ahead of us, for we could no longer see our quarry, as they had disappeared for the time being among some low foot hills. Following on we soon came to the scene of action. The English had gone to earth at a small homestead . . . Across their front ran the dry bed of a spruit, [stream] . . . we climbed the bank and were soon blazing away our first shots in war.
>
> The troops replied vigorously, but they were able to devote comparatively little attention to us, for by now the countryside was buzzing like an angry hive, with men arriving from every direction, and the end was but a question of time. After a few minutes a Creusot gun of the Transvaal *Staatsartillerie* unlimbered and opened fire. The very first shell stampeded all the troop horses . . . I saw a white flag go up at the kraal, and another at the farmhouse, so I hastened to be present at the surrender. By the time I got there the soldiers had thrown down their arms and were falling in under their officers. Their leader, Colonel Moller, stood on the stoep [veranda] looking pretty crestfallen, but the private soldiers seemed to take the turn of events more cheerfully.[21]

Thus, having surrendered, they earned their regiment the mortifying nickname of 'Kruger's Own'.

Despite the Boers being far from beaten, Britain, badly needing a triumph, declared 'The Battle of Talana' a victory; indeed, for a while 20 October was celebrated as a public holiday throughout the Empire.[22] The Boer retreat from the field of battle was, in fact, more a tactical withdrawal, and it became plain to Yule that being severely outnumbered by an enemy equally well-armed and, in addition, extremely mobile, he could, as earlier feared by White, be cut off from the rest of the British force centered in Ladysmith 50 miles away. His casualties so far were over 250 men, not counting the captured troopers of the 18th Hussars, whilst the Boers, unbeknown to Yule, had in comparison lost only 150. The telegraph line to Ladysmith was still open but Yule's request for reinforcements was flatly refused.

Meanwhile, another Boer force, under the command of white-bearded General Johannes Kock, who had fought the British as a 13 year old at the Battle of Boomplaats, had exceeded their orders and bypassed Dundee with the aim of taking Elandslaagte railway station situated between Dundee and Ladysmith. There were also, unbeknown to Yule, thousands of Boer horsemen about to descend in a pincer movement that would close around Dundee. Yule had but one course to take: ungallantly abandon the town and leave the inhabitants to their fate. However, such were the feelings of mutual fellowship between frontier folk at the time, that Yule could confidently abandon not only the citizens to the Boers, knowing they would be treated with due respect, but with the same confidence, he left behind the dying Penn Symons. However, as the citizens were to discover, there was little Boer chivalry as far as goods and chattels were concerned. Deneys Reitz became concerned at the general behaviour including his own:

> . . . Soon 1,500 men were whooping through the streets, and behaving in a very undisciplined manner. Officers tried to stem the rush, but we were not to be denied, and we plundered shops and dwelling houses, and did considerable damage before the commandant and field cornets were able to restore some semblance of order. It was not for what we got out of it, for we knew that we could carry little or nothing away with us, but the joy of ransacking other people's property was hard to resist, and we gave away to the impulse. . . . There was not only the town to be looted,

but there was a large military camp standing abandoned on the outskirts, and there were entire streets of tents, and stacks of tinned and other foodstuffs, and, knowing the meagre way in which our men were fed and equipped, I was astonished at the numberless things an English army carried with it in the field. There were mountains of luxurious foods, comfortable camping stretchers and sleeping bags, and there was even a gymnasium, and a profusion of other things too numerous to mention.[23]

Yule and his command, in intense darkness and pouring rain, had stealthily departed Dundee during the second night following the battle, leaving their tents standing and camp fires burning. They did not leave via the main road to Ladysmith, if it could be called a road at all, but, aware of a Boer presence along the railway line, headed east to Ladysmith by a much longer and more arduous route that would take the column on a forced march over hills and through flooded rivers. The rain relentlessly soaked clothing, kit and countryside, turning the route into a knee-deep mud wallow in which many of the draft animals succumbed and died. However, Yule's nocturnal departure had given him a half day start on his unenthusiastic pursuers who would have preferred to have remained with their more fortunate comrades, warm and dry, looting Dundee. Finally, after a few half-hearted skirmishes imposed upon them by the Boers, Yule and his men marched—or, more accurately, staggered—into Ladysmith where they, with the rest of the garrison, would remain besieged for many months to come.

Meanwhile, another battle had been fought and won. Kock's 1,000-strong commando had, in fact, bypassed Dundee and had taken the little hamlet of Elandslaagte with its railway station, coal mine and what was described as a hotel, only 18 miles from Ladysmith. The commander of Kock's advance party, Commandant Francois Pienaar and his men, bearded and festooned with bandoliers of ammunition were ferocious in appearance but were, as it transpired later, good-hearted and sociable fellows.

The first that Ladysmith knew of the capture of Elandslaagte was the receipt of a frantic telegraph message from the station reporting it had been captured. The Boers had opened fire on a train bringing it to a halt and had taken the crew prisoner, including the telegraphist, locking them in a room which happened to be the telegraph office. The telegraphist immediately wired Ladysmith with the frantic appeal: 'What shall I do?'

It was the last message from Elandslaagte. The Boers, however, seemed to have gone about the capture of the station in an almost convivial manner. The proceedings were made even more jovial when it was discovered that the captured train contained, amongst other things, a generous cargo of whisky. This resulted in the prisoners, whom the Boers had just captured, being put on parole and joining their captors in the *Travellers' Rest Hotel* for a night of revelry and song with everyone lustily joining in the choruses of popular ballads, played on the piano by an Englishman by the name of Galthorp. The evening included renderings of both *God Save the Queen* and the *Volkslied* in Afrikaans. Thirty-six hours later the death and wounding of many of those present would assert the reality of war.

When Kock arrived at daybreak, accompanied by the rest of his commando, he found Pienaar and his advance guard still suffering from the night's indulgence and the station undefended.[24] Kock's force was a mixed bag consisting of 500 mercenaries of the German and Hollander corps with roughly the same number of burghers of the Johannesburg Commando, amongst them Dr Coster the State Prosecutor, De Wit Hamer the Town Clerk of Pretoria and several Englishmen including a Major Hall. Major Adolf Schiel, a former conscript in the German cavalry who had immigrated to South Africa as a young man and now commanded the German Corps, was so enraged by the drunkenness and lack of discipline that he ordered, to the dismay of many, every bottle of whisky to be smashed.[25]

Meanwhile, in Ladysmith, Lieutenant-General Sir George White had sent out a cavalry patrol which confirmed the presence of Boers at Elandslaagte. White then put preparations in hand for a strong reconnoitring force to advance on the enemy, recapture the station and reopen direct communications with Dundee—Yule having yet to abandon the town at the time.

Early in the morning of 25 October, at the moment Yule was departing Dundee, Major-General John French arrived with his staff officer, Major Douglas Haig, both keen cavalry men and rising stars in the British Army. French, who was then 37, had had a brief naval career of two years as a midshipman but had left the sailor's life for the cavalry becoming adjutant of the 19th Hussars in which capacity he distinguished himself during the 1884–5 expedition to rescue General Gordon from Khartoum. He had also rewritten the British Army's cavalry manual. Haig, the staff officer, was well-connected socially having married one of the Princess of Wales' ladies-in-waiting. He was also secure financially as his father was the proprietor of a Scottish distillery.

The arrival of French and his force did not come as a complete surprise to the Boers: Colonel Schiel, commanding an outpost close to the British assembly point, had seen the British advancing and sent a frantic message to General Kock that arrived, more or less, at the same time as the first British shells from the Natal Field Artillery (NFA) began to drop around the station. In the ensuing panic, many of the British prisoners captured the day before made their escape, including Mr Harris, the general manager of the mine, and Mr Mitchell-Innes, one of the directors. Soon the British shells all but demolished a Red Cross wagon, which could not be distinguished as there was no wind to stiffen its distinctive flag, whilst another missile blew to smithereens a railway truck containing a consignment of imported furniture destined for Mr Harris' wife.[26]

General Kock, however, had already safely established his headquarters amongst some low lying *koppies* (hills) which formed the northern end of a horseshoe shaped ridge one and a half miles south-east of the station. Here he laid a strong defensive position and entrenched two of his 15-pounder canons and a Maxim gun—the Boers maintained that Kock's only artillery were two Maxim-Nordenfelt guns, those, in fact, captured during the Jameson raid.

The British troops spread out in battle formation, with the 5th Lancers going forward towards the south or furthest end of the ridge where Kock had his camp, driving in Boer horsemen who, on reaching cover, dismounted and opened fire with their Mausers. The Boers' 15-pounders, manned by professional soldiers of the *Staatsartillerie*, were not slow in joining in, and soon shells began to fall amongst the advancing British infantry who took cover while the NFA responded to the Boer guns. However, it soon became apparent that the little British muzzle-loaders could not compete and were hopelessly outranged. Fortunately for French, many of the Boers' shells failed to explode but when one missile hit and disabled an NFA ammunition wagon, which luckily did not explode, French decided the force at his command was inadequate and ordered a withdrawal back to Modderspruit, keeping picquets in his wake to forestall any sudden Boer counter-attack.

Once out of range of the Boer artillery, the telegraph line to Ladysmith was tapped and reinforcements requested, who finally arrived at about 2pm. The troops already at Modderspruit had spent an idle morning after the withdrawal. Arriving by rail and road and accompanied by General White himself, with his personal escort of Natal Mounted Rifles (NMR), a fair-sized army was assembled. It consisted of approximately 1,300 cavalry made up from the 5th Lancers, 5th Dragoon Guards, Imperial Light Horse (ILH) and NMR; 1,600 infantry from the Devonshire Regiment, the Gordon Highlanders and the Manchester Regiment; and over 550 artillery men with 18 guns. The Boers were completely outnumbered in both men and guns but it was too late for them to withdraw.

Colonel Ian Hamilton, in overall command of the British infantry, had a score to settle with the Boers which had been outstanding for 19 years, ever since his wrist had been shattered at Majuba leaving his hand withered and claw-like, a wound subsequently applauded by the young Winston Churchill as a 'glorious disfigurement'. Hamilton addressed the assembled infantry with a stirring speech, assuring them that news of their victory would be shouted through the streets of London by the following day. The troops responded with cheers and calls of: 'We'll do it, Sir, we'll do it!' With the hurrahs over, most of the day had already gone, and the attack began in earnest.

Schiel's detachment, which had scouted forward, had lost its way and was now nearest to the advancing British, who commanded both the railway line and the road to the station. At about 3.30pm the cavalry, escorting a battery of Royal Field Artillery (RFA), advanced on Schiel, who had begged Kock for one of the Boer guns to no avail. The RFA unlimbered, opened fire and in an unequal fight dispersed the Germans, sending them scurrying towards the Boer camp. The cavalry followed, sabring some of the Germans. They were accompanied by two batteries of RFA which finally clattered across the railway line, close to the station, where they halted briefly and were at once bombarded by the enemy. Then, spurring on closer, they halted again, unlimbered and opened fired on the Boer guns.

At the other end of the horseshoe-shaped ridge, to the south-east, the British battle plan was taking shape: the Manchesters, Gordon Highlanders and dismounted ILH began to climb up amongst the boulders that straddled the ridge from one end to the other, pushing the enemy before them back towards the Boer camp and their gun positions. Both the Gordons and the ILH had a score to settle with the Boers: the Gordons their defeat at Majuba 20 years before; the ILH, who had been raised from English *uitlanders*, the recent forfeiture of their Johannesburg livelihoods.

It was bloody work for the infantry as Boer marksmen began to take their toll. At the other end of the horseshoe, about 1,000 yards out from the *koppie* that concealed the enemy guns, the Devons began to advance, although not in the close formations taught at Aldershot but in a disburse-ment devised by Hamilton. It was almost scattered order, the men widely spaced thus making difficult targets for the enemy up ahead. Nevertheless, suffering a hail of rifle fire and shells from the Maxims at 800 yards, the Devons went to ground behind the shelter of numerous large anthills that covered the open plain, to await the result of the flanking movement of the other regiments that was progressing along the horseshoe ridge from the south-east.

However, the closer the flankers came to the deep depression that split the horseshoe ridge, just before it rose again to the *koppie* concealing the Boer camp, the fiercer the opposition became. The Gordon Highlanders, suffering the most, and with half their officers already killed or wounded, were desperate to escape from the crack and the whine of the Mausers, the sound of approaching death, so they could use their bayonets to get to grips with the enemy and wreak retribution. However, it was not to be. A barbed wire fence of a farm brought them to a halt and in desperation they tore at it with their bare hands. At last they were through, only to be frustrated by Schiel and his Germans who, having retreated from their earlier position, had now arrived and with great courage attacked the British right flank. However, before doing so Schiel, who must have kept a bottle of the whisky he ordered destroyed, said to his Germans: 'Gen-tlemen, before we ride further, let us, one last time, drink a toast as good Germans to our most gracious Kaiser.' [27] It was fighting almost muzzle-to-muzzle at 100 yards, making it impossible to miss. The British came to a sudden halt and their attack hung in the balance. It became a personal battle with antagonists on either side seeking out individual foes and to add drama and confusion, the late afternoon had become as dark as night as great purple-black clouds towered in the sky, their edges illuminated blood-red and gold by the sinking sun whilst thunder boomed and vivid lightning paled the flash of the guns. It was a classic battle setting as though some dark force of nature had suddenly provided a fitting back-drop for the carnage taking place on the ridge below.

As the British faltered, Hamilton rode into the thick of the battle, urging the men up and on. The pipe major of the Gordons stepped forward into the rain that now fell in torrents, his pipes pealing *The Charge* which was taken up by the infantry bugles. Once more the British line surged forward, over the boulders of the final slope, whilst the ILH dealt with the last of the German Corps, killing most and wounding the rest, including Schiel who was taken prisoner. He later wrote:

The enemy lines of marksmen were only some hundred yards distant. From their uniforms we noticed they were Scots. From both sides a murderous fire ensued and a new disaster struck! A detachment of the Imperial Light Horse appeared on the extreme right flank of the enemy . . . Three times they pressed forward and three times they were beaten back. We fired as fast as we could. To miss was almost impossible . . . [28]

Likewise on the plain the Devons, hidden by the torrential downpour, charged the ridge, arriving on top to capture or kill the gallant Boer artillery men who had stuck to their guns to the very last. G. W. Steevens of the *Daily Mail*, who was present, wrote:

The pipes shrieked with blood and the lust of glorious death. 'Fix bayonets!' Staff officers rushed shouting from the rear, imploring, cajoling, cursing, and slamming every man who could move into line. Line—but it was a line no longer. It was a surging mass of men—Devons and Gordons, Manchesters and Light Horse all mixed up, inextricably; subalterns commanding regiments, soldiers yelling advice, officers firing carbines, leaping, killing, falling, all drunk with battle, shoving through hell to the throat of the enemy. [29]

Then, suddenly a white flag was seen (so fact or legend has it) and, intermingled with cheers, the *Cease fire* was sounded. It was in those relaxed seconds, an escape from tension and fear, that the Boers counter-attacked with about 60 men led by Kock himself. It will never be known whether the white flag was a deliberate deception or whether, perhaps, it was displayed, unknown to Kock, by some subordinate. In any event, it was a counter-attack delivered at the perfect psychological moment, and once again the British whirled back and victory hung in the balance. However, the odds were against the Boers and, outnumbered, they were overwhelmed with Kock being mortally wounded.

The battle over, the elated infantry raised their helmets and, bareheaded in the pouring rain, shouted what was to become the British battle cry: 'Majuba! Majuba!'

Down on the plain on the far side of the ridge, the Boers were in full retreat. Many men of the commando, like Kock himself, had brought their wives, retainers and wagons along, so the retreat was a jumbled affair of conveyances and mounted burghers, all hurrying north-west over the railway line above the station and out towards the hills beyond. A rather pathetic and helpless enemy, but an enemy nonetheless who had yet to surrender. Level with them the Lancers and Dragoons of the British cavalry drew up into line. The mistakes made by the 18th Hussars at Dundee would not be repeated. This was the moment that every cavalry-man had waited for: the years of training, sword and lance drill, were all about to find their purpose. Here before them was the enemy who, until a few moments ago, with Mauser and Maxim, had been doing his best to kill them. The cavalry trotted forward into line, and then began to canter, then the shrill trumpet sounded and with wild cries they plunged into the Boers. With lance and sabre they speared and hacked their way through the fleeing columns. Some Boers stood and fired, bringing down horsemen as they came, and then, throwing down their arms begged for mercy. However, that was not to be the way of things, and a charge once started is brutal, terrible and impossible to stop. The Boers were shown no mercy and the maddened troopers, once through the column, turned and charged back through again with equal vengeance.

The charge of the Lancers and the appalling wounds they dealt were widely condemned. A British doctor treating a rare survivor of a lance thrust wrote:

> It is the only one I have ever seen, it went right through him and out of his chest [He was obviously struck in the back, most likely whilst he was on the run] and when he pulled back drew out a large piece of omentum, a fold of peritoneum connecting the stomach with other abdominal organs. This I had to remove and I am rather curious to see how he got on.[30]

A private of the King's' Royal Rifles who witnessed the charge recalled:

> It was a great but terrible sight to see those horsemen hew their way through the Boers. Three times they rode right through the Boers, hacking, cutting and slashing. We had suffered pretty severely and I suppose we got our backs up a bit. Any how we got even with Joubert's men.[31]

An officer of the Lancers described the chase:

But now the opportunity for which they [the cavalry] had waited had come . . . as they topped the rise which had concealed them, they found the Boers crossing their front at a distance of a few hundred yards. The Boers endeavoured to get away, but in spite of a donga to be crossed, and the bad, rocky going, the big English and Wales horses of the Lancers and Dragoons were soon amongst their little ponies. For over a mile did the two British squadrons ride through the enemy, spearing some forty of them. Then rallying, the troopers wheeled about and galloped back again through the still streaming crowds of fugitives. Many Boers endeavoured to fire their Mausers from the saddle but after the first onset of the cavalry, the Burghers were straining every nerve to gallop away from those terrible lance points. Then the scattered troopers were rallied. The men fell in and cheered madly. There was something awful in the dramatic setting of the scene. The wild troopers forming in the thickening darkness, with their reeking weapons bare; the little knot of prisoners, with faces blanched with fear herded together at lance point; the dim patches on the veldt, which denoted the destruction which had been dealt . . . [32]

Another lancer related the following to Donald Macdonald:

Some of them [the Boers] fell on their knees with uplifted hands, praying for mercy. 'I have five children' screamed one of them. 'For God's sake spare me!' The lancer raised his point and passed on, but on turning, saw the man he had spared in the act of reaching for a Mauser rifle. He turned back, ran him first through the muscle of the arm as he sought to shield himself, and then through the body. 'At the last minute I tried to let off one poor devil. He was white with fear' said the lancer, 'but my horse knew his business too well and the lance point found.'[33]

The British were also accused, correctly, of looting—just as the Boers would be looting in Dundee. However, it is unlikely that the exaggerated enemy claims were true: old General Kock, mortally wounded, was found the following morning, naked, all his clothing having been stripped off and stolen.[34] The Boers blamed the British, no doubt unfairly: there was a coal mine nearby and where there is industry there is labour.

The rain and darkness mercifully put an end to the pursuit. To the

Boers the use of edge weapons was uncivilised, savage and abhorrent, a legacy of past encounters with the Zulu. They swore that they would never forget the Lancers, and would kill every one without mercy who fell into their hands. It was a British victory but a costly one: somewhere in the order of 40 British killed and 180 wounded. The Boers suffered almost a third of their force killed, wounded or captured.

By the time the cavalry returned, it was completely dark and still pouring with rain. A dreadful night of privation and cold faced Briton and Boer alike. The plight of the wounded on both sides, lying in the wet and darkness, was pitiful and many would not receive comfort until after daybreak. This was the reality of war, not the raucous sing-song of the night before.

At that moment Yule and his 4,000 men were still in Dundee, having won a short-lived victory and he was yet to abandon the town. He and his troops in fact attempted to engage the retreating remnants of Kock's defeated commando.[35] With the victory at Elandslaagte the railway was back under British control and Yule only 45 miles up the line. However, General White, who had witnessed the Battle of Elandslaagte, believed his command was about to be cut off by an overwhelming number of the enemy and decided to withdraw into Ladysmith, thus squandering a great opportunity. Between the dark and dawn, and into the next morning, the victorious, rain-soaked and mud-caked British troops, many bloodied and wounded, made their forlorn way back to Ladysmith. The elation of their triumph had evaporated and there appeared to be nothing of value to be had for the sacrifices made.

At that moment the RMS *Dunnotar Castle* was about half-way to Cape Town. The young officers on board were close to frantic that the war would be over—in Britain's favour of course—before they had a chance to join in as they, like the revellers at Elandslaagte Station of the night before, knew no better at the time.

General Sir George White, a winner of the Victoria Cross 20 years earlier, was now, at 65, indecisive and at a loss how best to use the advantage of his victory. He had 13,000 troops and ample supplies of every sort. Should he and his staff make plans to attack? Or should he abandon Ladysmith and get his command back across the Tugela River as Buller had advised before leaving England? Perhaps, fearing that he could be caught in the open by his mobile enemy, whose numbers he believed to be increasing daily, White finally decided to remain in Ladysmith and there await the Boers and deal them a mortal blow as they approached.

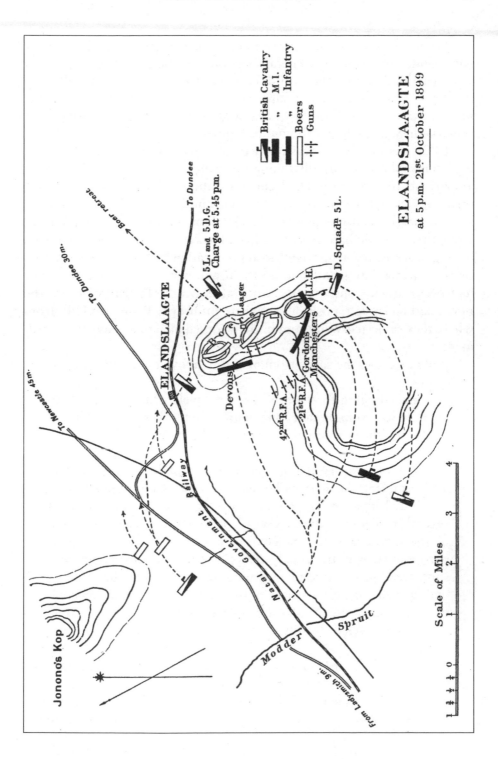

ELANDSLAAGTE
at 5 p.m. 21st October 1899

British Cavalry
" M.I.
" Infantry
Boers
Guns

When news of Kock's disaster at Elandslaagte reached the Boer command, Commandant-General Piet Joubert, the victor of Majuba 20 years earlier, and now the overall commander of Boer forces, called on the Free State burghers for support and soon the commandos came hurrying down through the passes to swell his ranks. As Deneys Reitz later remarked: 'Something was bound to happen.'

By 29 October, White was ready to launch an attack on the encroaching enemy who were rapidly taking up strategic positions on the distant approaches to Ladysmith. He decided to gamble all his troops and in one throw knock out the enemy. On the morning of the 29th, he led out an army of seven cavalry regiments, 11 regiments of infantry (not all at full strength) and seven batteries of artillery. However, the fast-moving Boers, having observed from afar the British preparations or having been advised by their sympathisers and spies in the town, were no longer where they had been earlier. Consequently, when at dawn the British attacked, the Boers had taken up a position elsewhere on nearby Pepworth Hill, from where they subjected White and his bewildered men to a heavy bombardment.

Reitz describes the scene from his camp above the battlefield:

As for the English force on Nicholson's Nek, orders were sent to the Free State commando, coming up from the west to attack them . . . But for the next hour or two we could spare them no thought, for tall pillars of dust were rising from Ladysmith, and soon long columns of infantry debouched into the plain before us. The Transvaal State Artillery had dragged a 6-inch Creusot gun ['Long Tom'] up Pepworth Hill, a mile to the left, and they had installed several smaller guns there as well, and all these now began to fire on the approaching troops. I expected to see the shells mow great gaps and lanes in the enemy ranks, but instead of this our first shots were spent in finding the range, and by the time the columns had opened out, and, in place of the havoc which I had expected, the firing only caused smoke and local disturbances of earth, while the infantry gained steadily on.[36]

Unexpectedly, in the midst of the battle, a locomotive from Durban rattled up the line bearing six naval guns and their crews. However, they were also unable to silence the Boer artillery. It was left to the gunners of the Royal Field Artillery to cover the infantry who were now retreating in disorder, while the burgher marksmen dotted the veldt with khaki dead.

Meanwhile, another battle had been fought: Colonel Frank Carleton, with about 1,000 infantry drawn from the Gloucestershire Regiment and the Royal Irish Fusiliers and with artillery support, had been sent to occupy the hills dominating the pass over Nicholson's Nek, a route into Ladysmith most likely to be used by the Free State burghers answering Joubert's call for assistance.[37]

Carleton and his men had set off from Ladysmith in the dark but had not made the hills by daylight. Close to dawn they were passing through a gully when, out of the gloom, boulders came bowling down from above, scattering the troops and completely unnerving the 200 mules carrying, in dismantled sections, the mountain guns and ammunition. The column immediately believed it was under attack. The mules broke loose and with their loads still on their backs galloped off in all directions—later in the day, Reitz some miles away, caught two mules as they galloped into his camp, one still carrying a mountain gun barrel on its back. The forward troops, hearing the thunder of hooves, were convinced they were in the midst of a Boer assault and opened fire, causing mayhem and casualties.

Christiaan de Wet, the future Commandant-General of the Orange Free State forces, fought at Nicholson's Nek as an ordinary burgher. He later recalled how he had taken command during the battle and with a force of no more than 250 men, drawn from the Heilbron and Kroonstad Commandos, and the Johannesburg police, had moved under cover towards the advancing British infantry and had used their sharp shooting skills to devastating effect.[38]

Deneys Reitz remarked:

> Both sides were maintaining a vigorous short-range rifle contest, in which the soldiers were being badly worsted, for they were up against the real old-fashioned Free State Boers for whom they were no match in sharp shooting of this kind.[39]

By noon the British could no longer sustain the rate of casualties being inflicted; a bugle call was heard and those soldiers who could stand walked towards the Boers in surrender. Down below on the plains, the burghers could see the rest of the British forces that had been sent out against them that day. The troops with which White thought he would deal the Boers a knock-out blow were streaming back towards Ladysmith in disarray. The burghers waited for the order to mount up, pursue and destroy—destroy like the British Lancers and Dragoons had so effectively done at Elandslaagte. However, Commandant-General Piet Joubert would give no such instruction and, when pressed to do so, admonished his subordinates by saying: 'When God holds out a finger, don't take the whole hand.' Thus unmolested White's army was allowed to escape into the dilapidated little town of corrugated iron houses, two hotels and a few other buildings of note. It had every aspect of a frontier town and would have looked equally at home in rural Australia or on the American plains. Its rather peculiar name derived from a foible of Sir Harry Smith for naming real estate after his family: Ladysmith honoured his wife and if that were not honour enough, he had similarly named another town in the Cape, spelling it 'Ladismith' to avoid confusion; he also kept his wife company by naming yet another town Harrismith.

As the remains of the broken and crestfallen British infantry shuffled back towards the town, the dismayed civilian population panicked and hastened their way to the railway station, carrying what they could, anxious to depart before the Boers surrounded them completely, the last train carrying amongst others Major-General John French and Major Douglas Haig.

At about this time Buller stepped ashore at Cape Town.

Ladysmith would not be an easy place to defend being overlooked and entirely circled by a chain of hills on which the Boers would install their guns; the most fearsome being a 155mm Creusot that could fire a 46kg shell a distance of over six miles.

Joubert's younger, but subordinate, generals urged him to exploit his triumph by bypassing Ladysmith and pressing on to Pietermaritzburg and Durban, thus forcing Britain to accept a negotiated peace before more imperial troops arrived. With this prospect in mind, men of the Wakker-stroom, Heidelberg and Krugersdorp Commandos crossed the Tugela with a Maxim-Nordenfeldt and began roving east of the riverside village of Colenso, which had been abandoned.

CHAPTER THREE

....

THE ARMOURED TRAIN

The dismayed and disillusioned Empire badly needed a restorative: a victory—or some dashing deed of British valour that would renew the Empire's confidence in its soldiery. Such a deed was about to be enacted. The publicity that would be accorded to the hero would, with the coming of the years, influence the history of the world.

Among the passengers who had travelled aboard RMS *Dunnotar Castle* at the same time as General Buller, but not accompanying him, was a young war correspondent by the name of Winston Spencer Churchill who was working for the London *Morning Post*. He was an intensely ambitious man who had a year or two previously, whilst an officer in the cavalry, seen much action in both India and the Sudan. Leading a life that required a greater income than that of a junior officer, he had taken to reporting battles rather than fighting in them and was now amongst the most highly paid of the correspondents in South Africa. Although a civilian, Churchill dressed in semi-military attire and carried a broom-handled Mauser pistol, a weapon with which he had managed to save himself from an extremely grisly end when his regiment, the 21st Lancers, charged and blundered into a horde of fanatical sword-wielding tribesmen.[40]

The small British force that remained between the Tugela and Pietermaritzburg had fallen back to Estcourt, 30 miles from Colenso, where an armoured train had been constructed from a standard railway engine festooned with lengths of marine rope (thus earning it the name of *Hairy Mary*) and armour-plated cattle trucks complete with loop holes. This vehicle left Estcourt each morning, a prisoner of the rails on which it travelled, to scout towards Colenso and then return: a task that could have been done with more efficiency, whilst drawing far less attention, by a small patrol of mounted infantry. On the morning of 15 November 1899, the train was commanded by Captain Aylmer Haldane of the Gordon Highlanders, an old friend of Churchill's from his India days, who gave permission for Churchill to travel aboard.

Haldane's description of the locomotive and its purpose was less than complimentary. He wrote that it departed '. . . on a fruitless mission' and observed how relieved the occupants looked when 'they climbed over the sides and congratulated themselves that their turn to form the freight of this moribund engine of war would not come around again for at least some days'. [41]

The train had made several previous sorties without sighting the enemy and on one occasion had steamed right into the silent and deserted town of Colenso. Today it would carry men of the Dublin Fusiliers in the foremost two trucks, which were preceded by a flatbed carrying a 7-pounder canon, while the two rear trucks held a detachment of the Durban Light Infantry. Bringing up the rear was an unarmoured carriage containing a repair gang and equipment. In the middle of this cavalcade huffed *Hairy Mary* and its coal tender. In all there were about 120 men.

The morning dawned grey and drizzling with the visibility varying as drifts of mist lifted and fell. As they neared the little deserted railway station at Frere, they paused to talk with a patrol of two Natal Mounted Police, who advised that no sign of Boer activity had been spotted so far that morning. Perhaps somewhat relieved—except for Churchill who would have been hoping for something more dramatic to write about—they chugged on, now uphill towards Chieveley, another deserted railway station. There was still no sign of the enemy. Finally, arriving at Chieveley, they drew to a halt and as they did so a large number of men, clearly Boers, were seen speeding towards the train. They were obviously intent on cutting off its retreat, whilst further up the line, on a low hill that dominated any further advance, the slopes were seen to be alive with moving figures. It was clear that a powerful force of the enemy was preparing to confront the armoured train.

The great disadvantage of an armoured locomotive now became clear: it could not manoeuvre and seek ground to its advantage. It was a prisoner of its iron road and its only alternatives were to either go forward or retire. Haldane would have been aware that one of the first acts of the war had been the destruction by the Boers of a similar armoured train at Kraaipan near Mafeking. He would also know that two weeks earlier the last train to escape from Ladysmith had been ambushed close by, and the carriages riddled with 'Pom-Pom' shells. Haldane halted the train and a telegraphist made contact with HQ at Estcourt. The order was given immediately to return to Frere, and once there to await events. The engine was put into reverse and now with the trucks containing the repair gang and tools to the fore, and the 7-pounder gun bringing up the rear, *Hairy Mary* began to gather speed on the down-hill run. However, Haldane and his command had seen but part of the Boer incursion. During the brief minutes that it had taken the train to travel between Frere and Chieveley, Boers of the Wakkerstroom Commando had piled boulders on the rails at a point where there was a sharp curve in the line. They had also taken possession of a hill that dominated the railway and had set up three field guns and a quick-firing Pom-Pom Maxim.

The Boer preparations were complete. Haldane was about to fall victim to a near perfect ambush: a catastrophe which had been predicted for some days by every private and subaltern in the British camp. General Sir Redvers Buller was later to describe the reconnaissance of the armoured train as 'inconceivable stupidity'.

At 600 yards the Boers opened up with all their guns supported by Mauser rifle fire. Churchill describes the moment:

> . . . Within a second a bright flash of light—like a heliograph, but much yellower, opened and shut ten or twelve times. Then two much larger flashes; no smoke nor yet any sound . . . then, immediately over the rear truck of the train a huge white ball of smoke sprang into being and tore out into a cone like a comet. The iron sides of the truck tanged with a patter of bullets . . .[42]

The driver involuntarily put on full throttle to dash through the gauntlet of fire and the train rattled down the incline, half took the bend and crashed with momentous impact into the waiting boulders. The leading truck containing the ganging tools left the rail, broke its couplings and somersaulted through the air to land bottom side up beside the line. The following truck with its detachment of Durban Light Infantry followed, but the restraint of its couplings broke its momentum, twisting it in the air to land on its side, scattering the infantry men hither and thither. The third truck was also impeded by couplings on take-off, and it too landed on its side, ejecting its contents of Fusiliers along the line and down the embankment. Haldane, Churchill and the rest of the force, after the shock of the impact, found themselves bruised, but for the moment otherwise unharmed. Churchill with wry humour recalled: 'We were not long left in the comparative peace and safety of a railway accident.' [43]

Before coming to a halt, the train had left the Boer guns behind and now their artillery men raced to close in, accompanied by swarms of Mauser riflemen who were fanning out to surround the stricken locomotive. The men exposed on the open flatbed were the first to come into action, gallantly getting off three rounds from their antiquated, muzzle-loading canon before it received a direct hit which blew it off its mounting and into the bush beyond. The shortcomings of an armoured train became immediately apparent: although it gave protection against bullets, it was a fallacy that its armour would keep those within safe from shellfire—during the course of the engagement four shells passed right through Churchill's truck, luckily all failing to explode until they had passed out the other side. Nevertheless the Fusiliers, rallied by Haldane, began to return the Boer fire through the loopholes of the truck causing some discomfort to the enemy artillery men.

It must be remembered that Churchill was there merely in the role of civilian newspaper correspondent and as such, by the rules of war, was bound to take no part in the battle around him. To deviate from the rules and act aggressively against the enemy would jeopardise the protection of his status and, if caught actively engaged in combat, he could be tried and executed: it would not help his case that he wore an officer's uniform, less rank and insignia and titles, and carried a 9mm Mauser automatic pistol, complete with two additional magazines of 'Dum-Dum' (soft-nose) bullets, a type of ammunition that had been outlawed at the Hague Conference five months earlier. However, in the excitement and fury of the moment, Haldane unwittingly placed his friend in great danger by formally putting him 'on duty'. It was agreed that whilst Haldane directed the fire of the survivors, Churchill would endeavour to clear the line and prepare the way of escape.

Clambering down from the comparative safety of the embattled truck, Churchill ran the length of the train with shells droning and exploding overhead while bullets clanged against the iron boxes. Those of the infantry who remained uninjured were giving a good account of themselves, sheltering amongst the wreckage and keeping up a steady fire. However, clearing the line appeared to be a task for a team of giants. The only solution with the slightest prospect of success was to use the engine as a battering ram to slam the wrecked trucks off the line.

The driver was still in his cab but even as Churchill made towards him a shell burst overhead spraying hissing shrapnel in all directions. One splinter caught the driver, cutting his face, and he fled to shelter, recounting indignantly for all to hear that he was a civilian not paid to be killed by bombs. Churchill, using all his considerable powers of persuasion, assured him that he was now safe as no man can be hit twice on the same day; furthermore, he told the driver if he got back into his cab and obeyed orders, he was sure to receive a reward for distinguished gallantry.

For the next hour or more, Churchill constantly exposed himself to the enemy fire as he directed the driver, rounded up volunteers, persuaded them to leave the safety of their defences and, with them, pulled and heaved at the couplings and wreckage. All the while the engine, wheels spinning and screeching on the iron rails, lunged backwards and forwards, attacking the dead weight of the obstructions. At last, by a miracle it seemed, the line was clear. The engine moved forward, but dismay was to be the reward for hope as the footplate of the engine stuck fast against a protruding corner of a derailed truck and forced the engine to a jarring halt. Shells now began slamming into the locomotive but luckily all missed the bullseye of the boiler. However, with the woodwork of the firebox ablaze, all seemed lost. The driver, mad with frustration and fear, and risking the derailment of his vehicle, took the locomotive back for one final charge. At full throttle *Hairy Mary* hit the obstructing truck, staggered giddily, swayed to overturn, passed the obstruction and slithered back on the rails, free at last. However, only the engine and tender were clear. With couplings broken, Haldane's truck was still a prisoner behind the wreckage. There it would have to stay. Bundling the wounded on the engine and tender and with the infantry trotting alongside, it looked as though all but the dead would make it to safety. Haldane's objective was now to reach some abandoned houses at Frere and there to make a stand.

Churchill was still in the cab, hemmed in by the wounded, as the locomotive moved off. The Boers, seeing their quarry escaping, immediately surged forward, intensifying their fire and began to inflict casualties on the retreating infantry. One of the first to fall was the officer commanding the detachment of Durban Light Infantry. Without the protection of the wreckage, others were hit in quick succession. Up to a quarter of the force was killed or wounded in a few minutes. The retreat turned into a rout and the engine driver, now in the grip of panic, forgot the jogging infantry who achieved some shelter from his locomotive and, opening the throttle, left them far behind. Churchill struggled to disengage himself from the overcrowded cab but only managed to do so on reaching the nearby houses of Frere. Jumping down he ran back along the line with the intention of collecting the retreating soldiers, but, unbeknown to him, in the meantime one man had, without orders, run towards the Boers waving a white handkerchief, causing confusion and uncertainty. Others, believing the order to surrender had been given, also gave themselves up and with all resistance dwindling, Haldane was taken prisoner. British casualties numbered 70.

Bewildered that he had encountered no one, Churchill continued to double back, running through a cutting with steep sides—virtually a tunnel without a roof—when he was suddenly confronted by two men, '. . . Tall figures, full of animated movement, clad in dark flapping clothes, with slouch, storm-driven hats, poised on their rifles hardly a hundred yards away'. [44]

Boers! Churchill turned and ran. Two bullets followed him, fired almost simultaneously. He sprang up the sides of the cutting with shots smacking into the damp earth beside him. He was up and over and as he paused for a moment in indecision another Boer, mounted this time, galloped to confront him. Churchill thought to kill him and, feeling for his pistol, realised that during his earlier excursions he had stripped off his belt and holster, leaving them in the railway cab. How lucky for him that he had done so: as a civilian, being captured in possession of a gun could have been his death warrant. The Boer stood silent and forbidding, seated on his 'stock still' horse with his rifle aimed unwaveringly at Churchill's chest. There was no option. Churchill put up his hands. He was a prisoner of war.

. . . .

CHAPTER FOUR

COLENSO

Between 20 and 23 November 1899, the Boers, becoming ever more daring, infiltrated Natal as far as Estcourt and beyond to halt at a farm called *Willow Grange*, less than 45 miles from Pietermaritzburg and only 100 miles from Durban.

Joubert had accompanied the invaders but, as he made clear to all his subordinates, he was unhappy with the situation despite having engaged a large British force. He had fought at night while thunder and lightning boomed and hissed, hammering friend and foe alike with hailstones as big as chicken eggs, the lightning killing men on both sides. The British had retired into Estcourt leaving, it seemed, the way open for an unopposed advance on Pietermaritzburg. Urged by Louis Botha, and other young commanders, not to squander their advantage but to put spurs to their steeds, Joubert instead preached caution: a British Army corps was rumoured to be on its way and, what is more, the Tugela River, 50 miles to the burghers' rear and in flood from the heavy rains, might well cut them off from their comrades. Therefore, reluctantly obeying the old farmer/warrior, the burghers turned and, in the rain that still poured relentlessly, they rode back the way that they had come. In the weeks that followed, Joubert would be censured for what was seen as his timid conduct by not pursuing the enemy and ignoring the sound advice of his subordinate commanders. It was later rumoured that at a council of war, held at Kroonstad in March of the following year, Joubert was sentenced to death and was given the choice of either being shot or voluntarily taking poison. It is a certainty that Joubert's death by natural causes, a week after the council of war, gave rise to this wild rumour.

Where was Buller while this was going on? The British hoped that he would appear through the rain and mist, indomitable and with a huge, equally indomitable, army behind him. His whereabouts were being kept secret, as far as it was possible to keep anything hush-hush in spy-infested Cape Town. Few troops had landed as yet except for those who had travelled on the *Dunnotar Castle* but, not many sea-miles away, there was an armada of vessels containing so many troops afloat that the number would be unequalled until the Gallipoli campaign of 1915.

Buller's quandary was how to juggle the distribution of this multitude of armed might. Kimberley lay besieged 650 miles to the north, and likewise Mafeking, a further 350 miles beyond, while 1,200 miles to the north-east the Boers had chased the British Army into Ladysmith and had locked the door. The original British plan, devised and approved in London, was for Buller's juggernaut to disembark at Cape Town and march north, crushing all before it; but that was before the defeat of White's army. Now Buller's priority, first and foremost, was to relieve White and to release the 13,000 British soldiers before they were forced to capitulate. However, there were, of course, other pressures: Cecil Rhodes with all his influence and wealth, was still locked up in Kimberley while many British Cape Afrikaners were seething with sympathy for their Transvaal and Orange Free State cousins and were but a step or two away from revolt.

As can be seen, South Africa is a place of vast distances and in 1899, once away from the railway, the only transport was almost biblical: the ox wagon. For the Natal campaign alone, Buller would require close to 1,000 vehicles, with ten to 16 oxen needed to pull each one. As Deneys Reitz had remarked earlier, the British Army had a profusion of other things too numerous to mention. The campaign equipment of an infantry battalion of roughly 1,000 men weighed nine tons while the regimental ammunition reserve weighed over one and a half. Ninety tents, each accommodating 16 men (this assumes only two-thirds of the battalion would be sleeping at any one time) weighed over four tons which increased in weight to five and a half tons when wet. The officers did not travel light either. Saddles, polo-sticks, chests of drawers, cricket bats, crates of champagne and, in Buller's case, an iron bathroom, increased the column's load.[45] Winston Churchill, for instance, had shipped with him aboard the *Dunnotar Castle* 26 bottles of wine, 18 bottles of ten-year old whisky, six bottles of brandy and a further six crates of brandy each containing a dozen bottles.[46] The British were inclined to look on the Boer's freedom of movement as a rather unfair advantage, one correspondent remarking:

> On point of mobility, General Buller's infantry could not compare with the Boers who were to a man mounted, who slept in the open and needed no transport system as is required in the British Army. While the British soldier was moving five miles the Boer could cover fifteen.

There was, of course, a price that the Boers had to pay: for much of the time they survived on dried meat (*biltong*) and black coffee laced with sugar. For cover, they had perhaps a bit of canvas tied to a branch for a windbreak.

The hundreds of thousands of beasts, the oxen and mules, that hauled the British transport, also had to be fed but it would have been a logistical impossibility to supply them with fodder. Therefore, the British convoys were required to govern their speed by the time it took for the oxen to graze. It was well-known that to deprive a beast, especially an ox, would result in it taking revenge and dying. A British soldier reminiscing many years later, recalled:

> We used to take great convoys of ox wagons, perhaps two miles long . . . Each loaded up with all the necessities of life. The Africans didn't drive them with reins, they walked alongside . . . and they had great long whips and they'd swished them round and give them a jerk [that gave off a sound like a pistol shot]. If one of the team couldn't go any further they would just unhook him and pull him out of the way of the column—perhaps pull half the flesh off his poor ribs while they were doing it and then put a bullet through his brain. The mounted escort would be a mile or so away on the flanks and likewise in front and to the rear. The rear guard was the most dangerous place as the Boers used to follow our columns and dash up and smite them. It would take a large body of Boers to attack a convoy and you would see a long way off in that clear atmosphere. The Boers had spies, a lot of Africans were spies for the Boers.[47]

By 9 November, the armada carrying Buller's Army Corps of 50,000 men began to arrive in Cape Town and there the 2nd Infantry Division, under Major-General Henry Hildyard, was diverted to Durban.[48] Buller had, under the circumstances, made the only possible decision: he broke up his Army Corps. Two more divisions, one commanded by Major-General Hart and the other by Major General Lyttelton, quickly followed Hildyard on their way to Durban.

The task of relieving Kimberley would be given to Lord Methuen, who was directed to follow the plan which had originally been allocated to the whole Corps, that of rounding up and crushing all Boer resistance as it marched north. However, the military colossus had been split into several pieces and Lord Methuen would find his march confronted by Boer generals more skilful than he. As for Mafeking, it would have to wait.

It would be a war between tortoises and hares as about 90 percent of the British forces so far were infantry, despite Buller knowing better than anyone the value of mounted men. Twenty years earlier, in the Transvaal and then in Zululand, Buller had served in, and had later commanded, the colonial Frontier Light Horse, a unit of tough horsemen once described as:

> . . . rough, undisciplined and disrespectful to their officers, fiercely slovenly and the veriest of drunkards . . . but looking what they were, just the rough and hardy men to wage a partisan warfare against an active enemy . . . The steeds they bestrode were as hardy as themselves.[49]

However, 20 years later, the horsemen sent out from England, the Imperial Yeomanry, would be of a more refined disposition. It was a gentlemen's corps, formed almost 100 years earlier, recruited from the upper and middle classes. Initially the War Office had refused their services but, with many reverses following one after the other in South Africa, it quickly changed its mind and there was a stampede to join. The terms of enlistment were service for one year or for as long as the war lasted. Officers and men were to bring their own horses and tack, be between 20 and 35 years of age, to be of good character and to be good horsemen and good marksmen. In the latter two categories they were soundly bested by the Boers. A few weeks after landing, Lord Methuen was to write of them:

> I found the men forming the rear screen, which consisted of the 86th Company Imperial Yeomanry, very much out of hand and lacking both fire discipline and knowledge how to act. There

seemed to be a want of instructed officers and non-commissioned officers.[50]

A 19-year-old yeomanry trooper, fresh out from Kent, the 'Garden of England', later remembered:

About 4 or 5pm. you stopped and watered your horses, fed your horses and put your saddles in the proper place. . . . You always had to stop somewhere where there was water. If you were lucky enough to be near a stream or a river—which was hardly ever— the cooks had to go to the mud hole. Wherever there was a hollow tree was a mud hole . . . that would be full of rushes and they would part the rushes, push the dixie down till they could get to water and then fill them out of there. When they parted the rushes, the water of course, was like soup, it wasn't fit to drink. . . . Four biscuits a day was full ration, but if you were short of rations you would only get three and if you were very short you would live on two a day. For your main meal when you were on trek, I think the cook would cook some water in a dixie a third full, boil it up, chuck a handful of salt in if he happened to have some—and don't forget the cook's hands were never washed from day to day—and they'd slice chunks of dead bullock and chuck them in, chunks cut off like rough cricket balls. Now one trek we went on we didn't have biscuits, I don't know why, we had sacks of white flour and the issue was a pound a day of dry flour per man. Just dry flour, that's all. You'd get to water with which to mix it into a thick paste . . . roll it out in your hands, you'd got nothing else to do it with and of course your hands were not washed for perhaps days on end, pat it down to about the size of the palm of your hand. When you patted it out it wasn't sloppy, it was three parts dry but wet enough to hold together into a 'chapattie'. You would lay that on hot glowing cow dung and when it was done one side, pretty well black with burning, you'd turn it over and do the other side and out of your pound of flour you could get half a dozen 'chap- atties'. At first we did not know what 'chapatties' were but it was a name given to the cakes by soldiers who had been in India.[51]

For the first three weeks after Buller had stepped ashore in Cape Town, he had done little but attend to the overwhelming administrative demands of his vast army. Despite the staggering number of decisions to be made, Buller had come to a conclusion regarding the most difficult one of all: he had resolved to take over command in Natal himself, leaving Methuen and his subordinates to deal with Kimberley.

There was to be much criticism of Buller for 'abandoning' Cape Town as some put it. He was also said to have an empathy with the Boers. A few days before his arrival Milner, the High Commissioner, who had avidly promoted the war and had done much to ensure that the earlier peace negotiations were unsuccessful, received a letter marked 'Personal and Secret', warning him that Buller had been influenced by Lieutenant General Sir William Butler, an Irishman with Boer sympathies, and an old comrade of Buller's. However, it is likely that Buller, as was the case with many Britons, did not need to be swayed in order to feel an empathy with the foe. This was in contrast to many British soldiers who, in earlier contact with the Boers, had berated their race with spiteful arrogance:

> A Boer . . . he is endowed with the appetite of an ostrich and the freedom from nicety of a vulture. To the weak he is insolent, brutal and overbearing, to the strong he is either cringing or takes refuge in stupidity and stolid sullenness.[52]

Buller had no such feelings; indeed after the Battle of Hlobane in 1879, he had been deeply affected by the loss of Piet Uys, whom he held in great respect:

> We have lost . . . Mr. Piet Uys, whose name you must have often seen in the papers since the war began to attract interest at home. He was my guide, counsellor and friend; his loss is a most serious one to all South Africans and is irreplaceable to me. He really was the finest man, morally speaking, I ever met. . . .[53]

In a report Buller added: 'One so courageous and so sagacious I shall never see again.' One historian wrote of Buller's appointment as General Officer Commanding, South Africa: 'Seldom can a General have approached his greatest challenge with less enthusiasm.'[54] However, Buller would do his duty.

Finally, on arrival at Frere railway station through which Churchill and Captain Haldane had passed two weeks earlier aboard the armoured train, Buller was greeted with a sight seldom to have been seen before: the surrounding fields now contained a 'tent town', accommodating 25,000 troops and mountains of equipment and supplies.

Undoubtedly every man present, from the lowest private soldier to Buller's subordinate generals, was cheered and assured by the commander's implacable presence: 'Good Old Bulldog Buller'—He would sort them out. It could be said that he even looked like a hefty bulldog: his lean campaign figure of earlier wars was a thing of the distant past as his fondness for good food and champagne had enlarged his girth, giving his uniform the appearance that it was a size too small. He too had brought a goodly supply of comforts with him: a whole cargo of champagne, code-worded and crate-labelled 'paraffin'—a subterfuge, it was rumoured, that resulted in his bubbly being purloined and replaced with lamp fuel.

Buller now faced the Tugela. Joubert's attempt of a blitzkrieg ride to Durban had, it seemed, been no more than an idle threat and the burghers had retired irresolute to the far side of the river, destroying the iron railway bridge at Colenso and thus underlining their loss of resolve to press on to the sea. Its destruction confirmed it was the Boers' intent to thwart the relief of Ladysmith and by so doing force the British into a negotiated peace.

The British camp at Frere was 12 miles south of the Tugela, just far enough to be out of range of the Boers' Creusot 'Long Tom'. By late November, Buller began to move his own guns forward to positions where they could reach the Boer defensives on the other side of the Tugela. The approach to the river from the south was across an open plain through which flowed the Blaauwkrantz River which supplied the British with water; this was a place of tragic memories for the Boers as it was here, 60 years earlier, that hundreds of men, women and children were massacred by the Zulu impis of King Dingane.

It was a country of ancient conflicts that had once been inhabited by the amaNgwane, a clan of the Nguni people, who had been conquered by King Shaka in the 1820s. The remnants of their stone cattle *kraals* would now be used by both current adversaries in the construction of Sangars and other makeshift defences. Before the amaNgwane, there had been the Bushmen who had ventured from their eyries, high up in the Drakensberg Mountains, down into the plains to hunt at a time when great herds of game inhabited the veldt. More recently, the amaHlubi, another tribal people, had taken up residence, but they had fallen foul of the British colonial government and, after a minor war, had been moved closer to the mountains whose jagged outline, topped with snow for half the year, dominated the western skyline. There the Tugela River had its birthplace, dropping almost 4,000ft. in one spectacular single fall, before reaching the plain and widening into a broad moat separating northern and southern Natal.

Across the Tugela on the northern side, the plain disappeared into weird shaped and scattered hills that, in most other parts of the world, would individually be regarded as mountains. Each would have had a local Zulu name but shortly many would acquire other names connected with the conflict to come; more importantly, many of the hills—or *koppies* in Afrikaans—were literally lapped by the Tugela, giving the Boer defenders the advantage of height and concealment.

The British Army knew little about the country surrounding them. Although Ladysmith had, for the last 20 years, been regarded as the Aldershot of Natal, there were few, if any, military maps available. The army would have to make do with farm survey plans.

At first, Buller rejected the idea of a frontal attack through Colenso and on 8 December cabled Lord Lansdowne, Secretary of State for War, to that effect. Buller had decided to take his army and march west, unavoidably in view of the enemy for part of the way, and attempt a crossing of the Tugela approximately 50 miles west of Frere, at a place called Potgieter's Drift. On 11 December he ordered the advance, but early next day changed his mind. News had arrived of the horrendous British defeats at Stormberg, where close to 700 men had surrendered, and Modder River in the Cape, where 480 casualties had been sustained. This news must surely have influenced his decision to inflict a much needed British victory on the Boers as soon as possible. A 50-mile flanking march with hundreds of wagons could take a week. Having changed his mind, he decided on an immediate three-pronged frontal attack across the river at Colenso and forthwith telegraphed White in Ladysmith that an assault was imminent.

Since Ladysmith had become encircled, things had initially gone better for the besieged than anticipated. Although there had been a mad panic by some, mainly white riffraff from Johannesburg, to escape at all costs, pushing women and children out of the way in order to secure a seat on the last train, most resolved to stay and do their bit. Soon they could plainly see the Boers at work placing their guns on the surrounding hills; likewise the Boers could observe the besieged sailors from HMS *Terrible* ballasting their guns with which they would reply to the Boer bom - bardment.

The Anglo-Boer War has been called the last of the gentlemen's wars and perhaps to a limited extent it was, for the Boer gunners at first made little effort to hit the town or private houses, restricting their fire to military targets. Reading reports of the damage done and the casualties inflicted, it is surprising how ineffectual the Boer bombardment was. The defenders also, like others before them, were amazed at the poor stopping power of the Mauser rifle and its nickel plated bullet: one British gunner was hit just to the side of his heart, the bullet exiting under his shoulder blade, but was shortly fit for duty.[55] There were also numerous cases of bullet wounds through the lungs but as a surgeon remarked: 'There is a little haemorrhage, but they soon begin to look all right again.'

Since the beginning of the siege, British cavalry and mounted volunteers had been constantly involved in engagements with Boer patrols, and this type of fighting had continued on a daily basis. By 4 November, there was serious concern that the town might be overrun and a request was sent to General Joubert asking permission for the women and children to be given safe conduct out of Ladysmith. This was refused but Joubert offered the alternative of a safe camp, inside the encircled perimeter, where any person who had not taken up arms against the South African Republic could obtain refuge. A meeting was called to consider the proposition and one Archdeacon Barker, a speaker more eloquent than the rest, proposed that:

> Our women and children shall not go out under a white flag. They shall, with the men, remain under the Union Jack and those who would do them harm may come to them at their peril. [56]

His uplifting, if misguided, words carried the vote and most people went home happy.

The shelling continued with the town itself now receiving its share of missiles. However, the *Staatsartillerie* did not have it all their own way. It was noticed that the Boer gunners stationed on what had been christened Gun Hill were the most active and it was resolved, on 8 December, seven days before Buller made his attempt to cross the Tugela, to make a night assault on the enemy gun position. Major-General Sir Archibald Hunter, who should have been with Buller as his Chief of Staff but had been caught in Ladysmith, gathered together 500 mounted men of the local Natal volunteer regiments, plus 100 troopers of the Imperial Light Horse, and, leaving the town at midnight, reached the bottom of Gun Hill two hours later. Placing 100 men to cover his rear, Hunter, with the Natal Carbineers,

Natal Mounted Rifles (NMR) and the Border Mounted Rifles (BMR) began to climb the almost perpendicular hillside that rose above them. Close to the top, the volunteers removed their boots and in silence had all but reached the crest before they were detected by the indolent Boer guard. The cry of, 'Come on, Boys!' was enough. The Boers ran helter-skelter whilst the Royal Engineers exploded charges of gun cotton in the breech of not only the 'Long Tom' but also a howitzer. Then, on making their way back to Ladysmith, the raiders encountered another Boer unit and captured two Maxim Pom-Pom guns. At dawn, to the jubilation of the population, the expedition marched into town in triumphal procession, carrying with it the shattered breech blocks and dragging the two Maxims. The night's work was even accorded a report in the enemy capitol:

> Pretoria, 9 December: The British at Ladysmith scored a success between 1 and 2 in the morning. A body of men crawled up a ravine and carried one of the koppies constituting the Lombards Kop Boer position on which one big Creusot and one Howitzer were put out of action with dynamite, after which the force retired. Major Erasmus and Lieutenant Malan will be court-martialled in connection with the loss of the cannon. Besides the big guns the Boers also lost two Maxims.[57]

While the Ladysmith garrison was keeping the flag flying and embarrassing the enemy, Buller launched his attack on Colenso. The right-hand prong of the assault contained the Mounted Brigade, commanded by 48-year-old Colonel The Earl of Dundonald, an old Etonian, a Lifeguards officer and a comrade of Buller's from his Sudan days including the Battle of Abu Klea. He had gained particular fame as a result of his epic ride bringing news of the death of General Gordon and the fall of Khartoum. He had recently made his own way out to Natal in the hope that Buller would find him a position and this Buller had done with alacrity. The mounted brigade was composed of 1st Royal Dragoons, 13th Hussars, Bethune's Mounted Infantry, Thornycroft's Mounted Infantry, South African Light Horse and a composite regiment of local volunteers.

Fifty-five-year-old Major-General Geoffrey Barton commanded the 6th Infantry Brigade. He had campaigned in the Ashanti War of 1873, the Anglo-Zulu War and, having served in China, would have been well-acquainted with Buller. In addition, he had served in Egypt during 1882. His brigade was composed of 1st Royal Welsh Fusiliers, 2nd Royal Irish

Fusiliers, 2nd Royal Scots Fusiliers and 2nd Royal Fusiliers who would form the right prong of the infantry advance with Dundonald's Mounted Brigade on its right flank.

The 2nd Infantry Brigade, comprising the centre prong, was commanded by 54-year-old Major-General Henry Hildyard who had been the first of Buller's subordinate generals to reach Natal after being diverted from Cape Town. It was the men of the 2nd Brigade who had engaged the Boers at Willow Grange. Hildyard had not seen as much active service as most of his fellow brigade generals. Before transferring to the army and the 71st Highland Light Infantry, he had spent five years in the Royal Navy. Later he served with his regiment in Cyprus and Gibraltar before seeing action in the Egyptian Campaign of 1882. His 2nd Brigade was composed of 2nd Royal West Surrey Regiment, 2nd Devonshire Regiment, 2nd East Surrey Regiment and 2nd West Yorkshire Regiment. The division's task would be to advance directly towards Colenso village.

The 4th Infantry Brigade was commanded by 54-year-old Major-General Neville Lyttelton, another old Etonian and a very athletic officer who had won the 100 metres track event at school. Like Buller, he had served against the Fenian Raiders in Canada. He had also seen active service in Egypt and latterly in the Sudan. His brigade was composed of 2nd Scottish Rifles, 3rd Kings Royal Rifle Corps, 1st Rifle Brigade and 1st Durham Light Infantry. Lyttelton would give support to Hildyard's and Hart's brigades.

The 5th or Irish Brigade, commanded by 55-year-old Major General Arthur Fitzroy Hart, had been allocated the position of the left prong. Hart had seen active service during the Ashanti and Anglo-Zulu Wars. He had also been on Colonel Wood's staff during the so-called First Boer War of 1880 and would thus also have known Buller well. The Irish Brigade was composed of 2nd Royal Dublin Fusiliers, 1st Connaught Rangers, 1st Border Regiment and the 1st Royal Inniskilling Fusiliers.

Artillery support, including the naval guns brought up from Durban, was under the overall command of Colonel Charles Long of the Royal Field Artillery. The total fire power included two 4.7 inch and four 12-pounder long naval guns, and two batteries, the 14th and 68th Royal Field Artillery, each consisting of six 15-pounder guns, with each gun being drawn by six horses as were the ammunition limbers. An additional battery, No. 72 RFA, was attached to the Mounted Brigade.

This considerable army of over 22,000 men, had been designated the South Natal Field Force, the command of which had been given to a 60-

year old Irishman, Lieutenant-General Cornelius Francis Clery, a dandy and an eccentric who, to enhance his appearance, regularly dyed his whiskers. He was another Zulu War veteran but there any past association with Buller ended, as he had no other ties of campaign comradeship, unlike other general officers. Nor, like others, could Clery claim the bond of being an old Etonian. Clery had spent much of his military career as an instructor of tactics at Camberley Staff College but little on active service, and he had never commanded troops in action. Although he would issue the orders of battle in his own name, they were given entirely at Buller's direction.

Opposing the South Natal Field Force, on the opposite bank of the Tugela, was an invisible enemy—or perhaps there was no enemy there at all? There was no evidence of gun emplacements, trenches or rifle pits which would be essential if the Boers were to challenge Buller's crossing. All was silent and unruffled by activity. However, the burghers, now under the generalship of a younger man than Piet Joubert, had been hard at work constructing fortifications. Working only during the hours of darkness and covering the evidence of their labour with foliage and brushwood, they had built a series of bastions and, at river level, facing the drifts and the still undamaged iron road bridge, several miles of trenches. They had also sunk, so it was rumoured, and anchored in the bed of the river where the attackers would have to wade, coils of barbed wire.[58] The brilliance of their camouflage and concealment was described by one disgruntled British correspondent as 'devilish and unfair'.

The new Boer General, 37-year-old Louis Botha, was himself a Natalian by birth, having been raised in Greytown for the first few years of his life. However, his family had moved to the Orange Free State before Botha had reached his teens. He was mostly self-educated and, apart from skirmishes with the Zulus, had little military experience until the recent encounters with the British and the raid he had led against Willow Grange. His vitality and personality would have to compensate for his lack of experience.

Manning the defences were a number of miscellaneous commandos, mostly bearing the names of the towns and villages from which they hailed: Wakkerstroom, Utrecht, Standerton, Krugersdorp, Vryheid, Bethal, Boksburg, Carolina, Utrecht, Vrede, Heidelberg, Zoutpansberg, Ermelo, Middleburg and the Orange Free State. There were also detachments of the Johannesburg and Swaziland police.

One Boer position, in fact, was to be found on the south side of the river. The 260-foot Hlangwane Hill was a prominence that dominated Colenso, two miles away, and overlooked the British right flank. Botha saw Hlangwane as a position that must be held but, for any commando to stay isolated with the river at its back cutting it off from its comrades, was not to be contemplated. At first, after a British bombardment, the burghers refused to occupy Hlangwane and their reluctance to do so was supported by their commander, Commandant Briel. However, Botha, aware of its strategic importance, played a trump card by telegraphing President Kruger and gaining his support. The Boer commandants then drew lots and it was the daring Wakkerstroom Commando, who had captured the armoured train, that pulled the short straw; 600 strong they crossed the Tugela and climbed Hlangwane just as Buller prepared to launch his assault.

As mentioned earlier, many of the British officers and men present, including Gatacre and Wauchope, newly arrived in the Cape, had a year or so before been fighting the Dervishes in the Sudan. Buller and Dundonald had fought the legendary Fuzzy-Wuzzys earlier, likewise Barton and Long. They, and the men who had accompanied them in the Sudan, would be well aware of the awesome power of the modern killing machinery.

The British casualties at the Battle of Omdurman were fewer than 100; Dervish casualties totalled 2,000 dead and 4,000 wounded. However, the foe the British faced at Omdurman was primitive and armed with no more than fanatical courage and fearsome weapons little advanced from the time of the crusades. Now the soldiers of the Queen were about to encounter an enemy whose weaponry was equal to theirs and who, although brave, would become renowned for stealth rather than fanatical courage.

The pouring rain and bitter cold, that had been the lot of Brigadier-General Yule and his column during their march from Dundee to Ladysmith, was past. Summer had arrived and by 4.30am on 15 December 1899, as the sun rose out of the plain into a cloudless sky, it was evident it was going to be a scorcher. Even at that early hour the troops groaned as they laced up their heavy boots and bound their legs with regulation woollen puttees, a type of cloth legging, knowing that in the heat of the day to come the puttees would do much to make life very uncomfortable. One good thing at least, the sun would be on their backs and glaring into the eyes of the enemy.

Buller had, through Clery, issued his battle plans the evening before. They were now to be implemented. On the far right Dundonald and his Mounted Brigade rode off to engage the forces on Hlangwane; the colonials with their slouch hats, bandoliers of ammunition and heavy moustaches, gave the column a brigandry appearance. As they rode, the dust, as fine as mist, was kicked up by the horses and turned gold by the rising sun, enveloped the column, casting the riders as silhouettes against the morning sky. Some have said it was an error to send mounted men to take a 'precipitous' hill, but Hlangwane, although steep, was hardly precipitous, as demonstrated by the Boers themselves who, under the command of J. A. Joubert (not to be confused with Piet Joubert), had reoccupied Hlangwane in the dark only an hour before Dundonald left camp. Furthermore, the objective was ten miles from the British lines over stony and uneven ground: a long march for infantry in the heat of midsummer.

To the left of the mounted column Barton's 6th Brigade, with its fusilier regiments, stepped out towards the Tugela. Its task was to support Dundonald and to protect Hildyard's 2nd Brigade of county regiments as they advanced towards Colenso. Hildyard's objective was to cross the Tugela by the iron road bridge and take the hills beyond. Barton was also to give support to Colonel Long's batteries of field artillery which in turn would support both brigades. Across the river, Colenso village and the iron bridge would be defended by the Krugersdorp, Heidelberg and Vryheid Commandos.

Lyttelton's Brigade of Light Infantry Regiments was to advance to a point, about a mile to the left of the road bridge, where it would be in a position to support both Hildyard's and Hart's brigades. The Irishmen had been instructed to cross the Tugela by a ford known as Bridle Drift. In the hills confronting the drift, waiting in complete silence and concealment, were the Zoutpansberg, Orange Free State, Middleburg, Ermelo and Police Commandos, commanded by Commandant Van Rensburg, General Cronje and General Fourie.

The naval gunners, under the direct command of Captain Percy Scott, RN, followed in the wake of the Royal Field Artillery. Scott also commanded HMS *Terrible* from whence the guns had temporarily been borrowed. The Boer artillery was the most modern and technically advanced in the world and drastically outranged the British field guns. Therefore, Scott devised a way to even the odds; two 4.7 and 12 long 12-pounder, quick-firing guns had been dismantled from his ships anchored in Durban Harbour and mounted on makeshift carriages ingeniously constructed in the Natal Government Railway workshops. He had found some 4-inch iron bars in a blacksmith's shop and likewise some iron plate. Following this discovery, and working round the clock, the guns were mounted and rolling within 48 hours.[59] They were drawn by teams of oxen handled by uniformed enlisted black civilians who, understandably, saw no reason to be shot or blown to bits themselves when the battle started. Both they and the oxen would be unwilling combatants.

On the British side there had been little reconnaissance. They knew the Boers were there but had no idea of their exact locations, defences or their number. It could also be said that the only action faintly resembling reconnaissance was a two-day bombardment of the northern bank by the big naval guns. However, even this failed to produce any reaction and, after expending hundreds of shells, Buller had no more idea of where the Boers were hiding than he had before a shot had been fired.

By 5am, the whole of Buller's army was on the move:

The scene . . . was one of unparalleled attraction as the sun peeped over the eastern hills and sent its rays down upon the embattled British legions, proudly marching on their way to combat. There would be death to many, possible defeat to all, in that huge disproportionate array of England's might and military pride, now sweeping on in majestic motion, like a resistless flood, over the resounding veldt. It was war in all its spectacular glory, as seen from where the little force of warrior farmers and beardless boys gazed with fascination but fearless eyes upon the wondrous living picture of 20,000 marching men; and war with all its horrors to the fathers and sons of families who looked upon the thousands of their country's foes whom they must in a few moments meet in the shock of deadly strife.[60]

Buller and his staff, armed with telescopes and binoculars, watched the breathtaking array of Britannic military might fade into the haze as it neared the river. The General had taken up a grandstand position about four miles from the Tugela from whence he could see the progress of all the columns. Dundonald's horsemen were now well on the way to Hlangwane and, despite the additional bombardment the hill had received since daybreak, the shelling had not so much as provoked a single rifle shot in return. The Wakkerstromers, who now occupied the hill, had not only managed to scramble a Creusot cannon to the top that very morning but they had also demanded the court martial for cowardice of Commandant

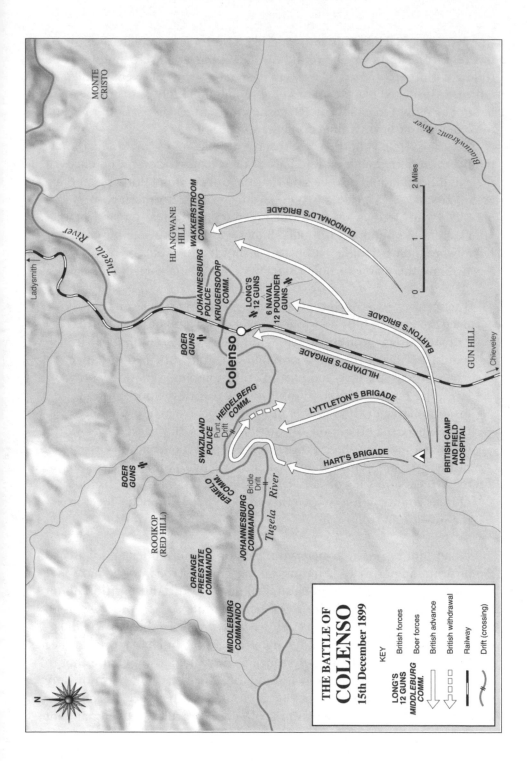

THE BATTLE OF
COLENSO
15th December 1899

KEY

LONG'S
12 GUNS   British forces

*MIDDLEBURG
COMM.*   Boer forces

     British advance

     British withdrawal

     Railway

     Drift (crossing)

Briel, the former commander of Hlangwane, who had earlier fled. By daylight the new defenders were well ensconced, having the benefit of the trenches dug earlier by Briel's men.[61]

Lord Dundonald's force included No. 7 Battery RFA, although shooting uphill would not do much harm to Hlangwane. Shortly before 7am the mounted column was in place a mile from the base of the hill. The men were dismounted and were formed into skirmishing order while the horses and their handlers took shelter in a donga.[62]

Five miles to Dundonald's left, the Irish Brigade was nearing the river. Hart, vainglorious and contemptuous of danger had, before leaving camp, subjected his soldiers to 20 minutes' drill—whether a punishment for some collective offence or merely to put some swank into their stride we shall never know. Now the brigade was advancing in 'quarter columns', that is the men were 'shoulder to shoulder', supposedly finding courage and comradeship in closed ranks as though they were marching on the French at Waterloo; to add to the illusion that the men were soldiering in a bygone age, there were officers on horseback waving their swords. Two months and several battles later, a correspondent wrote of Hart:

> . . . In the van rode an officer with polished straps and sword glittering in the morning sun. This was General Fitzroy Hart, and the troops were the gallant Irish Brigade . . .[63]

Although led by Hart, the brigade was being guided to the river by another, or perhaps two other persons; some accounts say this was a white man while others maintain the guide was a local Black, a spy in the employ of the Boers. In any event the so-called guide strode out in front of the brigade while Hart confidently followed. The objective was Bridle Drift, a crossing of the Tugela where, no doubt, Hart would have been assured his brigade could wade chest-deep. Perhaps it could have done so, but we will never know as the guide veered away to the right, taking the brigade into a bag-shaped, enclosed loop of land, with the river bank on three sides—a killing ground for a concealed enemy. Inconceivably, of the 4,000 men being led into this death trap, none had taken the opportunity to reconnoitre the intended crossing and thus avoid the slaughter that would shortly follow. Through his telescope, General Buller, four miles away, watched the Irish Brigade, still in quarter columns, march into the ambush.[64]

At about the same time, striding out to the left of the railway line and across the road to Ladysmith, Hildyard's column of county regiments had all but reached the road bridge over the Tugela that would lead them into the village itself. Half a mile beyond the village, in the Rooi Koppies (Red Hills) and Fort Wylie, which rose behind the river, the burghers crouched in their rifle pits and trenches, lying low beside their guns.

This was the formation of Buller's three-pronged attack, with Lyttelton's rifle regiments and Barton's Fusiliers, marching slightly to the rear, poised to render support as the need arose.

All the while since daylight, British guns had pounded the invisible enemy positions, the lyddite shells exploding in fumes of foul green and sulphuric smoke as though the very devil himself were at work and assisting from below. The first of the burghers to pull the trigger were those of the Wakkerstroom Commando on Hlangwane. From their position, the highest point on the battlefield, they could see the British advance laid out before them like a panorama. They had been ordered by old Commandant Van Rensburg not to fire until the enemy were only 500 yards away—he would tell them when to pull the trigger. The younger men, anxiously fidgeting with their Mausers, sweated for the order to fire. Suddenly, a Boer cannon barked back at the British guns and the burghers were no longer able to restrain the temptation to respond. It was taken as the awaited signal and all along the line the cannons, Maxims and Mausers, having been denied the opportunity to shoot back for so many days, now enjoyed an orgy of retaliation.

The first of those to suffer from the hail of bullets were the parade ground marching men of Hart's Brigade. As the wave of flying lead, fired from just across the river, shattered all before it, the division deployed—or was disintegrated—into some form of open order. The casualties were dropping quicker than could be counted but still there was no tangible enemy for the Irishmen to fight.

As Sergeant A. J. Windrum of the Royal Inniskilling Fusiliers later wrote:

> Company after company advanced on their position. The men, dropping like leaves, managed to get as far as the river, but could not cross it as it was too deep, and the enemy's advance trench was only 200 yards off. They could concentrate too heavy a fire on us to allow a bridge being thrown across it. . . It's all very well when you can see something to shoot at, but the beggars never show themselves.[65]

All was confusion, a military mass of men within the narrow confines of the riverine loop. Some shouted orders to advance, others shouted to retire. At one point a few men near the river bank, and perhaps within sight of Boers huddled on the other side, decided it was better to take death to the enemy than to be shot down in a riverside trap. They surged into the river and, as they did so, a 14-year-old boy, Bugler Dunne of the Royal Dublin Fusiliers, on his own initiative sounded *The Charge*, persuading his comrades by the blood-rousing notes of his bugle, to follow him across the river. Follow his comrades did but they were shot down. Dunne was wounded and survived but lost his bugle in the Tugela, giving Britain the opportunity to try her hand at public relations: Dunne was presented with another bugle by none other than Queen Victoria herself. His deed also evoked what must be the most inane jingle of the war:

> Bugler Dunne, Bugler Dunne, you are missing all the fun,
> And another chap is bugling where the battle's being won.
> Don't you hear the ringing cheers of the Dublin Fusiliers,
> Bugler Dunne?[66]

and so on.

H. W. Wilson in *With the Flag to Pretoria* reporting on the same incident, wrote:

> At last the Dublin Fusiliers reached the ford and attempted to cross. But the Boers had dammed the river, and in place of three feet of water there was seven. Yet, burning with enthusiasm and determination to get at their enemy, a number of men plunged boldly in. Several were carried down by their heavy rifles and cartridges; others were caught by the barbed wire which the Boers had placed in the stream. Only a handful reached the other side, climbed the steep bank, and, led by a colour sergeant . . . with the words, 'Let's make a name for ourselves and die!', doubled forward towards a kraal, a little way beyond the river.[67]

Having succeeded in fording the Tugela, they advanced on the *kraal* and one by one the men dropped wounded; no one reached it but the sergeant. Alone he could do nothing; so he turned and fled unharmed, and regained his battalion.

Although used as an excuse for Buller's devastating defeat at Colenso, it becomes obvious that the difficulties of the Boer defences were exaggerated by both the British Army and the war correspondents. It was reported in the press that the Tugela varied in depth from seven to ten feet with coils of barbed wire anchored to the bottom, yet the Dublin Fusiliers, laden with heavy boots, uniforms, rifle and 150 rounds of ammunition, were able to cross without either swimming or drowning. As will also be seen later in the battle, there were other examples of the relative ease with which the Tugela was crossed.

Buller must have been dumbfounded at the sight of Hart's column entering the loop. He immediately ordered an aide to gallop out and stop the advance but the courier was delayed by bad ground and the Irish Brigade continued its death march. Distraught with apprehension, Buller watched its annihilation as the men floundered to and fro, seeking either escape or an enemy to fight. A second messenger was sent and as he galloped with orders for Hart to withdraw at once, a large body of Boers, having forded the river, appeared with the obvious intention of making a flank attack on the retreating Irishmen. The situation was saved by General Lyttelton's brigade which was ordered forward with the cryptic message from Buller: 'Hart has got himself into a devil of a mess down there—Get him out!' As the Irishmen withdrew, the veldt inside the loop was strewn with the bodies of 500 of their comrades.

The centre prong of Buller's plan had also advanced. Hildyard's county regiments had stridden unwaveringly out towards the road bridge and Colenso village. Slightly to their right and rear marched Barton and his Fusiliers. At a steady trot, accompanied by the sound of jingling accoutrements and pounding hooves, 12 guns of Colonel Long's RFA overtook the infantry.

Hildyard's men reached the bridge and, with the feeling that many eyes watched their every stride, they cautiously began to cross. Some actually got into the village itself just as Long's guns, set out in parade ground order and with ammunition limbers to hand, opened fire at what was hoped to be the Boer defences. However, Long and his guns, positioned as though awaiting inspection, were at the mercy of the marksmen crouched in their elevated trenches on Fort Wylie and the Rooi Koppies. Fortunately for Hildyard, as we have heard, an unknown Boer, whether out of excitement or anxiety, could hold his fire no longer and the trap prepared for the county regiments was prematurely sprung. It had been Botha's plan to lure Hildyard's whole brigade either onto the bridge, or into the village where, cooped together like the Irish Brigade, they would be at the mercy of his hidden burghers. Thus, most of the brigade halted short of the bridge in open order, presenting themselves as difficult targets even for the skilful enemy. However, for Long and his artillery, it was a different matter. The guns were not equipped with armoured shields to protect the gunners and as soon as the horses were unharnessed, the men went about the drill-book firing procedure. This meant that over 350 men and 280 horses were in the open and positioned within easy range of the Boers across the river. Discharging seven rounds a minute per gun, Long's artillery opened fire at the still invisible enemy and in return received a retaliatory fuselage of 7,500 Mauser rounds in the first 60 seconds. It was a massacre brought about by ill-defined orders and Long's impetuosity. Long would blame Buller for the disaster and vice versa. Long's batteries, plus the two naval long 12-pounders, which were still to the rear of the RFA, had got too close to the enemy. Long would state that he had followed Buller's instructions but would later admit that in the prevailing visibility, he had gone further than he had intended. However, Buller continued to blame Long for the loss of the guns, the loss of which Buller further claimed was responsible for the catastrophic defeat which was now inevitable.

Buller had seen Long's cavalcade of artillery pass down towards the river where it had become lost from view. He had then heard the guns open fire but, within a short while, the bombardment had dwindled to a halt and he immediately called for an officer to ascertain the reason for the silence, informing the man that if the batteries were suffering from enemy fire they were to withdraw immediately. The officer returned shortly, reporting that all was well. Obviously he was lying and one can only assume that, on seeing the carnage, his courage failed and, rather than relaying Buller's orders, he had fled.[68] However, Buller, guessing the worst, set out with his staff towards the guns encountering two officers who had been with Long's batteries. They informed Buller that the guns had been abandoned, that every officer and man had been killed or wounded and that Long himself was in a critical condition. Buller and his staff then galloped on to seek out Hildyard whom Buller instructed to withdraw from the road bridge and to open fire on the Boer positions but on no account to engage in an attack.

Meanwhile, Dundonald's assault on Hlangwane, embarked upon with enthusiasm by the colonials, had, like the cool of the morning in which they had started, fizzled out under the scorching sun. Having left their horses behind with the handlers, the men in skirmishing order had advanced on the ominously silent hill. However, soon the distant clamour of Hart's disaster had reached both them and the waiting Boers; suddenly the crack and whine of Mausers warned the colonials that death was on the wing. The defenders, looking down on their vulnerable foe from the safety of their hill, joked between themselves. Their Maxim-Nordenfeldt was hammering away with such vigour that Ludwig Kràuse joked that it sounded like Old Dietzsch Krog, a builder from Pietersburg, putting up a tin roof. From their eyrie they clearly saw what must have been an element of the County Brigade making its way towards the scene of Long's disaster. It was being led by an officer with a dog that was mad with excitement, barking and jumping up and down at its master—distant targets for the Boers. Taking sighting shots and watching through a telescope they calculated the range as their bullets kicked up little plumes of red dust. Soon they had the distance and the Tommies began to fall. Then a troop of British cavalry, perhaps the Dragoons or Hussars attached to the Mounted Division, suddenly appeared below, making their way as though to bypass Hlangwane; the burghers held their fire until men and horses were only 100 yards away; 78 troopers were dropped from their saddles and a further 13 were captured.[69]

The colonials had made a gallant attempt to get to grips, hand to hand, with the burghers, but the dead and wounded that now dotted the plain between the donga and the foot of Hlangwane gave testimony to the marksmanship of the invisible defenders and the futility of the assault. Dundonald had called upon Barton for support but Barton, hearing of the disastrous attacks all along the river, refused to give assistance. The colonials either managed to reach the shelter of the donga where they had left their horses or lay prone for the rest of the burning day behind meagre outcrops of rock and shrubbery. Left behind were 136 dead and wounded.

Up on Hlangwane the burghers were also able to witness the destruction of Long's guns. Years later Krause, in admiration, recalled the bravery of the attempted rescue. Initially he wondered why the guns had become silent.

> . . . Why do they not speak? We turn our glasses that way, and the reason becomes clear. Every man around those cannon is down— killed or wounded. The earth around is covered with little tongues of dust where the Mauser bullets and the Pom-Pom shells strike. Look at that brave fellow, trying to ride in to save those guns, he

has hooked on one cannon—there, down he goes, his horse too. Another tries—and he too goes down. We see another approaching up a donga, he races in—he secures one of the cannon, he turns and races back, into the friendly donga. But now the Boers have their eyes on that donga, and the Pom-Pom shells drop all over it, and hurl to the ground the daring spirits who again and again would rush to save the guns.[70]

Buller and his staff pressed on to where General Clery had set up a temporary headquarters in a large donga some distance to the rear of the now abandoned artillery. Further out in a much smaller donga, and close to the silent guns, Long, wounded in the liver, lay rejecting any suggestion that the guns should be abandoned, ranting: 'Abandon, be damned! We never abandon guns!' In fact, for as long as the ammunition in the limbers lasted, the guns continued to fire. Long shouted, as one by one his men fell: 'Ah! My gunners! My gunners are splendid! Look at them!' Buller had also been slightly wounded, struck by a chunk of shrapnel, its force much expended.

The question asked was, was there a chance of retrieving the guns and saving them from the ignominy of capture? Losing guns in battle was tantamount to an infantry regiment losing its colours. Traditionally soldiers died to save the flag: a famous example having been enacted not 20 years earlier, and close by, when two officers lost their lives carrying their regimental colours from pursuing Zulus. [71] The guns must be retrieved. Buller called for volunteers. However, his first thought was to get the naval guns further back to safety but this presented a serious problem: the oxen had bolted as had most of the black drivers. Under heavy fire an NCO and a number of gunners, most likely from the ammunition supply teams of Long's batteries, hitched up some horses and, at a walk, took the naval guns away. Buller then turned to his ADC, Captain Henry Schofield of the Royal Horse Artillery, asking if he had a proposal and at the same time calling for volunteers from those who had found cover in the large donga occupied by Clery's temporary head-quarters. Only six men, Corporal Nurse and five other ranks, stepped forward. Buller then eyed the officers of his staff and also those of Clery's and said: 'Some of you go and help.' [72] Three officers did not hesitate. With Nurse and his men, and two teams of horses, Captain Henry Schofield was the first away. Seemingly leading a charmed life, he and his team galloped through a 'tornado of bullets' and, despite a gear jamming on the first gun that they attempted to rescue, two cannons were brought away, Nurse and the other men limbering up just 'as though it were a summer day outing'. Schofield had six bullets through his clothing but did not receive a scratch.

There were a few gunners sheltering in the small donga who, still unwounded, could have assisted with the manhandling of the guns but who made no effort to leave their precarious protection. The only volunteer to step forward was not a gunner at all but an infantryman, Private George Ravenhill of the Royal Scots Fusiliers who had, somehow or another, ended up in the small donga. He calmly held the horses and did not return to shelter until the gun was saved.[73] He was awarded the Victoria Cross but some years later, having been convicted of stealing six shillings worth of metal, he was sentenced to a month in prison and his name was removed from the VC Roll. However, before Ravenhill died, King George V declared the VC should never be forfeited: 'Even were a VC to be sentenced to be hanged for murder, he should be allowed to wear the VC on the scaffold.' Ravenhill's name was reinstated on the roll.[74]

Perhaps the Boers had been taken by surprise by the courageous audacity of Schofield's rescue team but, enraged at the loss of what they already anticipated to be their spoils of war, they were ready for the next rescue mission. Led by Captain Walter Congreve and Lieutenant the Honourable Freddy Roberts, son of Lord Roberts, they were shot down before they reached the guns. Congreve's clothing was struck twice, his riding cane shot in half and he was hit in the leg and, as he lay prone, his horse having been killed beneath him, a bullet entered the welt of his boot, coming out of the toecap and just missing his foot. Despite his wounded leg, Congreve managed to scramble into the small donga, dragging Freddy Roberts behind him. Roberts, who only moments before had set out on the suicidal ride '. . . laughing, talking and slapping his leg with his stick as though we were on the mall at Tashawar again',[75] now writhed in agony from a mortal wound in the groin. Congreve found plenty of company in the donga: a delirious Colonel Long with his second-in-command, Colonel Hunt; Colonel Bullock of the Devons (most likely the officer with the dog at whom Krause had shot) and a number of his men; the brave Private Ravenhill; several dozen gunners, wounded or otherwise; and Major Baptie of the Royal Army Medical Corps whose horse had been hit three times as Baptie rode to attend the wounded. All lay prone in the small donga, under the vicious sun, where they would have to wait, being driven mad by thirst for several hours until a truce was arranged and the wounded collected. However, ten guns still remained undefended and volunteers to effect their rescue came forward from the shelter of the big donga. Lieutenants Schreiber and Grylls, Corporal Knight and two gunners of the 66th Battery attempted to gather a team of unwounded horses, but before they could get a gun harnessed Schreiber was shot dead and Grylls wounded. The attempt was abandoned. One final venture was made. Corporal Warner of 14th Battery, who at that moment was behind the firing line procuring ammunition, was seen in the saddle of the lead driver clearly intending to gallop to the guns. However Buller, distraught at the loss of so many lives and especially that of Lord Roberts' only son, ordered Warner to halt saying that enough lives had been lost.[76]

It was about 11am. The battle had already been lost and won.

Buller gave the order for the British forces—those who could—to retire. In the attempt to retrieve the guns, including Major Baptie's ride to succour the wounded, seven Victoria Crosses were awarded and 28 distinguished conduct medals. For some reason Lieutenants Schreiber and Grylls were merely mentioned in despatches.

Buller was a shattered man. One correspondent, watching him and his staff dismount, wrote: '. . . The General climbed down limply and wearily from his horse like an old, old man. I thought he was wounded with vexation; I did not know he was wounded—badly bruised above the ribs by a fragment of shell.'

However, as far as the ordinary British soldiers were concerned Buller was still their General. Trooper Billings of Buller's bodyguard, reminiscing after the battle recalled:

All the time we were going along at a walk with General Buller in front, he did not seem to care a bit for all the bullets and shells, and I saw them bursting all around him; he never even turned his head, but walked on as if nothing had happened. I think General Buller is about the bravest man I have ever seen and he is also a very nice man to speak to.[77]

Buller also no doubt admired the British soldier so long as he was obedient, fought his country's battles and kept his place. However, Buller was strongly opposed to other ranks being elevated to the officer class. Only seven years earlier, when Adjutant-General at the War Office, Buller was asked to give his opinion with regard to commissioning out of the ranks and he replied:

I am strongly opposed to any scheme which would tend to increase the number of candidates from the ranks . . . To deliberately descend to debased articles when we can usually expect to get the pure ones would be a grave mistake.[78]

Perhaps Trooper Billings would have had second thoughts about his General, whose life he and the rest of the bodyguard protected, had he been aware he and his fellows were regarded as 'debased'!

The Boers, seeing the British withdraw all along the line, now started to cross the Tugela, either aboard their swimming horses or wading, holding their rifles above their heads. Those British who had not withdrawn and who were insufficiently incapacitated to be regarded as hospital cases, were expected to surrender. Such was the situation as the first cautious burghers approached Long's donga, whose occupants were unaware that those who could, should have retired. The burghers found not all those within, despite having lain there for close on six hours without water, were ready to surrender. A white flag was brought, beneath which the sides could parley, but Colonel Bullock would have none of it, ordering the Boer commander away and instructing his men to fix bayonets and open fire. Again the Boers sought to parley; the British donga, with Boer riflemen on all sides and a Pom-Pom to back them up, was little more than an open grave waiting to receive its dead. However, despite the entreaties of Major Baptie and other persuasive emissaries, Bullock would hear no word of surrender even when some of his men elected to become prisoners and departed of their own accord. Drawing his revolver, Bullock threatened to shoot the Boer commander; the situation was saved, as was Bullock's life, by an ancient burgher felling Bullock with a rifle butt.[79]

As the burghers grew bolder and more crossed the river, the British ambulances and stretcher bearers began their grisly task of gathering the dead and tending to the wounded. Although the year was 1899, it was a 20th-century battle field, the horror of which would, within a few years, be replicated all over Europe and the Mediterranean. It was not until well into the afternoon that many of the wounded were tended, by which time the flies had long since reached them: buzzing black nests, entrenched in every wound, repellent hordes investing every orifice of those wounded and those who came to their aid.

An American, surprisingly permitted to roam the battlefield with a camera—a camera he could not bring himself to use—recalled:

It was the most harrowing scene I ever witnessed. Khaki uniformed men lying about everywhere, deluged in blood, faces horribly distorted and swollen and black. A piece of shell had caught one in the head and opened up his brain. I was inexpressively affected by the sight, and after covering up as many faces as we could, turned away.[80]

And still the guns, starkly militant, with the dead gunners strewn resolutely in position all about, awaited their fate. Buller had forbidden any further attempts at rescue. His alternatives to saving the guns from the enemy were either their destruction, by blowing them to pieces with his naval guns—an act that could have been accomplished in moments—or waiting until nightfall and then mounting a new rescue mission. However, he did nothing, giving the burghers the opportunity to wade the river and stigmatising himself with the reputation of being the only British general to have lost ten guns without the enemy having had to place a hand upon them.

At about 4pm, Field-Cornet Joseph Emmett, a descendant of the Irish patriot Robert Emmett, and a brother of Louis Botha's wife, led a contingent of 200 burghers and Johannesburg Police commanded by Lieutenant Pohlman, to take Long's guns. Pushing and pulling by sheer manpower—exposing the false tales of the river's depth and the barbed wire anchored to its bottom—the guns that a year previously had helped to destroy the Dervish army were put aboard a train and taken to Pretoria, there to be exhibited to the gleeful and amazed populace as the spoils of war.[81]

So ended Black Week, as the defeats of Stormberg, Magersfontein and Colenso would come to be known; and Buller would be held responsible. As bad as his case was, it was he himself who then made it worse. Depressed, wretched and having failed utterly as a Commander-in-Chief in the war he most likely wanted no part of, he foolishly heliographed White the following day:

I tried Colenso yesterday but failed; the enemy is too strong for my force, except with siege operations and these would take one full month to prepare. Can you last so long? If not, how many days can you give me in which to take up defensive positions? After which I suggest you firing away as much of your ammunition as you can and making the best terms as you can.[82]

A further thought followed:
Also add to end of message: whatever happens, recollect to burn
your cipher, and decipher and codebook, and any deciphered messages.[83]

Lord Lansdowne also received a communication which advised him
it was Buller's view that he, Buller, had insufficient forces to relieve the
town, and he '. . . ought to let Ladysmith go, and occupy a good position
for the defence of south Natal and let time help us.'
Buller was advocating the surrender of Ladysmith: an ignominious
defeat, the captivity of 13,000 British troops and the enemy's seizure of
massive supplies of food, stores and ammunition. Not to mention the possible immense political repercussions—the feared uprising of the 'Dutch'
and an even more nightmare prospect of 75,000 rampaging Zulu descending on Natal. However, it is possible that Buller was already harbouring
a nascent and irrational thought that it was not he who had commanded
the Battle of Colenso and it was not he who was responsible for the defeat.
In 1902, a Royal Commission, comprising numerous imminent military, judicial and academic personnel sat in London to enquire into the
conduct of the war that had cost Britain so much in lives, money and prestige. On 17 February 1903, Buller was duly summoned to give evidence
and no doubt he startled his inquisitors by stating that it was not he who
ordered the attack on Colenso. He maintained:

On that evening [December 14th] I assembled my commanders,
and in the presence of them all explained to each his part in the
disposition for the morrow. Each commander with his troops was
to occupy a specific place, and to await the results of the general
bombardment before leaving it. On the morning of the 15th
December, the troops moved into their appointed positions.
    My intention was that they should remain there, out of fire
and at ease, while I ascertained by practise, the accurate range of
all the points from which opposition could be offered to our
advance.[84]

Buller continued to describe how, as the guns were taking up their
position, he happened to notice Hart's division had already left its starting
block and was about to enter the killing ground of the river bound loop.
He continued to relate how his messengers had tried to stop Hart, but to

no avail. Buller then produced a report signed by General Hildyard, of which he only read a few lines:

> The orders received were to seize the koppies north of Colenso when the bombardment had made itself sufficiently felt. Before this movement arrived the commander-in-chief informed me that owing to the loss of the guns the attack could not be carried out . . . [85]

Said Buller: 'I only wanted just to read that to show that there was no attack at all . . .'

Further questioning followed: "Had you' [he was asked] 'intended to attack?'

To which Buller replied: 'Fully. I had given all my orders the day before.' [86]

So Buller would have had the Commission believe that because he did not pull the trigger of the starting pistol himself and because the advance began prematurely—if, indeed, it really did—he was not responsible for the disaster that followed.

Would it, one wonders, have made any difference to the outcome of the battle if the British guns had thrown their ineffective salvos at the illusive Boer positions for another couple of hours whilst Buller's army stood by, its energy being sapped by the fiery sun? That would be for the Royal Commission to resolve three years later.

Shortly after the receipt of Buller's message suggesting that Ladysmith be abandoned, Arthur Balfour, the deputy Prime Minister, went to see Queen Victoria. Her Majesty was not amused and was deeply concerned for the morale of her Empire: She would not countenance despondency; she told Balfour: 'Please understand that there is no depression in this house. [Windsor Castle] We are not interested in the possibilities of defeat; they do not exist.' Having been so informed, Balfour decided to pass the message on to Buller by cabling a communication bordering on rudeness: 'If you cannot relieve Ladysmith, hand over your command to Sir Frances Clery and return home.'

Lansdowne, however, had to make an immediate decision and determined that Buller must go. However, who was to replace him? 'Bobs', Lord Roberts of Kandahar was the answer. At the age of 57 he was perhaps too old, but still full of vim and vigour and although only 5 feet 2 inches in height, he was the holder of the Victoria Cross and one of

Britain's most able generals—in fact, he had recently been appointed to the rank of Field Marshal. To his immense grief, his mortally wounded son would, within a day or so, die in the field hospital at Chieveley.

Lansdowne consulted the Prime Minister, and Roberts' appointment was readily approved. It was, however, an extraordinary step; it could be said clandestinely done, as neither the Commander-in-Chief of the British Army, Lord Wolseley, nor the Queen, were consulted. Wolseley's exclusion was significant as will be seen later. The man appointed as Roberts' Chief of Staff was a current British hero, though undoubtedly an aloof one; Lord Horatio Herbert Kitchener of Khartoum who, together with Long's guns, had smashed the Dervish Army and had avenged the death of General Gordon a year earlier. Buller would be allowed to remain as General-Commanding Natal with the possibility, in due course, of relieving the besieged garrison of Ladysmith.

Apart from the camera man from the USA, there was another American present, an official military observer, Captain Slocum, 8th US Cavalry. He impartially summed up the battle for his masters in Washington as follows:

> . . . A striking feature of the battle was the total invisibility of the enemy, not a Boer being seen during the fight.[87]

General Louis Botha, writing to President Kruger, began his brief victory report with the simple words: 'The God of our fathers has today granted us a brilliant victory.'

In comparing the number of British casualties against those of the Boers, it was more than brilliant—it was astounding. Impartial Captain Slocum put the British loss, killed, wounded or missing, at 1,167 whereas most historians agree that the Boer loss was fewer than 40 killed, wounded or taken prisoner.

....

CHAPTER FIVE

INSIDE LADYSMITH—
READY TO SALLY FORTH

What of the Ladysmith garrison and the civilians who had now been imprisoned in their tin town of heat, disease, danger and privation for 44 days? Could not the 13,000 soldiers have sallied forth, making a grand total, together with Buller's force, of 38,000 troops for the Boers to contend with? No doubt the besieged were as eager to fight their way out as the would-be liberators were to battle their way in.

Sir George White, aware that the relief force was just across the Tugela, 18 miles away, had exchanged messages with Buller on 13 December, two days before the battle. White had asked for the probable date of Buller's assault and had received a rather vague reply stating the actual date would depend on 'difficulties encountered', but would most likely be four days hence, on 17 December.[88] White asserted to the Royal Commission that he immediately assembled a formidable strike force containing the numerous cavalry regiments which had remained in Ladysmith. Buller felt that said regiments should never have been permitted to stay there, as their function as cavalry was so demeaned they were little more than a burden on resources—that is until the starving garrison began eating them—but that came later. On 14 December, White was ready to lead forth, in person, six cavalry regiments: the 5th Dragoons, 5th Lancers, 18th Hussars, Imperial Light Horse, elements of the Natal Carbineers and the Border Mounted Rifles, plus over 5,000 imperial infantry, five batteries of RFA and various support units.[89] However, White did not know whether the battle was on or off—or so he said. Admittedly, Buller had suggested the 17th as the day he would most likely strike, but as it happened he was two days early. Yet, how was it that such crucial information, the date and time of the attack, could not be communicated between the two armies? As we have seen, the 15th was a blazing hot day, ideal for the heliograph. It would also have been a fairly normal occurrence for a native runner (agent/spy) to have made his way through the Boer lines carrying the vital information.

If we try to imagine the scene inside Ladysmith early in the morning of the 15th, it is reasonable to assume we would conjure up a picture of Sir George White sitting on his charger, surrounded by his staff, about to address the beleaguered garrison: the infantry in their thousands; the Highlanders, the Fusiliers, the County Regiments and the Rifle brigade, each one proud of its name and traditions; the cavalry with the troopers astride their impatient horses, surrounded by the noise of jingling bits and stamping hooves, lances at the ready and swords drawn– a fearful spectre to an enemy whose memory of Elandslaagte was but a few weeks old— all in array with the townsfolk cheering and waving the troops on to fulfil the hope of delivery. However, it was not like that at all.

It was a day much like the other 44 that had passed by in boredom, fear and increasing hunger. Donald Macdonald, the Australian war reporter of the *Melbourne Argus*, who kept a highly informative account of the siege, makes no mention whatsoever of seeing White's strike force drawn up and ready to go forth. It seems impossible that an army of thousands could have been assembled within the confines of Ladysmith without all and sundry, especially a war correspondent, being aware of its existence. Following the siege of Ladysmith, White had been criticised for not doing more to assist the relieving force. When questioned by the Royal Commission in 1902 he replied that he had published:

> . . . a Special Natal Field Force Order on the 14th of December [ordering the assembly of the troops already mentioned] in anticipation of having the opportunity of helping Sir Redvers Buller's force . . . I dwell on this to show that I had before me intelligence which had led me to believe that an attack would take place on the 17th of December, that I got that information on the 13th of December and that I immediately issued that order with a view of having everything in readiness, when I got the opportunity of moving out, to assist as far as my means would admit, of the advance of Sir Redvers Buller's force.[90]

It therefore seems reasonable to assume from White's testimony that having received intelligence of an impending attack by Buller, and having 'immediately' put his strike force in readiness, White would have been eminently situated to assist the relief force the moment he was aware, either by signal, intelligence or the sound of battle, that the advance had begun. However, no action was taken and the strike force, if it ever were in fact assembled, was stood down. The official history of the Natal Carbineers, some of whom formed part of the strike force, merely comments: 'On the 15th [December] hopes of relief ran high in Ladysmith in consequence of firing heard from Colenso.' [91] There is no mention of a strike force.

Donald Macdonald also described the morning of the 15th:

It was three mornings since we first heard the canon [sic] of the relief column—'The deep thunder peal on peal afar'—and this morning (December 15) we heard the same distant rumble, no nearer, no further off. At daylight it was constant as a beat of a drum; at noon we heard it in fainter bursts. There was heavy fighting down there on the Tugela River, and we were out of it. Interlarded with the distant canon [sic] came rumour with tales more or less roseate, taunting us with tidings of victory in which we have no share. The first far away roar, the kaffir runners said, was the heavy English guns shelling the Boers out of their picked positions on the western bank of the river. They stood miles off, said the black scouts, and threw their great shells without the Boers being able to reach them in reply.[92]

However, he makes no mention of White's strike force (nor does the official history of the Imperial Light Horse[93]) and continues with a litany of glum observations commenting that only five days' supply of fresh meat remained for the garrison, even though the daily ration had been cut by over half since the siege began, and that Angora goats, once grazing the hillsides in their thousands, had all but gone. On a more cheerful note he mentions bread, cheese, pickles and especially Quaker Oats, were still plentiful.

The only reference this author has found that may collaborate White's testimony, is a diary entry, 13 December 1899, of Major G. F. Tatham, Natal Carbineers, (Ladysmith Siege Museum) who recorded: 'Mounted parade, heavy marching order, 8 p.m. Wagons etc. All parade and dismissed.' However, heavy marching order and wagons would be burdensome paraphernalia with which to attempt a lightning strike. The assembly time of 8pm and the date of the 13th are also baffling.

Macdonald also asserts that the bombardment of the town was unrelenting, if somewhat ineffectual in relation to the number of shells fired each day, and people became blasé rather than brave. There was almost a vague intimacy with the Boer gunners as often they could be seen as they went about their drill in preparation to fire. The *Staatsartillerie*, uniformed and trained by the German Army, were as smart and professional as their counterparts of the Royal Artillery but the burgher gunners of the commandos had their own method of doing things. Macdonald recorded:

> I watched them [the burghers] from Kings Post on Wednesday through a first rate glass [telescope]. The gunners came up on horseback, went through their work, and retired, perhaps a quarter of a mile to the rear, leaving one man to fire the gun. He had a fast horse and a long lanyard—about 200 yards I should say for he went quite that distance back before the gun was fired, then galloped off hurriedly to join the rest. They stayed under shelter for a time, and if our guns did not reply came slowly back again to the redoubt.[94]

Macdonald noted that he could count to 20 from the time the flash of the 'Long Tom' was seen until the missile struck.

Day by day, the population marvelled at their good fortune as morning after morning saw most of them still alive as though immune to shellfire. There were hairbreadth escapes to be related by one and all. During one such incident, Sir George White and his staff were sitting for a photograph when a 'Long Tom' shell hit the building and burst in the cellar, destroying the dining room where breakfast had just been laid. On the same day a missile made a direct hit on the Royal Hotel, penetrating a bedroom and exploding in the empty dining room. Another shell crashed into a child's bedroom completely taking a wall away, the child however, amidst the dust and rubble, was miraculously unhurt. However, a policeman in the street was not so lucky and was killed instantly by a fragment of the same shell. One poor man, enjoying the luxury of a bath on his veranda, was put to flight when a projectile from a 'Long Tom' ricocheted off a tree, struck the house without exploding and, spinning like a top, crashed into the bath, spilling the bather unharmed across the floor.

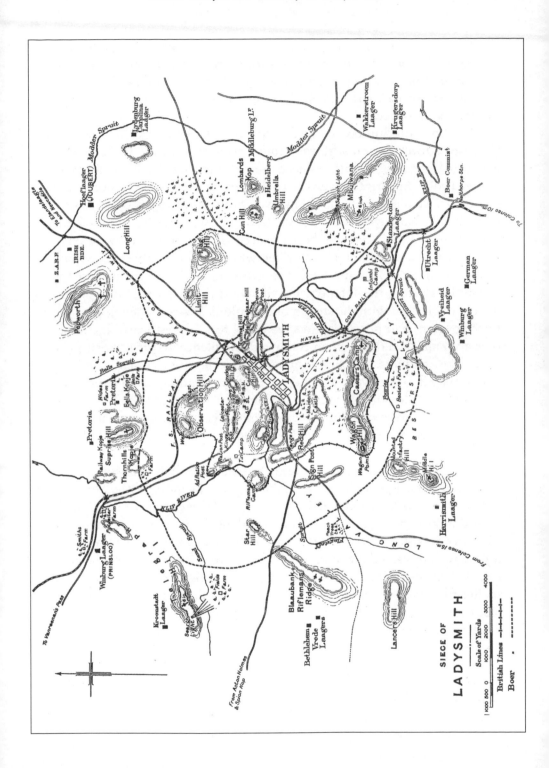

SIEGE OF
LADYSMITH

Scale of Yards

1000 500 0   1000   2000   3000   4000

British Lines ⊢⊢⊢⊢⊢
Boer ═══════

The burghers were not having it all their own way, though. Shortly before Buller's attempt to take Colenso, there was another night sortie against the Boer guns' positions. After the successful raid carried out by the colonial troops there was much competition amongst the Imperials to cap the locals' success.

At 10pm on Sunday 10 December, five days before the Battle of Colenso, a force drawn with the utmost secrecy from the Rifle Brigade began to assemble with the objective of destroying the Boer howitzer entrenched on Surprise Ridge. The raiding party was under the command of Colonel Metcalfe and was led by two scouts of the Natal Guides, local men familiar with every aspect of the terrain. It was decided to follow the plan of attack that had earlier been so successfully carried out by the colonials: 200 men would climb the ridge whilst 150 on either side would guard the flanks. The approach was slow and full of caution lest the enemy be alerted; the infantry, heavily shod in their issue boots, were unable to proceed with the stealth of the colonials who, when near to the Boer position, had proceeded in stockinged feet. Nevertheless, the imperials accomplished the climb in commendable silence, to the utter surprise of the Boer gunners. The first intimation that the riflemen had of having reached their objective was when one of the leading scouts suddenly realised he was looking straight up the barrel of a six-inch gun. The raiders froze in expectation of being blown to smithereens but, with no sound or movement from the foe, realised they were, as yet, undetected. Then, excitement and aggression taking hold, the riflemen surged forward, bayoneting the dumbfounded burghers seemingly before a sound was uttered. The occupants of the redoubt, 20 men or more of the *Staatsartillerie*, were quickly routed in the darkness and somewhat confused fighting—the Boers making little effort to stand against the lunging bayonets. The way was soon clear for the British artillery men and engineers to follow with tools and gun cotton with which to not only disable the guns but also demolish the magazine. Charges and fuses laid, the raiders took shelter from the blast that was about to follow but, as an anti-climax, the fuse to the guns was defective and only the magazine exploded with a roar loud enough to awaken every burgher for miles around. It took 25 minutes for the raiders to prepare another fuse and to lay the gun cotton, giving the Boers ample time to retaliate.

In ever increasing numbers the burghers came scrambling up the ridge so that the retreating riflemen were all but surrounded shortly after fleeing from the summit. It was assumed that the rattle of rocks, cascading down the slopes, caused by the hurrying Boers, had been dislodged by comrades guarding the flanks, and men shouted: 'Don't fire; we are Rifles', only to receive a Boer volley at close quarters. One officer was killed, another seriously wounded and a number of men put out of action, several being left for dead. A second Boer volley quickly followed with equal effect but before a third could be discharged Captain Gough shouted 'Fix bayonets', and, the gathering light illuminating the intervening ground, the rifles charged, scattering the burghers.

It was an expensive sortie: on the British side 11 killed, 43 wounded and six taken prisoner. The Boer loss was unknown until one British officer hit on the idea of checking bayonets for signs of blood. The inspection revealed that 96 burghers had been killed or wounded.[95]

Despite the number of British casualties, the tally was thought to be light considering the number of burghers present and the volleys fired. Having examined the Mauser rifles captured that morning, it was found that the Boers' somewhat erratic shooting was most likely due to their rifle sights being marked in metres as opposed to yards, the standard marking of the old, and much favoured, Martini-Henri single shot rifle that had recently been replaced by the Mauser. However, an even greater blunder had been made with the sighting of British rifles. Twenty-five thousand soldiers had gone to South Africa with the new Lee Enfield, the mechanics of which were the same as the superseded Lee-Metford except for the grooves of the rifling. The variation caused the weapon to shoot 18 inches to the right at 500 yards. Fortunately, the error was discovered during the last days of 1899 and the superintendent of ordnance factories in Britain immediately proceeded to make a back-sight that would rectify the blunder –whether or not it restored the British soldier's confidence in his marksmanship is not mentioned.[96]

By Monday 18 December the rumble of guns from the Tugela had become fainter: the relieving force was moving on. The Boers, having despatched Buller's army, were now able to turn their attention to forcing the surrender of the town. Six hundred shells were fired into Ladysmith that day. To make matters worse, the temperature soared to 104 degrees in the shade and when the humming, hunting mosquitoes, having made the night a misery, retired with the dawn, the flies took over, inflicting torment with equal ability, 'on every side death, sickness and despondency'.[97] It was a circumstance that the besieged would have to contend with for many weeks to come.

There was another dedicated diarist in Ladysmith, a civilian by the

name of James Bayley, who was engaged to a girl in England to whom he
wrote almost every day. His fiancée compiled his letters once the siege was
over. James was mostly concerned with his business, a furniture shop,
which he continued to run with various ups and downs throughout the
siege. He generally records the amount of the dwindling daily rations,
his Town Guard (TG) duties and the continuous bombardment. However,
he also mentioned that on 12 December, the TG were ordered by the
colonel of the Natal Carbineers to prepare for active service as all the
regular troops were required for service in the field; a reference, perhaps,
to White's intended strike force? Bayley also mentions that the price of
eggs was 18 shillings a dozen and that the town was rife with smell and
sickness.

. . . .

CHAPTER SIX

CHURCHILL RETURNS

Throughout the Empire the events of Black Week left Britain dumb-founded and humiliated. In just a few days, from being unassailably, in her Britannic might, the envy of the world, she and her generals had been put to shame by a largely uneducated, undisciplined army of bush farmers who had never seen a drill book, who would not know how to salute even if they had the inclination to do so and whose commanders had got no nearer to a Staff College than outlining tactics in the sand with a stick.

The feeling of gloom and doom was commensurate with a death in the family. Then, like a Victorian Superman, he returned. Churchill had escaped. His youthful face, his gay demeanour and his heroism were the perfect tonic. It was just what everybody from the lowest scullery maid to Queen Victoria herself needed. And this included Buller. If Britain was yet to be victorious, at least she now had a live hero. Churchill had been captured on 15 November, incarcerated in Pretoria, and now, on 24 December, he was back in Frere.

A few years earlier, when contemplating a future military career, he had realised that belonging to a regiment of Hussars would be an expensive business (Polo, pig-sticking, mess evenings and the like), requiring a lot of money of which, since his father's death, he and his mother had very little. Like many other young officers, he had hoped he would have the opportunity of active service and the promotion that commendable conduct under fire would provide. However, there was little prospect of this prior to the Anglo-Boer War; he had written:

. . . In 1895 scarcely a captain, hardly ever a subaltern, could be found throughout Her Majesty's forces, who had seen even the smallest kind of war . . . and there has never been a time when war service was held in so much esteem by military authorities or more ardently sought by officers of every rank. It was the swift road to promotion and advancement in every arm. It was the glittering gateway to distinction. It cast glamour upon the fortunate possessor alike in the eyes of elderly gentlemen and young ladies.[98]

The young Churchill, by pulling strings and by his mother's influence in high places, had likely seen more active service than anyone else of his age in the entire British Army but, even so, the promotion ladder had been a wearisome one to climb—so wearisome in fact that he abandoned it and set his sights even higher: a seat in parliament. However, in that endeavour he had been unsuccessful, losing a by-election for the Oldham constituency in Lancashire. Therefore, reverting to war correspondent and, in the hope that his despatches from South Africa would bring fame, fortune and a seat in parliament at the next election, he had set off in the armoured train. Risking his life, as he had done around the derailed armoured train, was one thing—risks had to be taken if the prize was worthwhile—but there were no glamour or prospects in being captured and spending the foreseeable future in a prisoner of war camp.

As the order was given to march, Churchill resolved to escape and called on the Boer commander to observe his status of a civilian correspondent, and set him free. However, his militant actions had been witnessed and he was marched off with the rest of the survivors who, wet to the skin in the unrelenting rain, and escorted by 20 or more mounted men, rifles at the ready, sloshed their way for six hours along tracks deep in mud before they halted for the night. During the march Churchill had conversed with a number of his captors in a most amicable way, causing him to ponder as he tried to sleep:

> Vexation of spirit, a cold night, and wet clothes withheld sweet oblivion. The rights and wrongs of the quarrel, the fortunes and chances of the war, forced themselves on the mind. What men they were, these Boers! I thought of them as I had seen them in the morning riding forward through the rain—thousands of independent riflemen, thinking for themselves, possessed of beautiful weapons, led with skill, living as they rode without commissariat

or transport or ammunition column, moving like the wind, and supported by iron constitutions and a stern, hard Old Testament God who should surely smite the Amalekites, hip and thigh . . . And then, above the rainstorm that had beat loudly on the corrugated iron, I heard the sound of a chant. The Boers were singing their evening psalm, and the menacing notes—more full of indignant war than love and mercy—struck a chill into my heart, so that I thought after all that the war was unjust, that the Boers were better men than we, that heaven was against us, that Ladysmith, Mafeking, and Kimberley would fall, and the Estcourt garrison would perish, that foreign Powers would intervene, that we should lose South Africa, and that would be the beginning of the end. So for the time I despaired of the Empire, nor was it till the morning sun—all the brighter after the rainstorms, all the warmer after the chills—struck in through the windows that things resumed their true colours and proportions.[99]

Having marched to Elandslaagte Station, the scene of the only engagement of the war so far that could really be classified as a British victory, the prisoners were bundled aboard a train, Churchill sharing a first-class compartment with the officers. However, he was about to revise his high opinion of all Boers in general and to reserve his admiration for those burghers of the veldt whilst condemning the spite with which the train was greeted at Pretoria Station. Gone was the camaraderie of enemies who had fought in a common battle. Churchill found himself in the grasp of unfriendly officialdom and, to his mortification, a scruffy unshaven police sergeant who grasped his arm and told him: 'You are not an officer, you go this way with the common soldiers.' However, no doubt as a result of many protestations, he was, with much relief, led away past the gawking populous to the State Model School, the place of the officers' incarceration, while the common soldiers were marched to a tented camp on the race course.

Churchill was taken prisoner on 27 November, escaped 27 days later and, aided by the most incredible luck and daring, was back in Frere, via Portuguese East Africa and Durban, by 24 December. The full story of his escape is too long to be recounted here, but it must be mentioned that the break from prison was planned, not by Churchill but by Haldane and a Sergeant Major Brockie. These two men were reluctant to include Churchill in their escape bid and in the event it was only Churchill who succeeded in getting away resulting in controversy in the years to come.

Churchill's triumphal arrival in Durban assured him of another chance to stand for parliament. He returned home to contest Oldham once again, and was greeted with rapturous enthusiasm.

> I received the warmest of welcomes on returning home. Oldham almost without distinction of party accorded me a triumph. I entered the town in state in a procession of ten landaus, and drove through the streets crowded with enthusiastic operatives and mill-girls.[100]

Churchill would sneak in with a mere 230 votes ahead of his opposition and immediately set off on a lecture tour describing the South African War, earning £3,782 in 35 days. In the USA, his average fee per night was £50 for a series of 50 lectures.[101] His political career was on the way. It was a career that 40 years later would cause his name to be synonymous with victory over the Axis Powers. It is no idle speculation that World War II would likely have been lost in 1940 if it were not for his inspired leadership. Yet, it was a career that may never have been realised had it not been for the blaze of publicity his actions at the armoured train ambush created. It may be said that the course of world events was determined at a bend of the railway line between Frere and Chieveley. It is a spot where this writer has often stood in contemplation of what might have been. Although Natal is spectacularly beautiful and many of its numerous battlefields are set amidst the most handsome scenery, the site of the armoured train incident is forlorn and ugly with no hint of its immense historical importance. There is a small memorial, no more than four feet square, enclosed by iron railings, that reads:

This marks the place
where the armoured train
was wrecked
and
the Right Honourable Winston Churchill
Captured by Boer forces
November 15, 1899.

....

CHAPTER SEVEN

THE GENERALS CONVERGE

Far away in England, in Autumn 1899, Sir Charles Warren was cycling back to his modest home in Ramsgate. He enjoyed cycling, it kept him fit in his retirement as did walking and golf. As he swung along the country lanes past the stark leafless trees of winter, he was thinking of Africa, pondering on his chances of securing a command against the Boers: not very good, he concluded. Being honest with himself, he reasoned that:

> . . . All the existing commanders of divisions were good men, and there were plenty more who might get selected before my turn came . . .[102]

So having given it much thought, he decided his best chance of getting to South Africa was to apply for a posting with the St John Ambulance Brigade. However, they suggested that before going any further, he should make sure the army had no plans for him. Therefore, he wrote to the War Office on 25 October (11 days after the Battle of Colenso) and to his immense surprise received, almost by return, a letter from none other than Lord Wolseley, the Commander-in-Chief of the British Army, saying that he had heard of Warren's illness and asked if he, Warren, was fit in every way for work. Warren, who had not been ill at all, commented:

> I felt capable of doing anything I could be asked to do, that I found my energy and powers of endurance were not in any way im-

paired, and I was quite satisfied I could do a hard day's work in the saddle as well as most young men in South Africa; I could walk thirty five miles against many of the best . . .[103]

A few days later, he saw Lord Wolseley. The meeting was not long in duration but its outcome would sow the seeds of the biggest and most controversial British disaster of the Anglo-Boer War. Warren was appointed to command the new 5th Division that was being assembled, ready for departure for South Africa before the end of the month. What he did not know was that he would carry with him a dormant commission that read: '. . . That in the event of any accident overtaking Sir Redvers Buller you are to take supreme command in South Africa.' This was just prior to Lord Roberts' appointment which, of course, changed matters completely.

We have to ask ourselves, did Wolseley know who Warren really was? Had he mistaken him for someone else? Is it likely that an officer who had been far from being a 'fighting general', and had been on the shelf for two years, spending his days cycling and playing golf, would suddenly, at such a crucial time, be given the second most important command in the British Army?

Some have described Warren's appointment as inexplicable. Unquestionably there are indications that Wolseley was under a misapprehension perhaps brought about by illness, overwork and advancing age. We have seen that, only six weeks later, without Wolseley's knowledge and as though he were a figurehead of no consequence, Roberts was appointed Commander-in-Chief in South Africa.

Five years previously Wolseley had out manoeuvred both the Duke of Cambridge and Lord Roberts to become the new Commander-in-Chief of the British Army. However, now, in 1899, his memory was inclined to blunder. Joseph Lehmann quotes that Wolseley could not remember the immediate past and that on receiving an old comrade whom he was expecting, he was likely to declare: 'I'm delighted to see you, no one told me you were coming!' Then after a break and a renewal of the interview, a surprised Lord Wolseley would say: 'Oh! How nice to see you, nobody told me you were coming!' It got so bad that there were times when he didn't even recognise his own secretary.[104]

Wolseley's lapse of memory appeared to have worsened further. Giving evidence before the Royal Commission in November 1902, he made the following replies to questions to which he should have been able to snap out the answers:

'I do not know.'
'I should think so.'
'I may have, but I cannot remember.'
'I do not know that . . .'
'I have no doubt I had. I cannot remember.'[105]

Whatever the circumstances of Warren's appointment may have been, it is certain that the animosity it would cause between him and Buller would do much to turn the next British attempt to relieve Ladysmith into another British catastrophe. Seldom had two commanders, appointed to work together, differed so greatly in background, service and opinion as did Buller and Warren. It is interesting to compare the diversity of their careers. Buller was the older by a mere three months. He came from an old and aristocratic family that could trace one line back to a John de Redvers, a companion of William the Conqueror; other ancient connections included the Dukes of Norfolk and the Earls of Devon. His was a wealthy family with estates in Devonshire and Cornwall, totalling over 5,000 acres. However, his generation of Bullers were a sickly lot: of his ten siblings, four died in childhood. The death of his mother, whilst Buller was in his early teens, affected him deeply. From private preparatory school, he attended both Harrow and Eton, but not Sandhurst; he entered the army by way of a purchased commission.

Warren's father had been a general, also by the name of Charles Warren who had served at Waterloo in the 80th Foot and had later fought in the bloody battles of the Crimea. While Buller was attending elitist public schools, Warren the younger received a grammar school education at Bridgnorth, later proceeding to Cheltenham before, unlike Buller, sitting the entrance examination for the Royal Military Academy, Sandhurst, which he passed with flying colours. From Sandhurst Warren, having sat further entrance exams, won a place at the Royal Military Academy Woolwich, a seat of learning for future engineer and artillery officers.

Having passed out from Woolwich as a Lieutenant of Royal Engineers in 1857, Warren was posted to Gibraltar to assess the defences of 'The Rock', a mundane and unexciting prospect. At the same time Buller had received a commission as an ensign in the elite 60th Rifles, his father having duly paid £450 to the General Commander-in-Chief at Horse Guards. The 'Sixtieth' as the regiment was known, had been raised 100 years earlier to fight the French in Canada and, unlike most British regiments, wore green jackets instead of red.

While Warren was carrying out a trigonometrical survey of the Rock, Buller found himself on the way to India where elements of mutineers were still active. On landing at Calcutta, he was assigned a convoy of women and children to escort on a 500-mile journey to his regimental station. Britain had recently acquired the island of Hong Kong and, with other European powers, had been endeavouring to enforce the importation of opium in to China, which the Chinese government had vigorously resisted, culminating in the murder of British envoys. An expedition of Royal Navy warships and troops had been assembled, including the 60th, and soon Buller and his comrades were off to the exotic East and briefed for combat. The Taku Forts, at the entrance to the Peiho River, were stormed in ferocious combat reminiscent of medieval times. Later the 60th confronted a charge of armoured Tartar cavalry. Finally, in 1860, Lord Elgin, as punishment for the envoy murders, gave orders for the burning of the Emperor's Summer Palace, consisting of scores of exquisite buildings and their contents. It was the all-clear for British and French troops to indulge in an orgy of looting—Buller included. Despite his condemnation of the war, which he made known by refusing to wear the medal awarded for the campaign, he did indulge in the plunder, taking a few choice pieces home for his siblings at *Downes*.[106] Then, after a pause, the 60th were off again. Instead of the heat, colour and mystery of India and the East, the regiment was destined to spend eight years amongst the frozen wastes of Canada.

Warren, during most of this time, had been either surveying Gibraltar or working at the Royal Engineers' depot in dreary Chatham. However, he too was about to be offered the chance of an exotic and extraordinary opportunity, although it would mostly lack all military merit. In Europe there was great interest in discovering the lost sites of the Holy Land. A society with many prominent people amongst its members, called The Palestine Exploration Fund, required a competent engineer and took Warren on loan from the British Army.

His instructions were to find

the Temple of Solomon . . . the date of the Dome of the Rock . . . whether the Church of the Sepulchre was built on the tomb of Joseph . . . What were the lines followed by the three walls at Jerusalem as described by the Jewish historian Josephus . . . Where were the gates of the city, referred to in the Bible . . . Where was the City of David, the Castle of Anatonia, the Palace of

The remains of British entrenchments on the Platrand. The Boer attack was made from the valley on the left. *(Author's collection)*

Buller's observation post on Mount Alice. Twin peaks is in the distance and the Tugela River is at the right of the middle ground. The crosses are memorials, not head stones; ironically one is to Buchanan Riddell and another to Buller.
(Author's collection)

Boer graves just beyond the crest line, on northern slopes of Spion Kop.
(Author's collection)

Boer entrenchments on the Rangeworthy Heights. Ntenjwa, the dark hill in the distance, was the headquarters of the British Cavalry Brigade.
(Author's collection)

The British main trench. Once the fighting was over it served as a convenient excavation for a mass grave. *(Author's collection)*

This photograph clearly illustrates how exposed the plateau was to the sweeping fire from Twin Peaks, which can be seen in the middle distance. The plateau was equally exposed to enemy fire from at least four other positions with, in addition, friendly fire from Mount Alice. *(Author's collection)*

Twin Peaks. The Kings Royal Rifles took cover in a large donga concealed in the left foreground, before scaling the saddle between the peaks. *(Author's collection)*

The memorial to the Wakkerstroom Commando, one of the most aggressive units of the Transvaal Republic. Its daring is reflected by the many names of those killed in their fight for freedom. *(Author's collection)*

The dismounted Imperial Light Horse storm the Boer position at Elandslaagte moments before a violent storm engulfed the battlefield in hail and rain. ('The Battle of Elandslaagte' from the painting by W. B. Wollen)

The defeat of Major-General George Pomeroy Colley and his troops at Majuba in 1881 was an added incentive for British retribution against the Boers. *(The Illustrated London News)*

Having defeated General Colley at Majuba, triumphant Boers celebrate and wave their Republican flag. *(Author's collection)*

After the initial skirmish at Elandslaagte, British forces withdrew and, having tapped the telegraph wire, called Ladysmith for reinforcements. *(The Illustrated London News)*

As early as 1876, the Boers had established a Krupp artillery battery manned by volunteers. It was the forerunner of the Transvaal State Artillery.
(With the Flag to Pretoria)

The charge of the 5th Royal Irish Lancers at Elandslaagte. The merciless charge, with lance and sword, weapons abhorrent to the Boers, was made as they were in retreat. Although the charge was justified within the rules of war, it caused an international outcry which Britain countered with this picture of the young trumpeter who, seemingly, had been the target of Boer machine gunners. Note the numerous expended rounds of ammunition. *(National Army Museum)*

British troops aboard the armoured train scan the passing countryside.
(With the Flag to Pretoria)

Men of the Dublin Fusiliers and the Durban Light Infantry attempt to rally
amidst the wreckage of the armoured train. *(Black and White Magazine)*

Winston Churchill, with his back to the camera and wearing a flat hat, arrives as a prisoner in Pretoria. The policeman in the foreground is undoubtedly the official who wished to imprison him with the common soldiers. *(With the Flag to Pretoria)*

Men of the Dublin Fusiliers, trapped within a loop of the Tugela River at Bridle Drift, are mown down by an unseen enemy. *(Authors collection)*

Winston Churchill, after his escape from Pretoria, poses in front of the armoured train wreckage. (*With the Flag to Pretoria*)

Boer commandos pose with their Mauser rifles. Note the clip loading of the magazine which differed from that of the British Lee-Metford rifle which was loaded one round at a time. *(With the Flag to Pretoria)*

Lieutenant-General Sir Redvers Buller was in overall command of British troops in Natal. *(The Illustrated London News)*

Lieutenant-General Sir Charles Warren, Buller's second in command, directed operations leading to and including the attack on Spion Kop. *(The Illustrated London News)*

Commandant-General Louis Botha commanded Boer forces at Colenso and Spion Kop and thereafter until the end of the war. *(Africana Museum, Johannesburg)*

Commandant-General Petrus ('Piet') Joubert. As a five-year-old child he accompanied his parents on the Great Trek. He fought in many native wars and defeated the British at Majuba. He died in November 1900, having handed over command of Boer forces to Louis Botha. *(Africana Museum, Johannesburg)*

Left: A studio picture of Bugler Dunn taken on his return to England. Queen Victoria presented him with a new bugle to replace the one lost during the attempted crossing of the Tugela River. *(The Illustrated London News)*

Below: In the middle distance Colonel Long's guns, with parade ground precision, deploy unprotected against a fortified and undetected enemy. In the foreground the oxen and their handlers, drawing the heavy naval guns, hurriedly seek shelter. *(Black and White* Magazine)

The Batttle of Colenso. The wounded are treated at a field dressing station before being carried from the battlefield. Note the Indian stretcher bearers.
(With the Flag to Pretoria)

Colonel Long's No. 5 gun. Within minutes of opening fire only two of the gunners were left alive, one running backwards and forwards with ammunition whilst the other fired the gun. Moments later they too were shot down. *(Black and White* Magazine)

There were several courageous attempts to rescue the 12 abandoned guns. At the cost of numerous killed and wounded men only two guns were successfully recovered. (*National Army Museum*)

Two resolute gunners stand firm as hidden Boer marksmen pick off easy targets. (*National Army Museum*)

Herod, the tomb of Bathsheba and other important places?[107]

Working in the most appalling conditions of choked up sewers, hindered by 1,000 years' of rubbish, dragging himself through claustrophobic tunnels, descending into ancient wells before the needle-sharp eyes of a million rats, Warren painstakingly drew his blueprints of an ancient world. However, the Palestine Exploration Fund was not the affluent organisation it had first appeared and Warren, with a wife and small children in England and only a spasmodic salary, returned to the army. His discoveries remained the key to further archaeological exploration in Jerusalem but although his achievements may have been of great moment to theologians, it is doubtful if his work in Palestine would have accelerated his military career. It did, however, earn him the sobriquet of 'Jerusalem Warren'.

When Buller returned to England in 1869, he had been away for 11 years out of a total of 12 years' service and, like Warren, had made little progress up the promotion ladder. Buller, on leave in Ireland but rather despondent, received heartening news of a potential war in Canada, the land he had so recently left.

Due to the fear of an influx of British settlers into the prairie lands of the Red River Territory, the local Métis, a people of mixed Indian and French blood, arrested the British Lieutenant Governor. Then, led by one Lee Reil, a mob of armed men seized Fort Garry, tore down the Union Jack and hoisted their rebel flag in its place. Buller had recently achieved sufficient seniority to purchase a captaincy but, as there was no vacancy in his own unit he was offered a transfer to the 1st Battalion in Canada. He jumped at the opportunity and finally, in June 1870, caught up with the punitive expedition which was under the command of the rising military star Colonel Garnet Wolseley.

At the time the normal road to Fort Garry would have been through United States territory, an easy route avoiding a maze of swamps and rivers. However, it was suspected that America sympathised with the rebels, therefore a military undertaking through North Dakota was out of the question. Wolseley had no alternative but to plan a scheme necessitating travel by rail, steamer, foot slogging and the construction of 200 specially built wooden boats that, in all, would take the expedition 1,200 miles through a largely unexplored wilderness. Here Buller came into his own: with the knowledge and strength gained as a youth in manual labour and carpentry on his Devonshire estates, he was as capable as any in lugging loads, digging roads, heaving on ropes, making portages and living rough. Wolseley said of him:

> It was here I first made his acquaintance, and I am proud to feel that we have been firm friends since. He was a first class axe man, and I think he was the only man with us of any rank who could carry a hundred pound barrel of pork over a portage on his back. He could mend a boat and have her back in the water with her crew and all her stores on board whilst many, under similar circumstances, would have been still making up their minds what to do. Full or resource, and personally absolutely fearless, those serving under him always trusted him fully.[108]

Perpetual rain, black-flies by day and mosquitoes by night added to the drudgery of the journey. On 24 August, as the flotilla of boats paddled their way across Lake Winnipeg, Fort Garry came in sight. Once dis - embarked, the rebel flag and cannons could be seen but, to the universal disbelief and disappointed of the 60th, the rebels had fled. There was no one to fight, no battle, just a long journey back. However, Wolseley had marked Buller as an officer with special qualities, a man he would seek out for future expeditions should they arise.

In 1872 Warren returned to military duties. He was posted to the School of Gunnery at Shoeburyness where he stayed as an instructor for three years. Thus, so far, in his career he had seen no action and, apart from the peril of being trapped underground and falling masonry that he had encountered in Palestine, he had not been exposed to danger or hardship. In 1876 he was posted to Africa for the first time. A major dispute had arisen between Britain and the Orange Free State regarding the rights to the diamond fields of the Kimberley area where, six years previously a diamond had been found in the mud brick walls of a farm house which had stood on the site of the future Big Hole of Kimberley, causing a stampede of diggers from all over the world to descend on the place. After protracted negotiations the British Government acquired possession from the Waterboer people and Griqualand West was ceded to Britain. Warren was ordered to survey and lay down a boundary line between the Orange Free State and Britain's new acquisition. He camped at Kimberley for many months and was subjected to ferocious thunderstorms, often preceded by choking dust.

Well pleased with Warren's work, Sir Bartle Frere, the South African

High Commissioner, appointed him Special Commissioner for Griqualand West. He was also promoted to the rank of Major and made a member of the Order of St. Michael and St. George. Warren was beginning to make his mark.[109]

Buller entered Staff College in 1872 with the objective of making soldiering his long-term profession and gaining the coveted letters PSC (Passed Staff College) attached to his name. However, in Buller's eyes there were even greater prospects within his reach: whilst on leave he heard news of another expedition that Wolseley was about to embark upon. As he had left no contact address, all Wolseley's attempts to find him had been to no avail. It was only by a stroke of good fortune that Buller was able to reach Wolseley just before he was replaced by another officer. The expedition was also Africa-bound, but to a very different part of the continent from the arid semi-desert where Warren was surveying the diamond fields. Wolseley was making preparations to sail for the jungles, heat and humidity of the West Coast, where Britain maintained a number of forts, specially established to protect her trading interests and her British subjects. During the previous century the coast, labelled 'The White Man's Grave' had been the point of departure for the slave trade, a trade that Britain had outlawed in 1807 thus wrecking the lucrative income of the inland tribes who caught the slaves in the first place.

By far the most powerful of these slavers were the Ashanti, whose name was a by-word for terror, torture and human sacrifice and who, by 1873, were beginning to raid out of their jungle labyrinth which separated their capital of Kumasi from the coast, and to attack British forts. The imperial government saw itself as the protector of the coastal people and the need for a punitive expedition became apparent. Wolseley and his staff, Buller included, prepared to sail for Ashanti land. Wolseley's band of favoured officers would in future become known as the 'Wolseley Ring' or the 'Ashanti Ring'; in the same way the chosen few of Lord Roberts would be known as the 'India Ring'.

Buller was appointed intelligence officer with the task of recruiting interpreters, informers and spies; and the all-but impossible mission of mapping the terrain through a jungle beset with swamps, snakes and poisonous insects and rife with disease. Nevertheless, he was soon heading teams who hacked their way inland, constructing where necessary a wooden road of tree trunks lashed together. Within days more than half the officers were laid low with fever, amongst them Wolseley himself, the future Field-Marshall Sir Evelyn Wood and the future Major-General Sir

George Colley who, as we have heard, was to be defeated and killed at Majuba.

On 5 January 1874, Wolseley's small army of sailors, marines, the West India Regiment, the Black Watch, artillery and various locally raised levies, began its advance on the Ashanti capital, fighting two major engagements on the way. On entering the city, horrific evidence of human sacrifice on an immense scale was found. However, the Ashanti army and King Kofi had disappeared into the jungle. Apart from the sickening evidence of human slaughter at the Palace of the Vultures, piles of riches were discovered: hoards of solid gold and silver ornaments which were duly carried away as compensation.

It soon became apparent that due to the alarming rate of sickness amongst all ranks, it was imperative to return to the coast. The putrefying corpses of tens of thousands of sacrificial victims had to be burnt and the capital of Kumasi was burnt with them. Buller had been in the thick of the fighting which had claimed almost 400 British troops, killed or wounded, but now, on the return journey, he became desperately ill. It took him many months of convalescing in Devon to regain his strength. For his contribution to the campaign he earned another medal, was promoted to the rank of Brevet Major and appointed Commander of the Bath.

Shortly after returning home, Buller's elder brother, James, died making Redvers the master of *Downes*, the Buller family country mansion and estate close to Exeter in Devon. *Downes* produced a massive annual income from rents and agricultural produce. As a landed squire, it would have been normal practice for a man to retire from the army and enjoy the life of a well-heeled country gentleman. However, the army as a profession had got into Buller's blood. He was appointed to the Adjutant-General's Department at the War Office and moved into London's social life, dining on occasion with the Prince of Wales. When the chance of active service came again he quickly put down his pen, swallowed the last dregs of champagne and headed once more for Africa. A war against the Zulu king was secretly under consideration and the newly appointed General-Officer Commanding Her Majesty's troops in South Africa, Lieutenant-General the Honourable Frederick Thesiger, later Lord Chelmsford, had invited Buller to join his team. However, before a war with Zululand could be arranged, fighting further south against the Gcaleka clan of the amaXhosa, in what became known as the 9th Frontier War, would require attention.

Buller sailed to Cape Town with Thesiger and his old friend and comrade Brevet Colonel Evelyn Wood. On arrival they departed at once for the combat area located in thickly forested and mountainous terrain in which the enemy inevitably had the advantage of surprise. The fact that the conflict between the amaXhosa and the colonial settlers was labelled the 9th Frontier War is an indication of how long both sides had been at each other's throats.

The 1/24th Regiment of Foot, who were destined to be massacred a year later, almost to a man, on the battlefield of Isandlwana, were, in February 1878, stationed in the northern Transkei and had encountered the amaXhosa on several occasions. A unit of mounted infantry had been recruited from local settlers by Lieutenant Frederick Carrington, an officer of the 24th, and under the name of the Frontier Light Horse (FLH), had on several occasions successfully skirmished with the enemy. Carrington was promoted and sent to Pretoria to raise further units. The vacant command of the FLH fell to Buller and his name would not only become synonymous with the regiment, the FLH would also carry him to military fame and fortune.

Warren and Buller were now destined to meet for the first time. Warren, many miles away in the Kimberley area, presumably under orders from Lord Chelmsford, was told to pack up his theodolites and raise a regiment of colonial horsemen. It is a little difficult to visualise Warren, the surveyor and engineer officer, as a rough, tough leader of Kimberley dropouts, drunkards and criminals guilty of varying crimes, but he undoubtedly was. He originally named them the *Dutoitspan Hussars*, but later changed the title to the Diamond Field Horse (DFH). That the unit fought in the Perie Bush there can be no doubt but Warren and his men were not destined to go on into Zululand. An uprising in Griqualand brought the DFH hurrying 120 miles back to Kimberley.

Many Griquas dispossessed by one government or the other, or by the giants of commerce, were in rebellion. Warren and the DFH arrived back in Griqua Town on 10 June having ridden 400 miles from King Williams Town in just under one month. With the Administrator, Major Owen Lanyon, Warren set off to engage the rebels, which he did successfully on four occasions. Finally, with the government force being split in two, and with Warren leading the smaller column which would include some men of the 1/24th, he pursued the rebels, numbering over 1,200, into a rocky canyon where they had constructed numerous barricades. The attackers found that they could go no further without incurring heavy loss and were forced to take cover for the remainder of the day. As night closed in, Warren ordered an assault on the cliffs, called Gobatsi Heights, that dominated the rebel camp and, dragging a seven-pounder cannon with them, the DFH set about the gruelling task of reaching the summit of the Heights.[110] However, it was not until midday that, to the complete surprise of the rebels, the DFH were able to open fire on the camp below, with the rebels scattering in all directions as the shells began to land amongst their barricades. Hauling up the canon had done the trick, but the fight was not yet over. Many of the Griquas were well armed and were competent shots. Dismounted elements of the DFH and Mounted Infantry were ordered down the cliff and before the rebels could take up a cohesive defence, both sides were forced to find cover. The fight from boulder to boulder lasted for five hours until, possibly running low on ammunition, the rebels fled, abandoning all their cattle and possessions.

Warren came out of the affair with accolades: he was mentioned in despatches and appointed Acting Administrator. However, within a few months Chelmsford had invaded Zululand and said invasion was closely followed by the British disaster at Isandlwana. Warren volunteered to take the DFH to Chelmsford's assistance but, having heard of the Zulu Army's success, the rebels were inspired and the country was once again on the brink of rebellion. The DFH were ordered to stay where they were. In the autumn of 1879, Warren was invalided back to England.

We now go back several months and return to Buller who, with Wood and the Frontier Light Horse, were on their way north to Zululand. Buller and his horsemen, forever scouting ahead and reconnoitring the country on all sides, were in the saddle for 16 hours a day. Living rough in all weather, subsisting on a diet of dried meat and army biscuits, meant that he was reduced to a figure of skin and bone, attired in clothes that hung on him like a scarecrow. One trooper remarked: '. . . If we were lying in the rain and the mud, hungry and without sleep, we knew Buller would be too.'

On 11 January 1879, Chelmsford's No. 3 column crossed the Buffalo River at Rorke's Drift and entered Zululand. Eleven days later, in one of the worst defeats ever to befall a British army, 22,000 Zulu warriors attacked the column's camp destroying everything that lay within it. At the time Chelmsford with half his force was endeavouring to find the Zulus whom many historians believe decoyed him from the camp.

Wood's column was 50 miles away to the north. It was the only one of the original five columns capable of remaining active against the enemy, and the FLH was the only unit with the mobility to engage the fleet-footed warriors.

Buller persuaded Wood that he should attack the Zulu stronghold of Hlobane Mountain. By now, many more mounted units, mostly colonials, had joined Wood's column, all falling under Buller's direct command. With this force Buller attacked Hlobane. It was an ill-conceived and poorly reconnoitred assault. It led to yet another disaster with a huge casualty list of horses and men. Furthermore, in the confusion of the retreat, Buller blundered, instructing one of his officers to retire in the wrong direction. Forthrightly, Buller wrote in his report that would duly find publication in the *London Gazette:* '. . . and to my careless expression must I fear be attributed the greater part of our heavy loss on this day.' [111] However, Wood, to protect not only Buller but himself, deleted the paragraph and recommended Buller for an immediate award of the Victoria Cross. It was a recommendation that was fully justified as Buller, riding back in the face of the enemy, rescued several dismounted men from certain death. However, it was an award that was not without resentment as similar acts of valour were performed by a number of men without reward or recognition.

The following day the Zulu Army, armed with many rifles captured at Isandlwana, attacked the column's camp at Kambula. Buller led out the remaining colonial horsemen, luring the impetuous warriors into the range of the British artillery and volley fire. After five hours of intense combat the courageous Zulus retired, pursued by the colonial horsemen led by Buller who, swinging a huge *knobkerrie*, (club) and striking left and right, was described as being: '. . . like a tiger drunk with blood.' [112]

With the final defeat of the Zulu Army at the Battle of Ulundi, Buller returned to England having earned the reputation of being the *beau sabre* of the Zulu War.

Although he was now a brevet lieutenant-colonel he still only received the pay of a substantive captain. It was proposed that he be appointed an ADC to Queen Victoria but as the lowest rank assigned to the post was that of lieutenant-colonel, application was made for his immediate promotion. However, the War Office required the sanction of the Lord's Commissioner of Her Majesty's Treasury in order to increase Buller's pay. As there was no vacancy in the British Army at that moment for an additional lieutenant-colonel, the Treasury refused to authorise the appointment of Buller to Queen Victoria's ADC. One War Office authority of an accounting disposition even supported the Treasury:

These regulations are as precise and imperative as words can make them—There is not a word as to give the Treasury any authority to deviate, or allow deviations from them, and I feel assured that if we sanction the promotion of Bt. Lt. Col. Buller as proposed, the audit office will pull us up and, in my opinion, rightly.[113]

It required His Royal Highness, the Field Marshall Commanding-in-Chief, the Duke of Cambridge, to hack a way through the red tape. Buller was duly invested with the Victoria Cross and for the next two years held posts in Scotland and Aldershot. However, he was soon back in South Africa.

In 1880, as we read earlier, Britain was humiliated by the Boers, culminating in the defeat at Majuba. Buller arrived in Cape Town the day Colley was killed and Wood, obeying orders from London, negotiated a peace with the Boers that British soldiers and settlers regarded as both humiliating and discreditable. With Wood often absent in Pretoria, Buller was appointed Administrator of Natal with the temporary rank of major-general. This was a skyrocket promotion for a soldier who had been but a substantive captain two years earlier.

War having being avoided, Buller returned to *Downes* in 1882 and in the following year, at the age of 42, he married Lady Audrey Howard, a widow of 37, and mother of four children.

In the same year, Warren, who since his return from Africa had held the appointment of Instructor in Survey and Practical Astronomy at the Military School of Engineering, received secret orders concerning an exciting assignment. In 1882, British interests in Egypt, including the recently opened Suez Canal which gave passage to international shipping, 80% of which flew the British flag, were under threat. In the lead up to conflict, a rioting mob in Alexandria massacred over 100 Europeans. Britain, in preparation for war, despatched Professor Palmer of Cambridge University, an expert Arabic linguist, on a clandestine mission to win the support of the Bedouin tribes at the southern end of and beyond the canal. Palmer, assisted by Captain Gill RE and Lieutenant Charrington RN and carrying £3,000 bribe money in gold, set out on camels, not only to win local support, but to cut the telegraph wires crossing the desert. They rode without escort and it was not long before rumours began to filter back to base that they had all been murdered, their baggage plundered and the gold stolen. The British Government decided immediately that an example must be made of the felons and concluded that Major Warren, with his knowledge of the Middle-East, was just the man to bring the perpetrators to justice.

Warren left Chatham at 12 hours' notice and having duly arrived in Egypt made his way to Aqaba. He found the local Bedouins singularly unhelpful and it took several weeks before he was able to discover the remains of Palmer and his party. With the aid of British troops, Warren captured and imprisoned several hundred Bedouin, holding them hostage until the names and whereabouts of the culprits were revealed. Fifteen were then captured of whom eight were convicted and hanged.[114]

While Warren was inflicting gunboat justice on the Bedouin, Britain had embarked on a war with Arabi Pasha and the Egyptian Army. The British fleet bombarded Alexandria harbour and then, during August, led by none other than Lieutenant-General Sir Garnet Wolseley, Britain began to land an army that would eventually total 25,000 men.

Buller was on his honeymoon when he received an enticing telegram— Wolseley would be delighted to have him on his staff but he would quite understand if Buller, under the circumstances, let the invitation pass. Buller bid farewell to his new bride and was soon on his way to Egypt.

Wolseley's objective was to get to Cairo and to do so he would have to destroy Arabi Pasha's army behind its formidable fortifications situated at Tel-El-Kebir. Buller was appointed Head of Intelligence with the task of evaluating and sketching the enemy defences. For two consecutive days, with only a small escort, he was in position, a mile from the enemy lines before the sun rose. On one occasion he found himself cut off from base by a large Egyptian cavalry patrol whereupon it became a race for life across the open desert.

Relying on Buller's assessment of the opposition's defences, Wolseley reasoned that a daylight advance would be at too great a cost in lives and therefore decided to attack at night. The plan worked to perfection, with many of the British troops being within the Egyptian defences before the alarm was raised. Nevertheless, there was bloody hand-to-hand fighting though, despite the stout resistance of the Sudanese soldiers, who formed part of the Egyptian Army, the battle lasted little more than one hour. With 2,000 Egyptian dead and 10,000 prisoners, the war was over and Buller returned to England and his interrupted honeymoon. He was awarded six months' leave and a knighthood of the Order of St Michael and St George.

While Buller had been engaged in a major conflict in Upper Egypt, Warren at the other end of the Gulf of Suez had fought a little-and-now forgotten war of his own. Having dispensed arbitrary justice on the

Bedouin he, with the assistance of British troops, attacked and took the port of Aqaba. Then he too returned to England where the grateful thanks of parliament and a knighthood, the same as Buller's, awaited him. Now Sir Charles Warren, he returned to Chatham for two years and then it was back to Africa again. White men of various nationalities, but mainly English and Boer adventurers, were endeavouring to establish individual national states such as Stellaland and Goshonland; the former already being ruled as a Republic, having its own national flag, and registrar of deeds. One prominent family were the De la Reys', later of Anglo-Boer War fame—Adolf de la Rey maintained it was he who had captured Churchill at the Armoured Train. Filibustering Boers, backed by President Kruger, were Warren's main concern as with Kruger's support they were likely to establish control over territory Britain herself wished to acquire. Appointed Special Commissioner and promoted to the rank of major-general, Warren raised 5,000 men and reached Mafeking ahead of Boer reinforcements, thus catching Kruger flatfooted. A negotiated settlement followed with Warren surveying and establishing a boundary that shared the territory between the Transvaal and Britain while the 'Free Booters', as they were called, rode away empty handed.

Warren, with a job well done, once again returned to England to receive the thanks of a grateful government and yet another decoration, the Cross of St Michael and St George.

With Arabi Pasha defeated and the Khedive restored to Egypt, the Middle East appeared set for a period of tranquillity. However, a charismatic and self-proclaimed prophet calling himself 'The Mahdi', raised an army and declared a Jihad, with the object of freeing the Sudan from Egyptian rule. A punitive Egyptian force, led by a British officer, Hicks Pasha, was wiped out to a man by the Mahdi's warriors. In February 1884, another Egyptian army, again led by a British officer, Colonel Valentine Baker Pasha, had an equally tragic fate. Britain now stepped in with an army of British troops who, no doubt much to their chagrin, were commandeered from troop ships on their way home along the Suez canal. Major-General Sir Gerald Graham was appointed Commander. At the time Buller was enjoying a blissful life in England when he was suddenly ordered to proceed to Suakin on the Red Sea, in order to take up the position of second-in-command.

Graham advanced across the open desert and, on closing with the Mahdi's forces, ordered his army of 4,000 men to form one great square, half of which would fall under Buller's command. The enemy, well-armed with cannons, rifles and a Gatling gun, mostly captured from previous encounters with the Egyptians, inflicted over 200 casualties on the British force, but the disciplined British infantry eventually put the Sudanese to flight. Graham decided to follow them into the desert and confront them at an outpost called Tamai. The formation of one single square was changed to that of two smaller ones. After a 15-mile march, the expedition came face to face with the Sudanese defences amongst hills and deep ravines. Graham commanded the foremost square and Buller the one obliquely to the rear. With still some distance to go to the first ravine, Graham prematurely ordered the front line of his square to charge. It was far too soon; out of concealment a horde of Dervishes—or 'Fuzzy-Wuzzys' as Kipling famously called them—poured into the broken square. For frantic minutes it looked as if the fate that had befallen Hicks and Valentine's armies was about to descend on Graham's desperately fighting men. However, Buller's formation, despite being attacked on all sides, held firm and poured volley after volley into the closely packed Dervish ranks, driving them back and out of Graham's square.

Buller was home by the end of April, his commander having written a glowing report of Buller's military ability to the Duke of Cambridge. He was also rewarded with promotion to the permanent rank of major-general. As on previous occasions, Buller's leave was of short duration. Major-General Charles Gordon, who had been tasked to evacuate all the Europeans and Egyptians from Khartoum, had become besieged and the whole of Britain was clamouring for his rescue. After a lot of military squabbling as to who would command the relief expedition, Wolseley finally got the job, immediately appointing Buller as his Chief of Staff. There was further disagreement as to the best and quickest way of getting to Khartoum. After much wrangling it was finally decided to travel by rail and steamer to Wadi Halfa and then to paddle over 650 miles up the Nile to the final destination. Four hundred whalers, manned by imported Canadian oarsmen, were especially built, each designed to carry a crew of 12 with all their kit. The river force would be escorted by a 1,100-strong camel corps. There was further bickering regarding the failure of supplies; blame was heaped on many heads. However, it was too late: Gordon had already met a martyr's death. All that could be done was to pack up and go home to a shocked and critical England.

Buller arrived back but not to the usual acclaim he and Wolseley had grown to expect. All the same, Buller was created a Knight-Commander of the Bath and in 1885 he went back to his desk at the War Office.

Like Buller, Warren was also back in England where he decided to venture into politics standing, unsuccessfully, as an independent candidate for the Hallam division of Sheffield. The army was inclined to frown on serving soldiers who attempted to become politicians, and Warren could have considered himself perhaps fortunate that the military fold was prepared to have him back. However, it was no plum job that he was offered. Governor of the Red Sea Littoral may well sound a grand title but, in reality, the strip of land running down the Red Sea, with Suakin as its port, was as remote and unpleasant a place as could be a soldier's lot. It was also dangerous with Hadendowa tribesmen firing into the town each night. On arrival and with what troops there were available, Warren set about making an insurgent-free zone, several miles wide, around the town. However, thereafter there was little else to do to occupy a major-general's time. A few weeks later, possibly due to his success in apprehending the criminals who had killed Professor Palmer and his party, Warren received a letter from the Home Secretary offering him the job of Chief Commissioner of the Metropolitan Police. It was a far cry from Suakin and Warren jumped at it.

It is difficult for us now to comprehend that the London Warren would have to police, the capital of the greatest empire on earth, was for many of its citizens a place of misery, with much of the population existing in conditions which the most wretched of the Empire's natives were not subjected to.

George Sims in *How the Poor Live* wrote:

This mighty mob, of famished, diseased and filthy helots is getting dangerous, physically, morally, politically dangerous. The barriers which have kept it back are rotten and giving way, and it may do the State a mischief if it be not looked at in time. Its fevers and its filth may spread to the homes of the wealthy; its lawless armies may sally forth and give us the taste of the lessons the mob has tried to teach now and again in Paris, when long years of neglect has done their work.[115]

The winter of 1885/6 was the coldest for many years and a mass meeting of the unemployed was held in Trafalgar Square. What was to be a peaceful protest turned into a riot with the mob looting shops through Mayfair and down Oxford Street. This was just prior to Warren's arrival and even more serious outrages were contemplated. Trafalgar Square was a favourite gathering place for the jobless, a place not only to express their grievances but actually to live in squalid camps. Threatening to take the law into their own hands, the shopkeepers of the West End made ready to hire gangs of thugs and clean the Square themselves. Sir Charles decided to beat them to it and with an army of 4,000 constables, 300 mounted police and the backing of 600 men from the Grenadier and Life Guards, the Square was cleared and 300 men arrested who would serve various terms of hard labour. Sir Charles was both praised and roundly criticised. However, he was to have an ally of sorts, an ally who would more effectively subdue the East End than all of Warren's constables: Jack the Ripper was soon to perform his first murder.

The terror wrought by the Ripper killings left the community with little else for immediate concern. As the grisly number of murders mounted, and thousands of police failed to make an arrest, Warren came under increased public criticism and was involved in frequent altercations with the Home Office. He also made himself somewhat of a laughingstock by importing two blood hounds that would, Warren hoped, track down the killer but the experiment ended in a farce. In the midst of all this upheaval in the capital, Warren was deeply involved in the organisation of Queen Victoria's Golden Jubilee procession through the streets of the city, later receiving a letter from Her Majesty expressing her 'entire approbation' and an award of Knight Commander of the Bath. However, despite all efforts, the Ripper was never caught and his identity still remains a mystery. Warren wisely resigned in the Spring of 1888.

It seems an extraordinary coincidence that Warren should have been offered, and had accepted, a policeman's job at virtually the same moment as a similar circumstance occurred to Buller. After a year at the War Office, following his return from the Sudan, Buller received a letter from the Secretary of State for War, requesting him to accept the post of

> ... Special Commissioner or Magistrate ... for the troubled areas of Ireland where the struggle for home rule, recent famine, avaricious absent landlords, unscrupulous agents and extreme poverty was creating a land rife for insurrection. Lawlessness, involving murder, arson, robbery and intimidation was already prevalent, the main perpetrators being armed gangs known as 'Moonlighters'.[116]

Buller accepted the job, not because he thought it would enhance his career—the opposite was more likely—but because he felt it was his duty. Unlike Warren, he did not have an army of thousands of policemen. He set about his task more as a detective than a military man, wearing only civilian clothes, refraining from armed escorts and, by having Lady Audrey at his side, installed a sense of security in the land. Arrests were made, there were no more assassinations and Buller's sympathy with the poor was patent. Within months he suggested his assignment had been fulfilled and that he should return to military duty, taking up the powerful position of Deputy-Adjutant- General, under Wolseley. However, there was to be yet another surprise. He was asked to remain in Ireland and to fill temporarily the post of Permanent Under-Secretary, a civil/political position. Although it would be of short duration, and for Buller of limited success, part of the package was a 'most charming' Georgian lodge set in the 2,000-acre Phoenix Park. Buller's contempt for hypocrisy and his outspoken opinions were not always welcomed; and, no doubt, it was with universal relief that he returned to the War Office.

Warren, much to his relief, was accepted back by the army and in 1889 with the local rank of major-general, was despatched to Singapore to command troops in the Straits Settlement. It was a backwoods posting but at least it was an independent command, although there was nothing in the way of military action. Warren recalls he was the chairman of a committee appointed to inspect and report on the police and that he was the district grand master of the Eastern Archipelago Masonic Society. It was also said that he spent much of his time in strife with the civil admin-istration. In 1895 he returned to England and took command of the Thames District Division, taking part in annual manoeuvres in the New Forest. Three years later he was put on the retired list and given the rank of lieutenant-general. As far as he could see his military career was over.

Buller in the meantime, for the last ten years, had ruled as Adjutant-General at the War Office, partly during the time of the Duke of Cam-bridge and partly under Lord Wolseley. It was written of Buller:

> Moreover, Sir Redvers was also an extremely able office-chief, clear headed, broad minded, and essentially dominant. The result was that in a few years he lifted the office of Adj.-Gen. to a plane perceptibly higher than that on which the other War Office departments stood, and for a considerable period he was, next to the Duke of Cambridge, distinctly the most powerful officer in the army.[117]

However, Buller also enjoyed the good life, good food and wine, and had a paunch to show for it. As the century drew to a close and war in South Africa seemed inevitable, Buller, past the desire for active service and further military laurels, especially if it involved fighting the Boers, no doubt hoped another man would be chosen to lead any expeditionary force. Twenty years earlier, in the confrontation of 1881, he had written: 'I never looked forward with any great keenness to fighting the Boers . . . and I really do like a good many of them, besides that they had in the long run justice on their side.' [118] Now it was even more apparent that a war with the Transvaal would be doubly unjust.

Whilst Buller would have been hoping that his campaign kit, including the tin bath and portable kitchen, would continue to gather dust in some attic at *Downes*, Warren was keeping fit and watching the post hoping that a message, summoning him to duty, would drop through the letter-box.

As we have seen, it was a reluctant and disconcerted Buller who was chosen to chastise the Boers and it was not until he had presided over one of Britain's most infamous military blunders that Warren, much to his surprise, was taken off the shelf to become Buller's second-in-command without Buller having any say in the matter. It is likely that Buller would have been scornful of Warren's record as a fighting soldier, especially in comparison with his own as he, Buller, had fought in all climates from the frozen wastes of Canada to the deserts of the Sudan; he had fought Tartars, Ashantis, Griquas, Zulus, Egyptians, Dervishes and Fuzzy-Wuzzys whereas Warren, the engineer, had but two or three minor encounters to his name, the most notable getting a cannon to the top of Gobatsi Heights and dispersing a rabble of rebels.[119] Whatever Buller's opinion of Warren may or may not have been, Warren was shortly to arrive and his grating personality would soon be felt.

CHAPTER EIGHT

....

INSIDE LADYSMITH—
THE FIGHT FOR THE PLATRAND

Sir Charles Warren set foot once again in Africa in early December 1899. It could be said that he was about to get the run-around. In London it had been decided that he should supersede Lord Methuen and that, on landing, he and the 5th Division should reinforce the Cape.[120] However, Buller had different ideas and countermanded the War Office's instruction. He sent Warren a telegram ordering him to proceed no further on his journey to Methuen but, instead, to make haste to Natal. Clearly Buller had had his fill of having his campaign being run by cabinet ministers and the War Office in London.

Despite his devastating setbacks, Buller decided to assert his authority as Commander-in-Chief South Africa, for the time being at least, and in no uncertain terms told the War Office that it would be folly to sack Methuen, or any other general, for one error—although, he conceded, such need not apply to himself. He was ready to go if thought desirable. He sent a telegram to London:

> . . . I cannot agree with the Commander-in-Chief and allow Methuen, who has done very well, to be superseded by Warren. Commander-in-Chief, comfortable at home, has no idea of the difficulties here. It would, I think, be a fatal policy to supersede every general who failed to succeed in every fight but I may say that, as I myself have since failed, I offer no objection in my own case . . .[121]

113

The War Office relented and Buller had his way. He bluntly informed Warren: 'Do not proceed: order is cancelled.' Thus, when Warren arrived at the dismal railway junction of De Aar, 500 miles from where he started and 150 miles short of his destination, he and his staff of travel-weary officers were met by a major carrying the order for Warren's return to Cape Town. Crusty and irritable at the best of times, Warren shouted: 'Am I a shuttlecock to be ranged about up and down the line?'

However, the die was cast and Warren and his team about-turned for the Cape. His brigade commanders were both soldiers of considerable experience: Sir John Talbot Coke, aged 58, hailed from a military family and, having attended Harrow and Sandhurst, had entered the army in 1859. Like Buller, he had served in Canada and had fought in the Sudan in 1889. Later postings were to Ireland and Mauritius.

Sir Edward Woodgate, at the age of 54, was one of the youngest and fittest of Warren's brigade commanders. Educated at Radley and Sandhurst, he had joined the army in 1865 and two years later accompanied Sir Robert Napier's expedition into Abyssinia. He then fought in the Ashanti War of 1873–4 and thereafter passed Staff College. During the Anglo-Zulu War he served as Colonel Evelyn Wood's staff officer and was present at the battles of Kambula and Ulundi. In 1896 he raised the West Africa Regiment and with it suppressed a rebellion. Both Coke and Woodgate were old acquaintances of Buller's who would have greeted them as friends and mess mates, all enjoying a camaraderie of past campaigns that Warren would have been denied. Coke's brigade consisted of: 2nd Battalion Somerset Regiment; 2nd Battalion Dorset Regiment; 2nd Battalion Middlesex Regiment; plus artillery and support services. Woodgate's brigade consisted of: 2nd Battalion Royal Lancaster Regiment; 2nd Battalion Lancashire Fusiliers; 1st Battalion South Lancashire Regiment; The York and Lancaster Regiment; plus artillery and support services.

The terms of service for the British soldier were 12 years: seven years with the 'Colours', which was invariably spent overseas in one of the Empire's many outposts, and five years with a reserve battalion in Britain. Many of the troops that were being sent to South Africa were a mixture of recruits and men who had already served their time with the Colours.

Only between 4% and 7% of men below the rank of sergeant were married. Despite scenes as depicted in illustrated magazines of young ladies bidding farewell to soldier husbands, such partings were few and far between. A soldier required permission to marry which was seldom granted.[122]

No doubt many of them, struggling to survive in some grim industrial occupation and living in one room swarming with family, would welcome the respite of adventure, camaraderie and a life free of domestic responsibility. Indeed, in the army even the newest private had rights such as a regulation number of cubic feet of space in the barrack room. So happy were some to get away from the restraints of home that one wrote: 'You can't believe how happy I was fighting against the Boers. I felt as if I were in a football match.'

In order to join the British Army at the time, the recruit was required to be between the ages of 18 (unless recruited as a boy-soldier: a bugler or drummer) and 25. He had to be of a certain height—which could not have been very tall as the average height of an Englishman in 1900 was five foot, six inches and Lord Roberts himself was only five foot, two inches. He also had to be unmarried and in this respect failure to declare his matrimonial status could lead to a two-year prison sentence.[123] Once accepted, the recruit was obliged to take the oath:

I, [so-and-so], do make Oath that I will be Faithful and Bear Allegiance to Her Majesty, Her Heirs, and Successors, and that I will, as in duty bound, Honestly and Faithfully defend Her Majesty, Her Heirs, and Successors, in Person, Crown, and Dignity, against all enemies, and will observe and obey all orders of Her Majesty, Her Heirs, Her Successors, and of the Generals and Officers set over me. So help me God!

How different to his Boer opponent who was, most likely, on average three inches taller, called to his commando at any age between 16 and 60, usually married and had a different God from the British: he of the Old Testament.

Warren finally got back to Cape Town on 20 December and, after a lengthy interview with Sir Alfred Milner, whose views on the war and whose opinion of the Boer people would have accorded with Warren's own, Warren and his staff embarked aboard the steamer *Mohawk* for the four-day voyage north to Durban. Warren, as on the voyage out, did not allow his officers to become indolent and recommenced, with the limited maps and intelligence available, engaging in war games as he had been taught at Staff College. On reaching Pietermaritzburg he immediately went to see Hely-Hutchinson, the Governor, and was perturbed to find an air of despondency hovering like a black cloud which, he believed as did 'everyone he spoke to', could only be dispersed by his immediate departure to the front:

> . . . Everyone seems to be of one mind, that I must go forward to restore confidence . . . It seems to have been their impression that General Buller has been telegraphing or talking about the dispirited condition of the troops, and this has got out and the troops are indignant. This is what came to me from all sources. I received letters also to the same effect, and I feel I must go up at once to see General Buller.[124]

Usually, defeated generals and their armies retreat from the battlefield, escaping the sight of their humiliation but, in the case of Colenso, Buller's army remained at Chieveley, ten miles from the scene of their defeat, with the heights beyond Colenso plainly visible and a constant reminder of their failure.

Buller was undoubtedly despondent as were some of his troops but now with the 5th Division about to arrive, he could prepare for the next attempt to relieve Ladysmith. However, he would have preferred the Division without its patronising commander. The contrast in confidence between Buller and Warren at that moment must have been starkly apparent. Buller had been chosen to thrash the Boers—for whom he had a fond regard and respect—but he would, no doubt, have preferred to have remained at home. Out of loyalty to Queen and Country, having engaged them in battle, he had been ignominiously defeated and a reputation built over years of soldiering had been lost overnight. Warren, on the other hand, had but a few weeks ago been spending his time cycling, attending the local Free Mason Lodge and wondering whether or not the St John Ambulance Brigade might give him a job. Now, like a miracle, he was a divisional commander and would shortly have the overall command of 26,000 men.

Therefore, it was with a jaunty stride that Warren arrived at Buller's headquarters on Christmas Eve. Warren recalled:

> I was shocked to find how he had taken to heart his reverse at Colenso. As an old friend [Whether they were, in fact, old friends, is doubtful] I endeavoured to cheer him up and told him that we would soon dispose of the Boers.[125]

Having given Buller that patronising assurance, Warren entered into a discussion as to where the next move on Ladysmith was to be. Buller revealed his intention of a flank movement to the west. Warren found himself confident enough to disagree, arguing that the route should be in the opposite direction past Hlangwane, the hill that had afforded the Boers victory during the recent battle, and which was still in their possession. Buller immediately turned on Warren barking: 'What do you know about it?' Warren, subdued, answered lamely: 'Through general knowledge and war games.' [126]

To be fair to Warren the rationale behind his argument was based on his knowledge of the Boers' eyesight. A burgher's vision, having lived his life in a land of vast vistas, free of pollution, was far superior over long distances to that of the British soldier whose eyesight had likely been inhibited by landscapes of buildings and street corners. Thus, the burgher was better able, as had already been proven, to pick off his enemy at a distance well beyond the capability of his foe. Warren argued the route to Ladysmith via Hlangwane would be confined by closely pressing hills where the Boers would be denied the advantage of their long-range vision. That, however, would be only one consideration in Buller's attempt to relieve Ladysmith. In the meantime the 5th Division, having landed at Durban, was being railed on to Estcourt. Now, well aware of the imminent arrival of British reinforcements, every Boer from President Kruger to the youngest boy with a Mauser, realised that time was running out. If they were going to take Ladysmith and perhaps sway Britain into a negotiated peace they must do so without delay. It was two months since the Boers had turned the key, locking in the garrison and the citizens of the town. Apart from the burghers with Botha's column, who stealthily guarded the northern bank of the Tugela, most of the besiegers had become bored, their thoughts turning to cattle, crops and their *vroue* (wives). Many had been given leave and, as the hot days dragged on, others just took a break and rode off home for a while. The fact that the commandos had besieged a British army had caused a sensation at home and, if possible, the folk, especially the ladies, wanted to see the phenomenon. So, boarding trains as though they were going on an excursion to the seaside, they came in their best attire from Pretoria and Johannesburg to gaze in admiration at the burghers and what they could see of the *Rooineks'* town (Redneck slang for a British soldier); most of all they wanted to lay a hand on the barrel of a 'Long Tom' so that they could return and relate to neighbours and kin how they had actually touched one of the mighty guns.

However, President Kruger required action and an end to the siege. At last he got Joubert, who had recently refused to drop dynamite into Ladysmith from kites because he could find no parallel for such tactics in the Old Testament, to agree to a full-scale assault. A French soldier of fortune, Colonel Georges de Comte de Villebois-Mareuil, one of many military men from a variety of nations who had joined the Boer cause, was despatched to assess the British defences.[127] He concluded that a table-top ridge of land, two miles from the southern outskirts of the town was Ladysmith's Achilles' heel. The Boers called the feature the Platrand, whereas it was known to the British as Caesar's Camp at its eastern end and Wagon Hill to the west. Colonel de Comte de Villebois-Mareuil drew up a comprehensive report of how the ridge should be taken, his plan being approved by the *Kreigsraad* (War Council) despite Joubert's objections, he being strongly of the opinion that he had insufficient men to launch a head-on assault against a fortified position.

Botha's column apart, it is likely that the number of besieging burghers never exceeded 6,000 and, on occasion, were as few as 4,000. However, Comte de Villebois-Mareuil, now much admired for his military judgment, received the full backing of the Boer commanders.

The Platrand was, as anticipated by the Boers, heavily fortified with rifle pits and redoubts. Nevertheless, the attack was planned to erupt at 2am on the morning of 6 January. The Vryheid Commando, with a hundred German *uitlanders*, were to lead the assault from the south; to their left, under Caesar's Camp, men of Utrecht and Wakkerstroom Commandos were to take up position while the extreme west of the line, under Wagon Hill, was to be covered by the Utrecht and Standerton Commandos. Meanwhile, in the town, there was the awful realisation that both Christmas and New Year had come and gone with Buller, it seemed, as far away as ever. His failure to cross the Tugela had completely demoralised White who was seldom seen outside his headquarters: glory had been replaced by grousing; the 'Ladysmith Spirit' was close to vaporising. White was taking no more risks. He felt safest with his infantry in their rifle pits, his artillery in their redoubts and the cavalry in their stables. There were no more night raids leading to expensive casualties despite the uplift to morale that they achieved.

Christmas had made no difference to the Boer bombardment. At an early hour the six-inch Creusot shells had come screaming over from Bulwana Hill. It was a disappointment: everyone had thought the Boers would have let-up for Christmas Day. Nevertheless, there were moments of humour: the men of the Natal Mounted Rifles had raided the Indian *dhukas* (shops) for Eastern finery and had dressed themselves and their mounts as some sort of sultan's mounted band, their instruments having been furnished from kerosene tins. The children had not been forgotten either: 62-year-old Colonel Dartnell of the Natal Police, who had guided Yule's column to safety, somehow managed to concoct some Christmas trees. It would, however, be difficult to get merry with brandy at £7 a bottle, whisky £5 and cigarettes at 4 shillings a packet.[128]

Although there were no casualties on Christmas Day, one man had been shaving when a shell flew between his face and the mirror, the shock-waves sending him reeling to the floor unconscious. A few days later Trooper Edmonds of the Border Mounted Rifles was not so lucky: a Mauser bullet hit him in the centre of the chest, passed through his lungs and out through his back; a little lower down another bullet also hit him in the chest and came out through his thigh. He lay for days close to death, his cot being close to the metal tent poles of the tent. One night his hand happened to touch one of the supports during the midst of a tropical storm which sent a bolt of lightning through both pole and the trooper almost, but not quite, finishing the work the bullets had failed to do.[129]

On the night of the 5th/6th, as the burghers were taking up their positions all along the lower slopes of the Platrand, a contingent of the ILH, with sailors from the Naval Brigade, under the supervision of 23-year-old Lieutenant Digby Jones of the Royal Engineers, were busy relocating a 4.7in naval gun on Wagon Hill. The work party was escorted by a detail of Gordon Highlanders. Already in position, in rifle pits and redoubts all along the ridge, were men of the Manchester Regiment to the east, the KRR and six field guns in the centre and the ILH on the western extremity. As the work party struggled to drag the naval gun to its new position, they paused several times and on each occasion heard the eerie singing of Boer hymns drifting up from the enemy camps below: a sure warning of a pending attack. However, the attackers were fewer in number than Joubert had ordered, many burghers having failed to respond. Deneys Reitz relates that about half the force he was attached to stood dejectedly behind the shelter of a river bank showing little inclination for the work in hand. When the field cornets ordered the advance, only about 500 burghers responded, the rest refusing to follow. Nevertheless, the burghers reached the Platrand crest without detection; the first indication of the assault was the clatter of dislodged stones and rustling footsteps. Then, close to the ILH redoubt, a voice called in perfect English: 'Don't shoot! We're the Ladysmith Town Guard.' For an instant the sentry hesi-tated, knowing in that split second he had been tricked and would be killed: a Boer volley followed and the sentry's fear became a fact. Imme-diately, the ILH returned the burghers' fire, and in places no more than ten yards separated the combatants, each side hugging whatever cover could be found, as they blazed away into the darkness. Reitz also recalled:

> . . . A further volley flared along the portholes [the loopholes of the fort] and before we had time to think, the attack had withered away. We saw the men go down in a heap, leaving only one man erect. The rest were either dead, wounded or had flung themselves headlong for as much cover as they could find . . . The man who still faced the enemy was Willemse [an officer of President Kruger's guard] and he, undeterred, ran up to the fort and tried to scale the wall. Bayonets were thrust at him which he parried with his rifle until a revolver was fired point blank into him.[130]

Lieutenant Walker of the ILH was fortunate that in the gloom he was able to drop his hand straight on to the Hotchkiss machine gun that formed part of his squadron's armoury. However, the Boers stayed firmly in position whilst Colonel Edwards of the ILH, standing upright to fire, miraculously remained unharmed. Wagon Hill and the rest of the Platrand must be held at all cost. If taken, the enemy would be able to bring their guns onto the southern slopes and fire directly into Ladysmith; indeed a number of the streets and houses would be within range of long-distance rifle fire: inevitably Ladysmith would fall.

At the moment of the Boer assault, only 70 men of the ILH, a small assortment of Gordon Highlanders and those at work shifting the naval gun, guarded Wagon Hill but, holding fast in the gathering light, flat on their bellies behind any cover that could be found, they kept the Boer onrush at bay. Donald Macdonald wrote: 'The Light Horse did many fine things in the campaign, but did never more for their country than during those few hours of darkness of January 6.'

John Kestell, the son of an English settler but now a Dutch Reformed Church minister and chaplain to the Orange Free State Commandos, later wrote:

> . . . The idea was that about 4,000 men should make the attack . . . [and] that after the storming party had taken the hill, reinforce-

ments would come from all sides to support them and thus carry out the attack . . .[131]

All along the Platrand the scattering of British outposts were hard-pressed by overwhelming numbers of the enemy, some of the best sharp-shooting marksmen in the world. G. F. Gibson wrote:

> It was dark and the Boers with their wonderful ability to make use of cover, had, it would seem by uncanny instinct, actually got into position where they could direct their fire over Wagon Point without themselves being seen . . .[132]

A finger, an inch of forehead, or a toecap at 50 yards, were targets that could not be missed. However, quality marksmanship was not a craft of the Boer alone: many troopers of the ILH were as frontier-born as the enemy and could shoot equally as well. Thus it was of cardinal importance that the art of concealment come a close second to marksmanship. Men on both sides, unable to actually detect an enemy known to be stomach-down behind a certain rock ten yards away, would gauge the likely path of a bullet deliberately aimed to ricochet and thus, deflected, find a target. So close was the struggle that in one mêlée Captain Mathias of the ILH, found himself amongst the enemy. The regimental history of the ILH records:

> . . . Breaking noisily into the Taal (Dutch) which he spoke fluently, he played the part of the fire-eater until darkness and opportunity enabled him to slip ahead of the attack and rejoin the remnants of his squadron . . .[133]

At the eastern end and in the centre of the ridge, the defenders were equally hard-pressed as, with the gathering light, the Boer reinforcements struggled up the steep boulder strewn slopes of the ridge. Kestell remembered:

> Everywhere above, in front of us, the flashes of the rifles leapt forth into the darkness and the sharp reports that followed, in such quick succession, as to give the impression of Maxims firing. All of a sudden a great long jet of flame, and instantly the thunder of cannon broke upon the startled air, and presently

behind us I could hear the shrapnel bullets falling on the ground. Then many of those who had not climbed the hill, turned and fled; but others rushed upwards and rapidly approached the cornice of the rocks . . .[134]

The valiant burgher vanguard of the attack who finally reached the crest of Caesar's Camp, found themselves face-to-face with strung-out picquets of the Gordon Highlanders—so strung out in fact that Colonel Curran, commanding officer of the regiment, had no idea that his section was under attack but was merely alarmed at the close proximity of the firing. Captain the Honourable R. F. Carnegie was sent off with a company of the Gordons to check the regimental picquets further east towards the Manchester Regiment redoubt on Caesar's Camp. Along the way he encountered Lieutenant Hunt-Grubbe of the Manchesters who, scouting forward towards the west, walked straight into the arms of the advancing Boers and was taken prisoner. Carnegie, unaware of what had happened, also decided to scout the crest. Advancing stealthily amongst the boulders, he suddenly saw the enemy and opened fire with his carbine, dropping one man as the Boers surged forward. Outnumbered, the British picquets, in a muddle of different regiments—Highlanders, Manchesters, NMR and KRR—fell back in confusion. However, on the plain below, Colonel Royston could see the action spread out high up on the hillside as plain as a diorama. Royston immediately ordered two squadrons of the NMR and the 58th Battery RFA to gallop forward in support:

Crossing the river the 53rd came into action at 6am. In the scrub north of Fly Kraal against a target such as was rarely given to gunners in this war of long ranges and guesswork firing. There, directly in front of them, at 2,200 yards range, was the slope of Caesar's Camp crowded with Boers dotted about in fancied security. In a moment the wicked shrapnel was bursting over them at its deadliest range. Welcoming the support, Carnegie at once led his Gordons forward. The gunners saw his move and lengthening their fusers, swept the Boers back along the slope in front of him. But the gallant Heidelbergers still clung to the cover of captured breastworks on the crest. Ordering a volley, Carnegie fixed bayonets and rushed in. The Boers stood up to meet the attack, Fired point-blank at the charging Highlanders and then, their hearts failing them, turned and leapt down over the boulders.[135]

Carnegie shot four with his carbine and was himself severely wounded in two places. However, if the Heidelbergers were in retreat they did not flee very far. They crept along the crest which brought them to a wide re-entrant—a trench formed by nature—and there, sheltered from the worst of the shelling, they went to ground, keeping at bay the advancing High-landers who, in turn, sought cover wherever it could be found amongst the scattered rocks. It was stalemate with everyone hoping to score a bull's eye without becoming a statistic of an enemy's scorecard.

It was deadly work which would linger on into the heat of the day when the rocks that had given shelter would become too hot to touch, when water bottles would become empty and when the sun would blister the skin and exhaust the spirit. It was a question of either lying low and waiting the darkness or moving and being shot. As for the wounded, they could expect to suffer for hours to come. Sergeant J. W. Laing of the ILH had his ankle shattered by a bullet during the first hour of the assault and had since lain bleeding amongst the rocks. Around midmorning, with his wound still seeping blood and with his position having been overrun by the burghers, his thirst had become unbearable.

> By this time the heat was intense and my thirst more so; in fact it became so bad that I had to place my finger on my tongue to hold it down to get my breath. Before this I had appealed to the two Boers who were firing over my head to give me a drink of water. At last, one of them who had a short beard handed me his water bottle—which was a British one—What relief I got from that drink! To my intense sorrow which I feel to this day, on handing back the bottle and while he was putting the strap around his neck, my unknown benefactor was shot through the face, and disappeared from my sight with blood gushing from his mouth. This he got for his kind and humane action which I shall never forget.[136]

The gallant burghers, led by such determined men as Jakob de Villiers, Zaccharias de Jager, Gert Wessels and many more resolute and grizzled warriors of the veldt, having gathered fresh support, rose up over the crest and pressed on to the British redoubt. Colonel Edwards of the ILH in admiration of his enemy's resolve wrote:

> Let it be ungrudgingly recorded that the enemy never lacked a

supply of enterprising and gallant men, ready to face certain death, to sacrifice themselves as leaders of forlorn hope. What they invariably lacked was the solid support of the mass of burghers. This was due to the inherent weakness of the commando system, where every man was, to some extent, a law unto himself and his own general with the resultant lack of discipline.[137]

Around the incomplete gun emplacement a struggle had begun. The escorting infantry had retired unnoticed, isolating Lieutenant Digby Jones of the Royal Engineers and his detachment. Suddenly Jones was attacked at close quarters. The first indication of the enemy was a volley fired over the parapet instantly killing an NCO. Jones immediately rallied his men and, with fixed bayonets, they counter-attacked forcing the enemy back down the hill. Shortly thereafter, when the infantry returned, he set about reinforcing the line of defence and was shot through the neck and killed. Nearby, Trooper Herman Albrecht of the ILH had a point blank encounter with three Boers. Led by Commandant de Villiers, they too had been attempting to seize the gun emplacement. Albrecht killed de Villiers only to be shot and killed himself moments later. Both Jones and Albrecht were posthumously awarded the Victoria Cross.

Once again the ILH were close to being overrun, outflanked and destroyed. Their call for reinforcements was little more than a death warrant for half a dozen men of the KRR:

> The only attempt to advance beyond the line of the outcrops held by the ILH while the Colonel remained on Wagon Hill, was the pathetically heroic and criminally wasteful dash made under orders, by Captain Bowen of the 6th KRR, and his company of six men. One officer and six men to clear an immensely strong natural position held by an overwhelming number of the enemy![138]

As the riflemen prepared for their impossible mission, Colonel Edwards asked Bowen what he intended to do. 'Rush the open ground and clear the enemy off that edge of the hill, Sir.' was the reply. Edwards attempted to dissuade him but Bowen, 'True to his training and tradition, insisted, simply saying he must make the attempt'. They stepped into the open with a cheer but, within a few yards the crackle of rifle fire and all were straddled across the rocks either dead or dying.

The artillery also joined in the duel. McDonald estimated that no fewer than 60 guns within the siege area were involved in the criss-cross clash of fire all around the town. The Creusot on Bulwana vengefully attacked 53rd Battery, still deployed on the open plain, but the skilled gunners limbered up and had trotted to a new position before the smoke had disappeared from the muzzle of the enemy gun: although the RFA gunners went about their business completely in the open, few of them suffered injury. This is was not the case for the Boer reinforcements as they were exposed to the shrapnel bombardment at 2,000 yards as they struggled up the open face of the Platrand:

> . . . Both percussion and shrapnel searched the hill from crest to foot. Stubbornly as they held their place against the Rifles, the shellfire was too much for them. The biggest rocks were useless against the downward blast and the hail of splinters, which searched every corner, and after the fight every corner of that bloody field was so horrible a spectacle. There were men lying there who apparently had not a whole bone in their bodies. They were literally torn to shreds.[139]

Thus the Burghers and the British remained in deadlock while brave Samaritans, like Chaplain Kestell and Surgeon-Major W. Davies, did their best to succour friend and foe alike*. Thus by late afternoon, as black/green clouds massed over the Drakensberg Mountains to the west, the final outcome of the battle remained in violent contention. Then the storm arrived. Born on a banshee wind that tore at the Platrand, sending spirals of dust twisting into the sky, it came with rain and a deluge of hail-stones as big as shilling pieces, whilst thunder and lightning boomed and crackled; the day became as black as night and a man could see no further than he could kick a stone. To the Boers it was a supernatural intervention. Disregarding the elements and the shock of freezing rain, they surged for-ward outnumbering the defenders and deploying to outflank the British redoubts. They came unseen through the hail and rain and when the storm began to subside, it seemed the defenders of Wagon Hill, with 30% of their number dead or wounded, would be overrun. Colonel Ian Hamilton,

---

*There had been an equally philanthropic British doctor by the name of Stark amongst the besieged, whose sympathies lay with what he considered to be the Boers' legitimate aspirations. Dr Stark's vowed intent was to administer aid to any wounded burgher who might be taken prisoner. It is ironic that he was killed outside the Royal Hotel by a Boer shell. [140]

who commanded the Platrand sector of Ladysmith's defences, had already called the Devonshire Regiment to fill the gap and, even before the arrival of the storm the Devons had begun their climb. At last, as they reached the crest line, there was a pause followed by Colonel Park's command: 'Fix bayonets', then, with a cheer, the Devons were over the top, the storm at their backs and the foe to the fore. Half blinded by the elements the burghers fired at the obscure figures and the glint of bayonets racing towards them: a volley was fired then another and another yet the Devons did not falter despite the toll of dead and wounded, driving Boers before them off the hill—that is the British version of the Platrand duel. Colonel Park later wrote to his wife:

> I have been through the most terrible experience since I last wrote. Thank God for his great mercy, that he has brought me safe through it . . . The first few yards we were under cover, but when we reached the top of the crest line, we were met by the most awful storm of bullets. I have never heard such hot fire in my life, and can only compare it with the crackling of a dry gorse branch thrown into a fire. . . . The men behaved splendidly; every man went straight and hard as he could for the enemy's ridge, and there wasn't the slightest sign of checking or wavering, though, as I ran, I could see men falling like ninepins on both sides of me; and then at last, to my intense relief, when we were within about fifteen yards of them, I saw the Boers suddenly jump up, turn tail, and fly down the hill for their lives, and the position was ours. After a minute or two, when we had got settled down in the position and I had time to look around, I realized that not only had we lost heavily in the charge but we were still exposed to a heavy cross-fire from both flanks, from which we suffered severely . . .[141]

Chaplain Kestell more or less confirmed Colonel Park's story; and the unfortunate wounded on both sides would lie for hours to come in their sodden frozen clothes.

> At last the sun set, and as it was clear to Commandant de Villiers that no reinforcements would come and as he had already lost a third of his men killed and wounded, he saw that it was impossible to remain there. He, therefore, told me that he would continue there a little while longer and withdraw when it became dark.

This took place at half past seven. We had been on the hill for sixteen hours under a most severe fire and now we retired; but we were not driven off by the Devons with levelled bayonets as I have read in an English book. We were not driven off the hill. We held it as long as it was light and when twilight fell Commandant de Villiers considered it useless to remain there. He stopped there until the last man had gone, then fired some shots, not however at the Devons advancing with fixed bayonets, but in the air, in order to make the English think that we were still all in our positions.[142]

Whatever version may be true, the Boers had failed in their endeavour to take the Platrand and the Union Jack still flew over Ladysmith not, however, due to the ability or inspiration of the British generals on either side of the Tugela, but due to the courage and tenacity of the regimental officers, the ordinary British soldier, his colonial counterpart and the citizens of the town. James Bayley's thoughts and experiences, which he recorded in the letters to his fiancée, were, no doubt similar to many occupants of Ladysmith.

Whilst I was lying in bed, my right hand man at the store died of fever. He had been going on all right, and we thought he would soon be about again, but something occurred one day in the hospital [Itombi] where he was lying which finally upset him so that his temperature went up, and he died. I don't know the full facts as it was only owing to a lad I have at the store, that I first knew Mr. Preace was dead. This lad came to see me one day and, boy-like, blurted it out . . . Many things have happened since the Christmas Day morning. The Boers have continued to shell day after day as usual, some days heavier than others, but on Sunday last they made for, I think, the first time in Boer history, a vigorous attack. It was from all accounts the most awful and bloodiest fight of the whole campaign. Some say it was worse than Elandslaagte and that was frightful. . . . I lay in bed and listened to it all from the beginning. It was hardly daybreak, about four o'clock in the morning, when the Boers attacked and rushed the position called Wagon Hill which has always been reckoned as our weakest point. The Manchester Regiment were in charge of it, but the Boers cleaned them out, and thus far got the Point [Wagon Point].

However other regiments came up, and the enemy were cleared off. Over and over again they tried to retake it but our fellows gave them beans. The fight lasted all day and a thunderstorm came in the afternoon, and added to the confusion, but still the battle raged, until darkness put a stop to it. We lost a hundred killed and many wounded, and the total Boer loss is estimated at two thousand. [A gross exaggeration] . . . I hear that our loss on Saturday was 120 men and fourteen officers killed and from 200 to 300 wounded. That shows what a terrible fight it was. Had the Boers only backed up their men on top of the hill it would have been a bad time for Ladysmith as they would have been able to command the town with their rifle fire . . . Alas the bravest lost their lives. You at home will hear of all the brave deeds in the fights, but we here know what happens. Many brave deeds were done on Saturday but some things too happened which are hardly to be spoken of. One Major called on his men for volunteers to take a position from which the Boers were pouring a heavy fire and six men stood forward. The Major went forward with so few and he and the six were shot before they got far. . . . Poor Tommy Atkins, it is a wonder the poor fellows have any backbone at all. Half starved, some with hardly any bottoms to their trousers, out in a scorching African sun during the day, and at night drenched with a deluge of rain, no tents or shelter whatever at many of the posts and thus he has to stick it and fight when it is necessary, or hang on until fever makes it necessary to go to the hospital. He is rather a different looking chap to the smart, upright Tommy you see strutting about the streets at home at holiday times but it is the same fellow nevertheless. . . . Good news was heliographed yesterday, and I am told the General had a notice put up. It was a message from the Queen and several other folk about Saturday's fight, also that Buller was pushing forward to our relief . . .

In actual fact, Buller was doing nothing of the kind. The sound of the ground-shaking bombardment that had stirred the Chieveley Camp at 2am, undoubtedly aroused consternation and curiosity in some; others turned over and went back to sleep. It was obvious to all that no plan was in place for immediate response to what must either be an aggressive attempt by the defenders to break out or by the Boers, finally to take the town.

Winston Churchill's reaction at that moment was probably typical of those who were not in a position of responsibility:

> It was two o'clock in the morning of January 6. The full significance of the sounds came with consciousness. We had all heard them before—heavy cannonading at Ladysmith. They were at it again. How much longer would the heroic garrison be persecuted? I turned to rest once more but the distant guns forbade sleep.[143]

Nevertheless, Churchill remained in bed until breakfast time, speculating as to what was happening 18 miles away. By 10:30am the uproar still continued and it was not until noon that a heliograph message was received, and leaked by the signals officer to his friends, revealing that the town was under attack from all sides but holding out. That was good news so those at Chieveley prepared to sit down to luncheon. However, they were interrupted by a galloper with orders for the whole force to fall in. Thus 11 hours after the first indication of the Boer attack, something was going to be done. There was to be a demonstration that would hopefully draw some of the attackers away from the town. The demonstration was an impressive affair with the cavalry sweeping forward, clearing the ground of non-existent foe men, with thousands of infantry and artillery following in their wake. However, it was only a demonstration as no plan had been put in place in anticipation of a Boer attack taking place and the Tugela was in flood, so it was not until 5pm that Buller's army faced the Boers across the river. It was at that moment that they were hit by the same storm of hail and rain that was engulfing the Platrand. How easy it would have been for such an assembly of military might, hidden by the rain and gloom, to have stormed Hlangwane in the same manner as the burghers were, at that very moment, storming the Platrand. However, perhaps without a thought to such a possibility, the opportunity passed and at 7pm all the troops returned to camp. The next morning the Ladysmith heliograph was able to confirm that all was well—but a price had been paid. British losses were 148 killed and 272 wounded: total casualties 420. The Boers officially gave their losses at 64 killed and 119 wounded.

Sir Charles Warren had, of course, arrived in time to hear the bombardment which, at Frere, his Headquarters, was a further five miles from Ladysmith than was Chieveley. In fact, it would have been the first time in his career that he had heard more than a single cannon fired in anger.

....

CHAPTER NINE

POTGIETER'S DRIFT

Buller was an obstinate man. Although he had been demoted to merely Commander of the Natal Field Force and had received orders, telegraphed by Lord Roberts from Madeira, not to take the initiative, he had every intention of doing so and, with the arrival of Warren's Division, he was ready to move. There were three possibilities:

1. East via Weenen and into rather unknown and rugged country, a route that would emerge close to Lombard's Kop in Lady-smith. It is likely that neither Buller nor Warren gave it serious consideration.
2. Back to Colenso, take Hlangwane, and proceed via the Tugela Heights, following the railway line through gorges and cuttings finally to emerge in the town itself.
3. Westward, following the Tugela upstream to where, by local accounts of the terrain, it would be possible to outflank the Boer entrenchments. As mentioned, there were virtually no maps.

On 29 December, as soon as Warren and his travel-weary staff had settled down, Buller paid him a visit to enlarge upon his plans for the next assault.[144] During the brooding days before Warren's arrival, he had firmly decided where it would be. Buller, sullen and aggressive, finding solace in the bottom of a champagne glass, would not be an easy man with whom to discuss alternatives. At about this time, in a candid moment with Churchill, he exaggerated the number of the enemy facing him and bemoaned his lot saying: 'Here I am condemned to fight in Natal, which all my judgment has told me to avoid, and to try to advance along the line worst of all suited to my troops.' Nevertheless, having decided on his line of advance he would stubbornly adhere to it no matter how strongly he might be persuaded to do otherwise. Buller's entire strategy at this stage had not been revealed—most likely even Warren did not know, but Buller now disclosed that he intended to strike westward to Springfield, (present-day Winterton) 22 miles from Frere, cross the fast flowing Little Tugela and turn north for the crossing at Potgieter's Drift nine miles further on. Once successfully over with his army he would be faced, three miles away, by a range of formidable hills. However, his left flank would be protected, almost to the foot of the range, by an inverted loop of the Tugela. It was there that battle would commence. Warren did not like the idea, likewise Lyttelton commanding the 4th Brigade. Warren later wrote:

> When I arrived in Durban on the 25th December 1899 Lyttelton begged me to come over and buck-up Buller, otherwise the army would go smash. Up to that point Buller was a consul of despair: he could not see his way to relieve Ladysmith. My business was to tell him it could be done and that I could do it . . .[145]

Buller had informed Warren that he wished to march on 6 January but not only had the Boer attack on the Platrand stalled any move on that day, Warren had objected that the enemy across the Tugela had yet to be demoralized by bombardment and, this far, the artillery attached to his division had not arrived. However, Buller, secretive in his ways, had already signalled White that it was his intention to start from Chieveley on the 6th with the object of advancing on Ladysmith via Potgieter's Drift and Lancers Kop, four miles west of Ladysmith. White had replied:

> If you will trust me with further details of your plan, I hope to be able to assist you in the latter stages of your advance on Lady-smith; but to do this effectively I should require to know on which line or lines, you intend to force passage of the Tugela.

Buller confirmed his intent and White replied with the plucky re-sponse: 'Do not hurry on date of starting on our account if recently arrived troops need rest, as I am quite confident of holding my own here.' [146]

However, Warren was still resolutely opposed to Buller's scheme and later wrote that it seemed most hazardous because in the broad valley, surrounded by high hills that the army would have to traverse between Springfield and the drift, the Boers might well have artillery hidden. As it turned out there were no guns—in fact, no Boers at all. Warren had proposed that before the advance commenced, he should attack and take the hills concerned but Buller dismissed his proposal objecting to Warren embarking on what he termed 'Alpine excursions'. [147]

By 3 January Warren's brigades had arrived at Frere and, having been denied the opportunity of assaulting Buller's 'Alpine' hills, Warren had them manoeuvre and, en masse, practise one of his favoured activities, that of taking cover from imaginary burghers.

On 8 January, Buller issued a general order for the advance to take place on the 10th. Apart from Barton's 5th Brigade, which would stay behind and act as rear guard, the whole of the army, amounting to 19,000 infantry, 3,000 cavalry, 60 guns, and support services which included a pontoon troop of Royal Engineers, would advance on Potgieter's Drift. The army was also accompanied by two harbingers of more sophisticated wars to come: an observation balloon, constructed to operate at the altitude of the English Downs and, therefore, without the 'lift' that had been hoped for but nevertheless invaluable; and, of even greater value, a number of steam traction engines—vague forbears of the tank? They proved to be an asset without which Buller's army would literally have become stuck in the mud.

As we shall see, there was to be much contention between Generals Buller and Warren, the latter now second-in-command of the Natal Field Force. Not only did their strategies for the relief of the besieged town differ to such a degree that feuding and wrangling would cost many lives, but every decision would be encumbered as Warren's attitude to the war and the Boer people was out of date and at stark variance to Buller's. Warren was to write, or have written on his behalf:

. . . Subdued by a distinct sense of disappointment and humiliation as one disaster after another occurred [Black Week] there was no acceptance of defeat, but a dogged determination that the war, being a righteous war, must at any sacrifice be carried to a victorious conclusion. The national honour had been wounded by the impudent invasion of British dominion beyond the seas, and that wound could only be healed by the complete subjugation of the invader . . . Never again must a British defeat by Boers be allowed to conclude the matter, to rankle and fester in a way so difficult for a high-spirited people to bear, even when disguised under the name of magnanimity. Defeat must only mean renewed effort and determination to succeed. We were in the hands of God, but, so long as we could send out a man [Warren being the man, it was implied] to fight, we were determined to go on, and, God willing, at whatever cost to end the matter, once and for all, in such a way that our wounded honour should be healed, the susceptibilities of our invaded colonies soothed, and the Boer taught to know his proper place, but as a member of a free and world-wide empire and a subject of the Queen . . .[148]

Before we accompany the two generals westwards to Potgieter's Drift and the disaster that would follow, it must be explained that Buller would leave Warren to 'get on with it' and abandon his responsibilities as overall commander. He would also heap blame on Warren for the failure of the battle to come. Worse still, Buller would fail to disclose to Warren the adverse report that he, Buller, would submit to the War Office regarding Warren's conduct despite it being the custom for any commander criticizing a subordinate, to first acquaint the officer with the intended accusation. When Warren two years later, became aware of what had occurred behind his back, he arranged for the publication of a book, the title, *A Vindication*, speaking for itself. It was published under the pseudonym of 'Defender', whose identity was revealed 100 years later by Owen Coetzer in his book *The Road to Infamy*. 'Defender' was, Coetzer believed, Captain The Honourable Hedworth Lampton RN, the officer who had brought the naval guns from HMS *Powerful* to Ladysmith where he commanded them throughout the siege. Lampton was the son of the Earl of Durham and had taken part, as had Warren, in the Egyptian War of 1882. Lampton's motive in agreeing to pose as 'Defender' if indeed he did, is unclear, especially so as it is blatantly apparent that Warren guides the author's hand no matter whom he may pretend to be. For instance, on returning to England in May 1900, only a few months after Ladysmith was relieved, Lampton was given command of the Royal Yacht until his appointment as Rear Admiral of the Mediterranean Cruiser Squadron, thus becoming the youngest flag officer of the Royal Navy.[149] It seems inconceivable that under such circumstances he would have had the urge or means of communication to research *A Vindication*, the first 54 pages of which do little but extol Warren's accomplishments whilst turning a blind eye on his less successful endeavours.

Unrelenting rain, similar to that experienced by Yule on his retreat from Dundee, had returned creating conditions not unlike those encountered by Napoleon's soldiers during their retreat from Moscow. However, instead of snow, Buller's army became bogged down in glutinous mud churned and trodden by 4,000 oxen, 3,000 horses, 2,400 wagon wheels and 19,000 marching men—or perhaps, more accurately, men who were attempting to march. From afar, 15 miles long, the cavalcade had the appearance of a gigantic struggling snake. J. B. Atkins, the war correspondent of the *Manchester Guardian* wrote: 'The hills seemed to melt like tallow under heat; the rain beat the earth into liquid and the thick, earthy liquid ran down in terraced cascades . . . '

Watching Warren's division march out from camp on what was only their first week in South Africa, Atkins continued:

> The passages through the spruits were nightmares—carts overturned in the water, wheels up, mules mixed up, fighting and kicked in their harnesses and half-drowning oxen, with their heads pulled down under water and heaving with all their mighty strength to the opposite bank, a gun or a heavy wagon stuck and the river traffic looping around it as water flows around an island.[150]

Up to 80 oxen had been harnessed to one wagon in a futile attempt to pull it from a quagmire, where it seemed likely to disappear forever, when a Puffing Billy was summoned. Full steam ahead and what bovine power had failed to do the traction engine accomplished single handed:

> They performed splendidly, climbing mountain sides and fording spruits with an agility not to be expected from their ponderous nature. They could haul twelve tons whereas the ox wagons could only carry half a ton so in hauling power the traction engine was calculated to be of equal value to forty wagons.[151]

Nevertheless, once away from the lifeline of the railway, and despite the inventions of a new age and fast approaching mechanized warfare, Buller's army was still dependent on transport that had changed little since the days of the Bible. There were 324 wagons in service, each wagon making two trips in order to haul the supplies from the railhead at Frere to the forward camp at Springfield. Amongst the provisions for the men there were lime juice, rum, groceries, disinfectants and 465,000 individual rations while the horses and mules had 11,000 feeds of hay and bran, at five pound per feed, set aboard the transport.

However, better weather was on the way and, if they were lucky, on occasion the soldiers would have farm milk and Natal beef to look forward to plus a dry berth at night as the wagons carried sufficient tents to house the entire army. Within a couple of days, any hint of luxury would be replaced by hardship. Even so, for the moment things were not too bad for most, and even better for the cavalry. The sun had come out, the clouds had disappeared and as the hundreds of horsemen trotted on their way past the squelching infantry, no doubt relishing the splatters of mud their horses' hooves threw up, they could see away to the west and straight ahead the great spectacle of the serene Drakensberg Mountains, the Barrier of Spears, rose to 10,000 feet, its myriad peaks and bastions sharp etched against the sky. What more could be asked than to be alive and astride a willing horse on such a morning? Tomorrow could look after itself.

The cavalry proceeded in open order; not close packed as though contemplating a charge. The pace also was most controlled: 'Trot march', 'Walk march', trot for a mile and then walk for another. Conserve your horses. Who knows what the day holds. The Cavalry Division had been tasked with proceeding ahead to Springfield where a substantial wooden bridge, on massive masonry piers, spanned the fast-flowing and sparklingly clean Little Tugela River. The bridge, capable of supporting the passage of more than 20 mounted men at a time, was expected to have been destroyed but, as the cavalry approached, to the surprise and suspicion of all, it stood unharmed. An immediate search was made for hidden explosives and to the even greater surprise of all, none were found. Dundonald, having been ordered to take the bridge had done so without firing a shot. What sort of cavalry man would he be if he did not press on? It had been planned that the infantry and the accumulation of wagons of Clery's Division would bed down at Pretorius' farm, six miles from Springfield, while Warren's Division would press on into the dark until reaching Springfield itself where the exhausted men would be subjected to a violent thunderstorm passing what remained of the night cold and soaked to the skin.

In the meantime, Dundonald and about 1,000 men of the Mounted Division had crossed the Little Tugela, the remainder of the cavalry staying behind to guard the flanks and rear of the struggling column of wagons. Dundonald was contemplating exceeding his orders.[152] He had command of 1,000 splendid horsemen and although the regiments which they formed would be mostly short-lived, they being disbanded at the end of hostilities, during their brief existence their names would become as famed as regiments boasting 200 years of history: Thornycroft's Mounted Infantry (TMR), led by Maj. Alexander Thornycroft of the Royal Scots Fusiliers, the unit now 500 strong, had been involved in various skirmishes since November and had played a leading role in the attack on Hlangwane Hill. The Earl of Rosslyn, in his capacity as a war correspondent for the *Daily Mail*, rode with TMR for three weeks and described them as:

> . . . such a clinking lot of officers, they were from all parts of our colonies—Australians as well as Englishmen. Hard as nails, keen on their work, fearless yet cautious, they are just the men we want . . . you will find men of business, men of money, and men of honour; and you would, of course, find as you do everywhere, the pot hunter, the fortune seeker and the black sheep . . .

There was also Bethune's Mounted Infantry, raised by Major Sir Edward Bethune, a British Cavalry Officer of the Afghan Wars. He had recruited his men in Durban where, before moving up-country, the other ranks had entertained the officers and their friends with a smoking concert giving renditions such as: *Yes, let me like a soldier fall*; a comic song, *Right before the Missis too*; a recitation, *The Field of Waterloo*; and, inevitably, everyone sang *We're Soldiers of the Queen*. Now, 500 strong, they too had been present at the attack on Hlangwane; The South African Light Horse, to whom Churchill had attached himself, comprised mainly dispossessed Johannesburg *outlanders*, but included adventurers from all over the world. It was 600 strong and commanded by Lieutenant-Colonel the Honourable Julian Byng, 'Bungo' as Buller affectionately called him. The regimental motto, of Zulu wording, *Usiba njalo nga pambili* meant 'Feathers always to the front', the significance being that each man wore in his hat, a long black tail feather of the Sakabula bird. For the same reason the regimental nickname was 'The Cocky-ollie birds'. Finally, there were the British mounted infantry, soldiers who could ride, drawn from the ranks of divisional regiments, who would, in time, become as proficient as their colonial counterparts.

Before crossing the Little Tugela, Dundonald had stopped short of the bridge. Shortly a scout arrived who, working ahead, had ridden several miles beyond the Little Tugela and reported not a Boer to be seen. Dundonald gazed at the country beyond: perfect for horsemen and Potgieter's Drift was only seven miles away. He could be there in an hour and, with luck, take the drift before the Boers knew what was happening. First the horses were watered. More scouts came in, and all reported the same thing: not a Boer was to be seen and the country was deserted. Dundonald waited no longer. He gave the order 'Mount up' and the horsemen filed across the bridge, spread out into open order and rode towards the Tugela and the mountainous hills beyond which the enemy, who were well aware of every British move, were frantically entrenching, using the spade, as a British officer remarked, as effectively as they used a rifle.

It is approximately 15 miles from Colenso to Potgieter's Drift and a further eight miles to Bastion Hill, making a total of 23 miles, as the crow flies, for what could be considered the length of the Boer defence line on the northern side of the Tugela. Beyond Bastion Hill, the Boer extreme right flank, the country flattened out, accommodating the farm and hamlet of Acton Homes and, over rolling country, a road led off east to Ladysmith, 25 miles away. The land immediately north of the river, the terrain that the British would have to cross, was dominated by a barrier of hills bearing such names as Rangeworthy, Tabanyama, Grootehoek, Spion Kop and Green Hill. Of course, in order to get at the Boers the British must first cross the river. In this they would be assisted by natural drifts that, depending on the state of the river, some of the men and animals would be able to wade. However, those dragging the supplies and guns would require pontoon bridges to affect a crossing. The British had a formidable task ahead. However, their numbers totalled 22,000 men with 60 guns whilst, opposing them, at that moment, there were probably fewer than 1,500 burghers between Colenso and Bastion Hill. Perhaps here General White's strategy of tying up the Boer Army to besiege Ladysmith was beginning to pay off.

Louis Botha had already begun sifting through his burghers facing Barton at Colenso, dispatching some west to oppose Buller's advance. Botha, due to illness, worry and overwork, was in a wretched state. As yet he had not moved his headquarters from Colenso and would, long before daylight, mount his horse and ride for three hours, supervising the construction of defences along the upper Tugela River, then ride back to

Colenso to organize the dispatch of supplies and dictate his report to Pretoria which, out of weariness, he did lying on his bed, frequently falling asleep as he spoke.[153] He had requested sick leave but President Kruger had replied: 'I regard your presence in the difficult circumstances on your front as indispensable. God will help sustain you in your onerous task.' [154] Botha's urgent call for reinforcements received an immediate response; although it was, nevertheless, limited to the manpower available. Young Deneys Reitz had obtained two weeks' leave but, on arriving in Pretoria, news of the British advance had already reached the capital. Reitz' father cautioned the young man to return immediately and do his duty. Arriving back at Ladysmith Reitz found that there was no lack of burgher volunteers for the Tugela line—anything was better than the boredom of besieging the town. Reitz and his brother were amongst those selected from the Pretoria Commando and within an hour they were off, complete with horses and a mule wagon laden with supplies, ammunition, pickaxes and shovels.[155] It was not long before the northern hills commanding the Tugela had taken on the appearance of a gold rush as with calloused hands and aching backs, the burghers dug deep and narrow trenches: each spade full of soil removed would, in the battle to come, be as valuable to their defence as a pouch of Mauser bullets.

Leaving 300 men to guard the Springfield Bridge, Dundonald's cavalry pressed on through a country free of all opposition arriving at Potgieter's Drift more than an hour before nightfall. They found a well-constructed redoubt with loop-holed walls that, if manned and held with determination, would have taken a considerable toll in time and lives. It too had been deserted. The heights above the drift, still on the southern bank of the river, were known as Mount Alice, named after the wife of the man who owned the farm on which they stood. They commanded one of the most panoramic views in Southern Africa. It was like standing on the edge of the world where one could peer out past the Drakensberg Mountains to the passes of the Orange Free State and the hazed extremities of Northern Natal. Nearer, when the heliograph flashed, or the sun caught the tin roofs of the town, Ladysmith, 25 miles away, confirmed its exact location. Coming closer, the Boer defence line of hills and *koppies* stretched from left to right as far as the eye could see while 1,000 feet below the Tugela wound its languid way across the plain, dotted here and there with native *kraals* and fields of cultivation. Nearer still, with its three islands, Potgieter's Drift itself was visible and, a few hundred yards upstream, the anchored ferry could be seen. However, alongside, the massif of Spion

Kop blocked further visibility to the west. What a platform from which to conduct a battle: it was a dais fit for Mars himself.

Dundonald, having sent messages to Buller advising of his success, had his troopers form a camp in which they spent a wet and anxious night. Yet, in the morning, they were confident that they could hold the drift and cross the river at will. However, through binoculars, as active as an army of ants, the burghers could be seen entrenching with relentless determination.

A day of inactivity followed the coup of taking the drift. However, to add lustre to their achievement, the South African Light Horse volunteered to capture the ferry. Thirty of them set off and while 20 or more lay guard amongst the riverside boulders, six men and Lieutenant Carlisle stripped off, plunged into the river and struck out for the ferry on the southern bank. All arrived safely and having released its moorings, the ferry, under long range Boer fire, was pulled to the southern bank. Other than Lieutenant Carlisle receiving a slight bullet graze, the action was a complete success.[156]

On 12 January, three days after the advance from Frere had begun, Buller himself arrived at Potgieter's Drift and such was his popularity, despite the reverses he had presided over, that Churchill wrote of his arrival: 'A few minutes later Sir Redvers Buller and his staff rode up to see things for themselves, and then we knew that all was well.' The ordinary soldier had similar feelings. Two battalions of infantry from Lyttelton's Brigade had followed hard on Buller's heels and any doubts that the drift might be recaptured were soon dispelled. Buller, like the god of battle, found a great boulder on Mount Alice—which was soon dubbed 'The Observatory'—where he sat silently for half an hour gazing at the Boer lines through his telescope. As he watched, a nearby soldier, looking in wonder at the panorama, said to his mate: 'We ought to have the Queen up here in her little donkey cart', to which his mate replied: 'Ah, we'd do it alright then!' Expectations were high; the betting between the officers was two to one that Ladysmith would be relieved by the end of the week.[157]

However, whatever was happening—if anything was happening at all—it was happening ponderously slowly. The 5th Division was still at Springfield where wagons were still arriving and where a village of tents sprawled across the plain. Warren, with his staff, rode to see Buller at Mount Alice and a disagreement immediately ensued. From his eyrie, Bulller pointed out his proposed line of attack across Potgieter's Drift. Warren wrote:

... I did not like it. It was exposed to gunfire from three-quarters of a circle, to which we could not effectively reply, and it was exposed to rifle fire from unseen riflemen at two thousand yards. Could there be a worse line of advance?[158]

The bickering and disagreement had begun.

When Buller sat on Observation Rock with his telescope, the panorama before him was his only map, the topography of the area never having been recorded except on farm maps which were notoriously inaccurate. At a future date, the lack of military surveys would come under the scrutiny of the War Commission when it would be astonishingly revealed that the vast majority of the farms in the Ladysmith area were owned by Boers who refused British officers access to their land. The chairman of the Commission incredulously asked: 'Do you mean that before the war, in our own colony, a British officer could not sketch the country?' General Hunter, to whom the question was directed, replied to the effect that had an officer insisted, he would have been summoned before a magistrate for trespass and the magistrate would have given a decision against him. Thus, despite the almost aerial view that lay before Buller, Spion Kop Hill obscured the extremity of the Boer right flank. However, having reconnoitred the enemy positions following Warren's visit, the limit of the Boer right flank had been revealed. Now it was Buller's turn to visit Warren. Having arrived at Springfield, both generals continued on to where General Coke and his brigade were camped. Warren proudly pointed out the *schanzes* (semi-permanent defences) which '. . . the whole brigade had been employed in making . . . of the most modern and up-to-date kind, a perfect defence.'[159] Coke's construction had obviously met with Warren's approval—perhaps even built at his instigation. Buller flew into a rage. He was marching to relieve Ladysmith, not making plans to defend Springfield. Coke got the rough end of Buller's tongue. 'For some reason unknown to me', wrote Warren, 'General Buller vigorously censured General Coke for his work, which he called folly. Of course,' Warren continued smugly:

. . . it may be said that the Boers are not likely to attack the camp—but who knows? We have to be prepared for all eventualities, and in any case it is important that the men should know how to build schanzes.[160]

Shortly after this exchange Buller gave Warren secret orders for the morrow. Warren was to have command of over half the army and most of the guns, whilst Buller would take on an umpire-like role from his perch on Mount Alice. Warren's precise orders were:

One: The enemy's position in front of Potgieter's Drift seems to me to be too strong to be taken by direct attack.

Two: I intend to try and turn it by sending a force across the Tugela from near Trichard's Drift [A further drift six miles upstream, westward from Potgieter's] and to the west of Spion Kop.

Three: You will have command of that force, which will consist of the 11th Brigade of your Division, your Brigade Division, Royal Field Artillery, and General Clery's Division complete, and all the mounted troops except four hundred.

Four: You will of course act as circumstances require, but my idea is that you should continue throughout refusing your right and throwing your left forward till you gain the open plain north of Spion Kop. Once there you will command the rear of the position facing Potgieter's Drift, and I think render it untenable.

Five: At Potgieter's there will be the 4th Brigade, part of the 10th Brigade, one battery RFA, one Howitzer battery, two 4.7 inch naval guns. With them I shall threaten both the positions in front of us, and also attempt a crossing at Skiet's Drift [A drift further to the east] so as to hold the enemy off you as much as possible.

Six: It is very difficult to ascertain the numbers of the enemy with any sort of exactness. I do not think there can be more than four hundred on your left, and I estimate the total force that will be opposed to us at about seven thousand. I think they have only one or at the most two big guns.

Seven: You will take two and a half days' supply in your regimental transport, and a supply column holding one day more. This will give you four days' supply, which should be enough. Every extra wagon is a great impediment.

Eight: I gather that you did not want an ammunition column. I think myself that I should be inclined to take one column for the two brigade divisions. You may find a position on which it is expedient to expend a great deal of ammunition.

Nine: You will issue such orders to the Pontoon Troop as you think expedient. If possible, I should like it to come here [Potgieter's Drift] after you have crossed. I do not think you will find it possible to let oxen draw the wagons over the pontoons. It will be better to draw them over by horses or mules, swimming the oxen; the risk of breaking the pontoons, if oxen crossed them, is too great.

Ten: The man whom I am sending you as a guide is a Devonshire man: he was employed as a boy on one of my own farms; he is English to the backbone, and can be thoroughly trusted. He thinks that if you've crossed Springfield flat at night he can take you the rest of the way to the Tugela via a road that cannot be overlooked by the enemy, but you will doubtless have the road reconnoitred.

Eleven: I shall endeavour to keep up heliographic communication with you from a post on the hill directly in your rear.

Twelve: I wish you to start as soon as you can. Supply is all in, and General Clery's Division will, I hope, concentrate at Springfield today. Directly you start I shall commence to cross the river. Please send me the 10th Brigade, except that portion which you detail for the garrison at Springfield, as soon as possible; also the eight 12-pr. naval guns, and any details such as ammunition column, and etc. that you do not wish to take.[161]

Having issued Warren with his orders, Buller, in rousing terms, then addressed the troops at Springfield, assuring them that they were about to march on Ladysmith, that they would raise the siege and that there would be no turning back. He rode around the camp extolling the men and wherever he went he was greeted with excited cheers, and calls of 'No turning back this time!' As yet, however, everyone believed they would be marching to Potgieter's Drift—not that it made much difference as one drift or another and what lay on the other side, were all the same to the rank and file.

Early in the evening of the 16th, as soon as it was dusk, the great concourse began to stir; the men were fed, rations issued and packs consisting of only one blanket, a waterproof and shed of all else except bare essentials, were shouldered. Quietly platoons formed into companies and companies into regiments. Tents were left standing, campfires remained burning and one company per regiment was left behind to create the illusion that the British camp still bustled with an army. With the hope of some sleep before morning, and guided by Buller's former farmhand,

the army set off on a 12-mile slog into a night that brought with it drench-
ing rain which in turn caused the usual chaos amongst the floundering
wagons. Nevertheless, entreated to 'Get a move-on' one moment and then
to slow down the next, the infantry arrived at the river before dawn,
believing they had accomplished, in difficult circumstances, that which
was not only their commander's goal, but also a situation that would
allow them to cross the river in darkness, thus depriving the enemy of easy
pickings. However, despite the breathless hurry from Springfield, there
now seemed to be no need for haste. One soldier wondered to his mate,
why it was that they were waiting; his mate replied bitterly: 'To give the
Boers a chance.'

Piling up at the drift was a convoy of wagons, later reported by
'Defender' 'to be 15 miles long'; rather an exaggeration it would seem as
the total distance from Springfield to Trichard's Drift was a little over 12.
Whatever the distance, there seemed no hurry to deploy, dawn revealing
hundreds of men and wagons sprawled along the southern bank of the
Tugela. The deceptions of camp fires left burning, tents standing and the
night march now appeared pointless.

Dundonald's brigade had also been ordered to join Warren's army
and they too had completed their ride in darkness, arriving at Trichard's
Drift in time to greet the general himself. Churchill later remarked:

One main feature has characterised the whole undertaking—its
amazing deliberation . . . A lightning blow had been expected and
everyone speculated because of delay: was it folly, incapacity or
even laziness?[162]

Finally things began to happen. The sappers arrived with all their
equipment and soon a bridge began to span the river: '. . . span after span
of pontoons sprang out at the ends as it lay along the bank. Very soon it
would be long enough to tow into position across the flood.'[163] By late
afternoon the zealous engineers would have completed a sister bridge
alongside the first, which would give passage to the guns, ammunition
columns and heavy transport. Warren was in his element. Not so much,
perhaps, because he was across the Tugela, but more so because he was
an engineer and he knew a thing or two about building bridges and he
would, after a lackadaisical start, get his convoy over in record time. In
doing so he no doubt hoped to acquire some of the rough soldierly admiration that the troops so readily bestowed upon Buller. On New Year's

Day, whilst in camp at Frere, Warren went on a walk-about shaking hands with every soldier he met and wishing them a 'Happy New Year'; when encountering groups of men he made 'a little speech'. On the way to Springfield he had helped manually to heave and haul the wagons in the mud.

> At first I was not recognised, but eventually the men began to know me and look for my help in emergencies, and in three days I was known and welcomed throughout our force. This was an enormous advantage to me, because in starting out on the campaign I thus became well-known to the men, though [he added primly] I knew none of them individually.[164]

Finally, having given two days to the task, by nightfall on the 18th, the whole force was across the Tugela and had moved three miles west from Trichard's Drift, where its position would have been vulnerable to Boer gunfire, to Venter's Laager, a large round hill that would give protection. Mission accomplished. However, instead of seeking contact with the enemy, Warren had lost the element of surprise by getting all his transport across the river in what he would hold to be record-time. He had also used up half his supplies which had been intended to sustain his army most of the way to Ladysmith and had given the enemy two days grace in which to reinforce its position. Buller had estimated the number of the enemy facing him to be no fewer than 7,000. Warren thought their number, in reality, to be a great deal more. The British Intelligence Office estimated the total number of Boers in Natal at 40,000; allowing for those besieging Ladysmith, for those facing Barton at Colenso and commandos on other duties. By British calculations Buller and Warren were faced by 20,000 burghers—it is more likely that when Warren arrived at Trichard's Drift, there were as few as 400 Boers with one field gun on the opposite bank, while 1,500 opposed Buller at Potgieter's Drift. By the 18th, the burgher forces had increased to 4,000 with five 75mm field guns and two Pom-Poms. Nevertheless, it was still a David and Goliath situation.

CHAPTER TEN

INSIDE LADYSMITH—
DEATH'S WAITING ROOM

After the Battle of the Platrand, the feeling in Ladysmith was not so much elation at beating the Boers and keeping the flag flying, as grief at their losses and regret that Buller would not be arriving as expected. Strewn around Wagon Hill and Caesar's Camp, the British and Boer casualties lay side by side. Some of the wounded had been there for 27 hours, first burned and blistered by a scorching sun and then subjected to a night clad in icy garments. Donald Macdonald, the war correspondent, toured the slopes of the Platrand in the early morning and was aghast at the grotesque contortions that agony and the elements had assigned upon the dead. A ceasefire had been agreed and the Boer Red Cross wagons were busy collecting their dead and wounded. Some bodies had been so pulverised that they could not be lifted. Macdonald wrote:

> About ninety of the Dutch [Boer] dead were taken off the hill they had come to capture. Thirteen of them could not be moved, they were in that pen of death where our shrapnel fell thickest, and, much as we in Ladysmith had seen the destruction of shellfire during this past ten weeks, we had witnessed nothing quite so appalling as that. These men could not be removed for burial— they were too shockingly mangled; so their graves were dug beside them.[165]

A cemetery for the British dead was selected on the slopes of the

Platrand that commanded a great vista of the distant plains terminating in the foothills of the Drakensberg. Each regiment dug a communal grave for its dead who were laid shoulder to shoulder. There were no coffins; an army issue blanket was thrown over each one before the stony soil was shovelled in and the bugler sounded *The Last Post*. They were all young men. Because of exposure, many of the wounded who would have lived, died. One illustration, as given by Macdonald, will suffice:

> By noon on the day after the battle the death toll of the ILH was twenty men; twenty-four hours later it had risen to thirty. There were, however, those whom luck had favoured and were still alive. One trooper had four bullets through his hat and a fifth that had slightly stunned him.[166]

Heartening news trickled through that the Boers regarded the battle as a national calamity and that the Free State Boers blamed the Transvaalers for their want of tenacity, confirming Reitz's description of the attack. That led in turn to the Transvaalers, later in the day, occupying a donga which proved to be a sitting duck for the Royal Artillery. Days after the battle the Boers were still searching for their dead as many bodies had been flushed away into Fourie's Spruit alongside the burghers' camp. During the storm this had turned into a torrent carrying all before it down to the Tugela. Macdonald came upon the bodies of two Boers who, from their appearance, were clearly father and son, leading him to ponder how often a Boer family must be deprived of all its men folk as, unlike the British, fathers and sons went off to war together.

In Ladysmith, enteric disease and dysentery were outstripping the toll of battle casualties. The Border Mounted Rifles who, at the commencement of the siege could parade 200 men, could now only muster 96. It was the same story with all the regiments: the ILH had gone from 475 troopers down to fewer than 150, and the Devons had only 500 fit men out of a regiment totalling 1,000. The worst cases found their way to *Death's Waiting Room* at Ntombi Hospital Camp. The rest, the lucky ones, sweated it out on a ground sheet, covered by an army blanket and, looked after by their mates, hoped for the best. Amongst those who had died of fever was G. W. Steevens, the brilliant war correspondent who had described so vividly General Yule's retreat from Dundee. Steevens had been nursed with great care throughout his long illness by a fellow war correspondent and artist, Mr William Maude of *The Graphic*. Maude had travelled widely in his profession including to Egypt, India and the Sudan. He wrote of the siege:

> We have had a horrible time of it, one I shall never forget as long as I live. The number of fine men that have gone under since the siege is simply appalling to think of. What with the deaths from shot, shells, starvation and disease we have but a shattered remnant of the fine force that came here last October.[167]

After the death of young Lord Ava, shot through the head on the Platrand, who had been an ADC to Sir George White, Maude, aware of the shortage of officers, offered himself in Ava's stead and was gratefully accepted for the post.

Within a few days of the battle, rations were reduced to a quarter pound of bread, half a pound of beef, half a pound of mealie meal and some sugar, tea, pepper and lime, issued three times a week. Any other titbits had to be scrounged:

> Tobacco was made from a 'woeful' mixture of peach and wild geranium leaves; 'well-seasoned' sausages dispel all thought of the horse that had provided most of the contents; butter, lard and cooking oil had long since finished but brave attempts were made to fry bread in coconut oil.[168]

It was said that had it not been for the peach trees that grew in profusion around Ladysmith and the nourishing fruit that dropped in abundance, Ladysmith would have succumbed to privation long before the siege was raised. As for the horses, those unfit for service were turned out either to fend for themselves upon the veldt, or to become items on the butcher's shopping list. Nevertheless, many an old troop horse on hearing the trumpet call 'Feed off', now reserved for only fit mounts, would hurry to the cavalry lines where, and without understanding why, it would be shooed away.

On the civilian side of things, James Bayley, who it will be remembered, had a furniture shop in Ladysmith and a fiancée elsewhere to whom he wrote almost every day, was greatly relieved that the 'Tommies' had won the battle of the Platrand, but did not seem particularly grateful for the sacrifices that they had made. Bayley was recovering from the fever, without having entered the perilous and tainted domain of the Ntombi

Hospital Camp. He had had the benefit of a private doctor and was able to tell his fiancée that he was now doing fine. In fact, he was going to attempt a few steps up the street to the barber to have his beard removed. He and a neighbour, a Mr Mitchell, had been treated by Dr Anderson, but Mitchell, so Bayley relates, neglected to take his medicine and quickly died. Dr Anderson prescribed eggs every day for Bayley but, at 18 shillings a dozen, they were, like most food stuff, unaffordable.[169]

On 17 January, the day that Warren would commence crossing Trichard's Drift, Bayley was awakened early:

> There is evidently a big battle being fought by the relief column. There has been tremendous cannonading in the distance since day-break and it has continued the whole day, it now being about twenty minutes to six.

By the following day fire from Buller's naval guns and howitzers had grown even louder:

> What a fight Buller's column must be having. It was after midnight last night when I got to sleep yet the cannon still roared and when I awoke before six o'clock this morning it continued. Thus it has been throughout the day. This afternoon about five o'clock it was very heavy, a continuous, roar, roar, roar. A balloon attached to the column was sighted here this morning.[170]

In fact, Bayley had had a very disrupted day. In the afternoon a messenger arrived bearing an envelope marked 'On Her Majesty's Service'. Inside was a note advising him his shop had been struck by a shell and that he was to hurry there at once to prevent looting. Bayley pocketed a revolver but on arrival found two policemen guarding the shattered lounge suites, the remains of a grand piano and other assorted items of furniture, many of which lay in the street. He was told that the looters, believed to be soldiers, had been hustled off. Bayley returned home to compose a claim to the government for compensation. He ended his letter to his fiancée in a despondent mood: 'We shall get something, but whether full value or not remains to be seen.'[171]

CHAPTER ELEVEN

TRICHARD'S DRIFT

The cavalry that had hurried through the dark and rain to rendezvous at Trichard's Drift before daybreak, were now kept hanging around until close on noon before they received the order to cross the Tugela. However, unlike the infantry, they were in for a wet passage. A quarter of a mile further downstream there was another ford by the name of Wagon Drift, held to be rather deep and dangerous as indeed it turned out to be. The big heavy horses of the 1st Royal Dragoons were through to the other side with little trouble but when it came to the South African Light Horse and Carbineers, whose mounts were little more than ponies, many were swept off their feet and it was considered lucky to get away with just a ducking. One unfortunate trooper of the 13th Hussars, weighed down with equipment, was swept away and drowned. For the rest of the day the cavalry did little but watch the growing mass of infantry, guns, oxen and wagons pile up like some great traffic jam along the northern bank of the river. So far not a shot had been fired from the column's 36 cannons. It was not until dawn on the 18th that infantry were ordered to deploy in skirmishing order towards the barrier of hills that, two miles from the Tugela, began to rise steeply to the Rangeworthy (Tabanyama) plateau, whose crest contained the lines of entrenchments that the burghers had earlier been seen frantically digging. It will be remembered that Buller's secret orders to Warren were to the effect that the Boer positions were too strong to be taken by frontal attack and therefore it was intended to turn the burghers' flank: 'You will of course act as circumstances require, but my idea is that you should continue throughout, refusing your right and throwing your left forward until you gain the open country north of Spion Kop', was the vague instruction. Churchill put it more concisely:

> The Boer-covering army was to be swept back on Ladysmith by a powerful arm, the pivoting shoulder of which was at Potgieter's, the elbow at Trichard's and the enveloping hand—the cavalry under Lord Dundonald—stretching out towards Acton Homes.[172]

Buller's orders, although vaguely worded, nevertheless revealed his preference to relieve Ladysmith by way of the Acton Homes road—but he stopped short of giving a direct order to take that route; if mistakes were to be made, let Warren make them and take the consequences. Once across the Tugela there were three roads to the besieged town. The closest to Ladysmith, and actually crossing Potgieter's Drift, was the Doornkloof road that passed to the east of Spion Kop. It was obviously not Buller's intention that Warren should use this route as he and his army were on the western side of Spion Kop. Two choices remained: either the Fairview/Rosalie road (henceforth called the Fairview Road) which commenced at Trichard's Drift and then rose steeply on to the Rangeworthy Heights and the Boer entrenchments or, the Acton Homes road, the main route from the Orange Free State, into which the Doornkloof and Fairview roads eventually entered for their final run into Ladysmith. Access to the Acton Homes road was one and a half miles west of Bastion Hill where it became the extremity of the Boer right flank.

As the infantry probed forward, Dundonald received orders to guard their left flank; thus a screen of horsemen, scattered over a six-mile front, began to deploy. The Composite Regiment, as it was clumsily called, consisted of elements of the ILH, South African Light Horse (SALH), Natal Carbineers, Thornycroft's Mounted Infantry (TMI) and the 60th Rifles Mounted Infantry. They led the way, 600 horsemen all told, followed by British regulars of the 1st Royal Dragoons and 13th Hussars. The colonials moved at speed towards Bastion Hill and, led by Major Graham, were rewarded by sighting a substantial body of the enemy moving along the Acton Homes road in the direction of Ladysmith. Using all the cover and dead ground that could be found, the colonials, as skilled as their enemy in the use of stealth, made it to the Acton Homes road unseen and just minutes ahead of their quarry. Once there they extended and, as the burghers rode into the trap, opened fire at 300 yards. There were about

200 Boers, many of whom fell at the first volley. Those at the rear of the commando managed to scamper away but for the rest their only option was to dismount and fight it out. However, with British reinforcements arriving at the gallop, the enemy was inevitably surrounded and after one or two false signs of surrender, a white flag appeared waving above the rocks and slowly and timidly the burghers appeared. The Boer toll was ten dead, eight wounded and 24 prisoners 'of the most formidable type'. The British suffered two killed and one wounded, a reversal of the usual outcome in an encounter with the Boers.

Churchill was on the scene within minutes and watched as the instinct to kill that had blazed during the battle, dimmed to pity for the wounded. Churchill himself was deeply moved by the sight of the Boer dead whereas minutes before he had gleefully watched the troops trying to kill them:

> The Boer dead were collected and a flag of truce was sent to the enemy's lines to invite a burying and identification party at dawn. I have often seen dead men, killed in war—thousands at Omdurman—scores elsewhere, black and white, but the Boer dead aroused the most painful emotions. Here by the rock under which he had fought lay the Field-Cornett of Heilbron, Mr. de Mentz— a grey haired man of sixty years, with firm aquiline features and a short beard. The stony face was grimly calm, it bore the stamp of unalterable resolve; the look of a man who had thought it all out, and was quite certain that his cause was just, and such as a sober citizen might give his life for.[13]

Apart from de Mentz the ambushed commando had been led by 'Rooi' Daniel Opperman who not only escaped but would play an important part in the events to come. The prisoners revealed that they had seen the regular cavalry moving forward from two miles away and had wrongly assumed them to be the vanguard of the British force. They blamed their misfortune on a volunteer Austrian, 'a cursed foreigner', who had been their forward scout and had failed to spot the ambush.

Dundonald's colonials had not only proved that they were as skilled as Boers in bush warfare but, by good fortune, had rattled the door to Ladysmith. Nevertheless, whatever initiative Dundonald may have grasped, Warren would make sure that it did not evolve. Inexplicably, he forestalled the cavalry—indeed the whole of the relieving army—from the possibility of liberating Ladysmith by way of the Acton Homes road.

Instead of reinforcing Dundonald as requested, Warren stripped the mounted brigade of 500 of TMI[174] and consigned the unit to guarding the British oxen behind Venter's Laager, a job more fitting for infantry. With the enemy only just holding its own along its extended miles of entrenchments, the possibility of a Boer raid on the British *laager* from any direction was most unlikely.

A short distance from the position held by the cavalry on the Acton Homes Road, was a single Boer gun and a number of rather isolated entrenched enemy marksmen. Dundonald had made an immediate request for an artillery attack on this position but Warren refused. Also, when Dundonald sent in for provisions, these too were denied by Warren who remarked to the transport officer: 'If I let them go, Lord Dundonald will try to go to Ladysmith.' [175] However, despite the lack of rations, the colonials held on to their foothold at Acton Homes until the following morning when Dundonald was ordered to see Warren whom he found at Venter's Spruit, exhorting some wagon drivers to greater effort in getting their vehicles across the stream. There was a fierce argument with Dundonald asserting that he was endeavouring to fulfil Buller's orders— it will be recalled that the cavalry was still at Potgieter's Drift when Buller arrived there on the 12th, when he would certainly have discussed his plans with his cavalry commander and friend, Lord Dundonald.

Buller would regret his failure to assert command and give Warren a direct order to attempt the Acton Homes Road as his first priority. Attempts to relieve Ladysmith by other routes would be doomed to failure, and the Acton Homes Road, although longer by about ten miles, was by far the easiest passage. However, Warren, sitting by the stream at Venter's, would not listen and silently, by gesture, rebutted every argument Dundonald made. Finally, he stood up and, yelling more advice at the wagon drivers, ended the discussion by saying: 'I want you close to me.' [176] After this argument, Warren ignored Dundonald, denying him any credit. 'Defender' gives Warren's brigade commanders the following number of mentions: Hildyard, nine; Lyttelton, nine; Hart, ten; Clery, 17; Woodgate, 30; and Coke, 40. Dundonald is mentioned only once: 'On 20th January the cavalry on the extreme left, under Lord Dundonald, demonstrated effectively.'[177] Warren would later assert that he, in fact, made a reconnaissance of the Acton Homes road but, as he would already have had Dundonald's intelligence and had made up his mind to pursue an alternative route, another reconnaissance would have been unlikely. In addition to the Acton Homes road being a longer route to Ladysmith,

Warren held that two miles beyond, there was a pass that was not only defended (as was every route to Ladysmith) but, due to its narrow passage, would delay his wagons. These he had been moving in six parallel columns, a formation he would have to dispense with if he were to advance at all. The Acton Homes road was one of the main routes from the Orange Free State to Natal and would have been an unlikely natural hazard. In any event, should the pass have proved to be a bottle neck of sorts, Warren had at his disposal engineers, tools, explosives and, including soldiers, drivers and natives, an almost bottomless source of labour. Twenty years earlier Buller, then a colonel leading a force of colonial horsemen, had reconnoitred the route of the second invasion of Zululand which took 200 wagons, similar to those in use by Warren, 100 miles over terrain that was yet to feel the crunch of a wagon wheel, the column making its road as it went and all the while subject to imminent attack.[178]

So much for the activities of the 18th! The next day was filled with wagon hauling once again as the column made its way to the shelter hill of Venter's Laager. 'Defender' called it 'a most hazardous proceedings' and stated that it was only due to Warren's careful management and the lack of initiative on the part of the enemy commander that there was no disaster. Warren now directed his attention to the possibilities of the Fairview road and found that it came within rifle range from the western flanks of Spion Kop and, so long as the hill was held by the enemy, that route would also have to be discarded. However, there was no other. If the Rangeworthy Heights were stormed the attackers would be faced with a wide empty plateau swept by a maelstrom of fire from the enemy trenches 500 yards away.

The activities that took place on the 19th are confused by the wrangling of Buller and Warren, each offering a different account. Buller, in a letter to the Secretary of State, written at Spearman's Camp (Mount Alice) on 30 January, 1900, said:

> The arrival of the force at Trichard's Drift was a surprise to the enemy who were not in strength. Warren, instead of feeling for the enemy, spent the whole day passing his baggage. During this time the enemy received reinforcements and strengthened his position. On the 19th he [Warren] attacked and gained a considerable advantage. On the 20th instead of pursuing it, he divided his force and gave General Clery a separate command: . . . Dundonald's movement was a decided success and should have been

supported by artillery, while Warren's infantry should have attacked the salient, which Dundonald's success had left exposed. On that night I debated with myself whether I should relieve Warren of his command.[179]

However, Buller, shunning responsibility, failed to do so.

On the evening of the 19th, Warren, a dictatorial and intimidating man, assembled his brigade generals and staff officers, and the officers commanding the Royal Artillery and Royal Engineers—everyone, in fact, except Dundonald. He pointed out there were only two roads by which transport and guns could proceed, either the Fairview or the Acton Homes roads. He told them he had rejected the latter because 'time would not allow of it'. Having received 'universal approval' from all present he sent the following message to Buller:

I find there are only two roads by which we could possibly get from Trichard's to Potgieter, on the north of the Tugela—one by Acton Homes, the other by Fairview and Rosalie; the first I reject as too long, the second is a very difficult road for a large number of wagons, unless the enemy is thoroughly cleared out. I am there- fore going to adopt some special arrangements which will involve my stay at Venter's Laager for two or three days. I will send in for further supplies and report progress.[180]

Warren did not reveal to his Commander-in-Chief what his special arrangements would be which is understandable as they were more the conception of a callous military adventurer rather than that of a com- mander of three brigades of British soldiers. Warren wrote:

All my life long I have watched events and their results—and have become more and more certain that to do anything well you must have practice and rehearsals. We allow this for cricket and football and golf and theatricals, but no one now seems to realise that fighting the Boer is an operation which required practice and rehearsals, just as in the case of games. The men were trained to meet European troops, but meeting the Boers with their good weapons of precision and their powers of shooting and taking cover, was a new experience to which our troops must get accus- tomed, while the advent of smokeless powder added to the intricacy of the operations. The troops I was taking into action were quite unfitted for immediately fighting the Boer. They had been kept entire apart from him, till he had become rather a bogey. They had not seen him yet, dead or alive . . . It was my mission to introduce Mr. Tommy Atkins [the nickname for a British soldier] to Mr. Boer, face to face. I wanted three days for what I called 'Blooding the troops'. I would no more think of taking troops, in the condition of our men as handed over to me, to assault a position, than I would take a team of cricketers who had no experience of football to compete in a football match . . .[181]

On the 20th he put his theory into practice by ordering a general advance. All day long the lines of British infantry moved forward.

Major General Fitzroy Hart, still courageous to the point of insanity, commanded the centre of the attack, leading the Dublin Fusiliers, or what was left of them, who were followed by the Border Regiment and the Lancashire Brigade. Viewed from afar the assault appeared to be a mass of khaki blobs weaving and ducking as they advanced, some dropping for cover and then rising to dart forward once more, others never to rise again. The body language of the attackers transmitted their fear and the danger of their task. However, on they went and Hart, like all other officers, now carried a rifle and had discarded his conspicuous badges of rank—perhaps he would have been happier waving a sword and wearing a red coat. However, the troops were being taught how to play the game and meet Mr Boer face to face. The score for the day's play was 34 British dead, 293 wounded and two missing.

Churchill later visited the 'Officers Mess' of the Dublin Fusiliers which consisted of a two-foot-high wall and a wooden box. On being asked how his regiment had fared in the assault, the colonel proudly replied that since October, the regiment had lost 450 men out of 900 and there were few of them left.[182]

In the evening the troops were withdrawn from the most forward positions to spend a bitterly cold night in the open. However, Warren's absurd theories were not applied to the cavalry, and those of the South African Light Horse who had escaped his net took and held the crest line of Bastion Hill adjacent to the Acton Homes road. One trooper, more agile than most, arrived at the summit first and there exposed and reckless, put his helmet on the end of his rifle, waving and cheering for all to see, friend and foe alike. However, the taking of the hill had been ominously easy; the reason was quickly revealed: 1,000 yards away, across an approach devoid of cover, a line of Boer entrenchments, hardly visible, opened fire. It was Warren's last chance to exploit an alternative route to the one chosen—the Fairview road and the passage past Spion Kop. Between 4pm and 5pm, nine companies and one battalion of infantry was sent to relieve the cavalry, and they kept in contact with the enemy throughout the night. No casualties were incurred.

The follow-up on the 22nd, described in General Hildyard's *Brigade Operations* is vague but what does become clear is there was no attempt to exploit the success of the SALH earlier in the day. Churchill had been riding on the flanks of Bastion Hill, witnessing the infantry advancing and expressing his regret that modern warfare was disappointing as a spectacle. He wrote at the time:

> There is no smoke except that of bursting shells. The combatants are scattered, spread over a great expanse of ground, concealed wherever possible, clad in neutral tint . . . rows of tiny brown dots hurried forward a few yards and vanished into the brown of the earth.

Not like the magnificence of Omdurman, he noted, with its flashing spears and waving flags. Then, turning his attention again to the present battle, he continued:

> . . . A great wave of infantry surged forward along a crest line. The patter of Mauser bullets swelled to a continuous rumbling . . . and presently the wave recoiled . . . There had been a check . . . Then the whole wave started again full of impetus . . . and we wished we were near enough to give them a cheer.[183]

However, the attack had not been aimed at Bastion Hill nor with a specific purpose elsewhere along the line—Warren was continuing with 'bloodying' his troops.

The SALH held Bastion Hill until the infantry arrived but, to ensure that Dundonald did not take the initiative, Warren placed the cavalry under the command of General Hildyard whose report of 20/21/22 January records:

By the personal order of the General Officer Commanding Field

Force, General Hildyard was placed in command of the mounted troops and was made responsible for the safety of the camp. In consequence of this the officer commanding mounted troops was directed to provide for the safety of the camp to the right bank of Venter's Spruit.[184]

This was a severe admonishment for Dundonald but Warren was taking no chances. The following day, the 22nd, the British assault faltered although the infantry still clung tenaciously to the crest lines of Range-worthy Heights and Bastion Hill, '. . . clustered in the steep re-entrance like flies on the side of a wall', as Churchill recalled. Each side fired away at the other with little chance of success while the Boer gun at Acton Homes, which Dundonald had requested Warren to attack with artillery, still pounded the British infantry with shrapnel. At nightfall the guns fell silent and Hildyard's artillery was withdrawn to Venter's Spruit.

Meanwhile, at the other end of the battlefield at Potgieter's Drift, below Buller's lookout on Mount Alice, Lyttelton's battalions of light infantry had been ordered to demonstrate against a Boer position still held by the burghers on the north side of the drift. The Scottish Rifles and the King's Royal Rifles led the attack, which was partly directed from an observation balloon until the balloon was hit by rifle fire and the observer slightly wounded. The Boers brought up machine guns which in turn came under fire from the British naval guns on Mount Alice. Additional artillery, two howitzers and a field battery, then engaged the enemy knocking out, Lyttelton asserted, the Boer machine guns. However, the whole force withdrew under the cover of darkness. The action resulted in 17 British casualties.[185]

On the 21st an uninterrupted bombardment of artillery fire was pounded out all day along the ten mile front, turning the tranquil Tugela valley into a nightmare of unrelenting violence. Warren's hesitation to strike with full purpose allowed Botha to deploy his guns and men to full advantage; his burghers, under the most hazardous conditions, all the while were extending their entrenchments 500 to 2,000 yards back beyond the trap of the forward crest lines. Nevertheless, the burghers began to waver under the intensity of the British bombardment as the missiles found their targets, smashing and tearing entrenchments apart with lyddite and shrapnel. Many burghers abandoned the trenches for the relative safety of the reverse slopes, whilst others deserted their duty completely. By the 21st General Botha realised that his burghers were deserting in greater numbers than reinforcements were arriving. Warren continued with his probing tactics but at sunset the distribution of the two armies had changed little as though in stalemate. Buller, although he could hear the pounding of guns and the rattle of musketry coming from Trichard's Drift, could not, much to his frustration and despite his panoramic view site, actually see what was happening as Warren's area of operation was completely obscured by the mass of Spion Kop. He, therefore, decided to ride again to Warren's headquarters; where he found, to his annoyance, that the artillery batteries had been placed all together straddling the Fairview road. 'Defender' believes that Warren on this occasion described to Buller the nature of his 'special arrangements' that he had alluded to in his message of the 19th. If he did so Buller makes no mention of it nor does he seem to have enquired what they may have been.

On the 22nd Buller once more visited Warren, accompanying the delivery of four howitzer guns, and personally directing where they should be located. Part of their task was to silence the enemy gun firing from Acton Homes. Buller was to write of Warren's performance so far:

> I suggested a better distribution of his batteries, which he agreed to, to some extent, but he would not advance his left, and I found that he had divided his fighting line into three independent commands, independent of each other, and apparently independent of him.[186]

Warren would later reply to this criticism:

> I omitted to state that during the afternoon of the 22nd the Commander-in-Chief proposed an attack upon the enemy's position on our left flank that night. [Acton Homes] I summoned at once the General Officers available, namely, Generals Clery, Talbot, Coke and Hildyard. General Clery who was in command of the left attack, did not consider it advisable to make this attack because, if successful, it would commit us to taking the whole line of the enemy's position, which he considered a hazardous proceeding, as we might not be able to hold it. In this I concurred, more particularly as it was evidently too late in the day to carry the operation out successfully.[187]

Buller then had his say:

Jubilant Boers wade the Tugela to carry off the abandoned British guns.
(With the Flag to Pretoria)

A Boer 'Long Tom', drawn by oxen, on the way to besiege Ladysmith.
(Africana Museum, Johannesburg)

General Sir Charles Warren, when a major commanding the Diamond Fields Horse, acts as a 'horse holder' during an encounter with rebels in Griqualand. *(The Illustrated London News, 6 June 1878, Author's collection)*

Traction engines did sterling work in pulling out bogged down British convoys. This cartoon suggests that the traction engine may have been the forebear of the tank. *(The Illustrated London News)*

FROM THE DAILY GRAPHIC 2 DECEMBER 1899

In and around Ladysmith many civilians spent their daylight hours in reinforced culverts, only appearing at night when the enemy bombardment slackened. *(Africana Museum, Johannesburg)*

Military shelters against the bombardment appear to offer more comfort than their civilian counterparts, but less protection. *(Africana Museum, Johannesburg)*

Above: The celebrated bayonet charge of the Devonshire Regiment at a crucial moment during the Battle of the Platrand. *(National Army Museum)*

Left: 'Spy', the famed cartoonist, gives his impression of General Sir George White. *(National Army Museum)*

Below: Men of the South African Light Horse stand guard whilst comrades capture the ferry at Potgieter's Drift. *(Authors collection)*

British transport crossing a pontoon bridge straddling one of the many streams encountered on the march to Trichard's Drift. (*Black and White* Magazine)

British cavalry crossing the Little Tugela en route to Potgieter's Drift. (*With the Flag to Pretoria*)

Men of the Lancashire Fusiliers embarking at Southampton for South Africa on 2 December 1899. Seven weeks later they led the attack on Spion Kop. (*With the Flag to Pretoria*)

The officers of Thorneycroft's Mounted Infantry. Thorneycroft is seated in the middle row with a helmet on his knee. (The Illustrated London News)

Boers hauling a
gun into position
using pure
manpower.
*(With the Flag
to Pretoria)*

The battle for Spion Kop crest line was brutal and unyielding.
(Africana Museum, Johannesburg)

The artist has accurately defined the plight of the British Troops. They are devoid of shelter and shelled from all sides by devastating artillery and rifle fire. *(Africana Museum, Johannesburg)*

The Naval guns on Mount Alice blindly open fire on Spion Kop causing British casualties. The Boer guns were immune from bombardment as they were entrenched on the reverse slopes of the hill. The rugged outline of Spion Kop is highly exaggerated. *(Black and White Magazine)*

Several observation balloons were brought out from England and proved very effective. Nevertheless, they and their crews were vulnerable to enemy rifle fire. *(With the Flag to Pretoria)*

The Kings Royal Rifles, despite being shelled by friendly fire, successfully stormed the Boer artillery position on Twin Peaks. Having achieved victory, Buller inexplicably ordered their recall. *(Black and White* Magazine)

A Boer commando at the foot of Spion Kop.
(Africana Museum, Johannesburg)

Wounded and
shell-shocked,
British troops
stumble down
from the summit
of Spion Kop.
*(With the Flag
to Pretoria)*

Officers of the Indian Ambulance Corps. Over 1,000 men served at Spion Kop. The Corps was raised by Mohandas Gandhi, seated centre, middle row. (*Africana Museum, Johannesburg*)

With the advent of motorized vehicles yet to come, mules and oxen drew the transport for both the British and Boer armies. *(Black and White* Magazine)

In the thick of the fighting to the very end, General Hart's Irish Brigade storm their way up the koppies to the Tugela Heights. *(Black and White* Magazine)

The British main trench on the morning following the battle. (*Africana Museum, Johannesburg*)

The aftermath of battle. The summit of Spion Kop was strewn with the shattered bodies of both Boer and Briton.
(Africana Museum, Johannesburg)

The Indian
Ambulance Corps,
nicknamed 'The
Body Snatchers',
go about their
grizzly work of
carrying away
the dead and
wounded.
*(With the Flag
to Pretoria)*

After 118 days, the Siege of Ladysmith is over. General Sir George White raises
his cap and calls for 'Three cheers for the Queen'. *(National Army Museum)*

I continually proposed to General Warren that he should attack the enemy's right, which was en l air and not strong, and which it was part of the original program to try and turn but I never suggested doing this hurriedly or without adequate forethought and preparation.[188]

Buller now calculated that the enemy were 15,000 strong whereas Michael Davitt, writing in *The Boer Fight for Freedom*, estimated that Botha's 40-mile defence line from the eastern side of Colenso to Acton Homes, contained no more than 6,000 men, but conceded that they were the best horsemen, able to move from one position to another at a moment's notice, and the best marksmen in the world. On the 23rd Buller rode yet once again to Warren's headquarters and pointed out that he had received no further reports, nor had Warren clarified what the 'special arrangements' were that he had alluded to on the 19th. Furthermore, Buller continued, Warren had kept his men continuously exposed to shell and rifle fire, clinging to precipitous hills, whilst supports were too close and provided no second line of defence; any panic could well send the whole line into utter chaos. Buller concluded that it was too dangerous a situation to be prolonged. Warren must either attack or Buller would withdraw his force. Withdraw could only mean retreat back across the Tugela. Buller again 'advocated' as he had done previously, an attack towards Acton Homes but still could not bring himself to issue a direct order. Warren replied to the effect that, with the agreement of his generals, he had decided to proceed with an assault along the Fairview Road and, in order to do so, it would be necessary to take Spion Kop. He had, he continued, ordered General Coke to make a night assault but Coke, not unreasonably, had objected most strongly to doing so without having first made a reconnaissance of the position.[189] That Buller did not counter Warren's proposal indicates his desperation to achieve action. His reluctance to attack mountains with the hope that their taking would provide a strategic advantage, was not unknown: in 1880 he had virtually foretold the tragedy of Majuba by remarking to Sir James Sivewright, of the Cape Telegraph Department, a day or so prior to the battle:

Does Sir George Colley know his African ground as we know it? He may be tempted to go up one of those infernal hills. Very well he'll climb one of them, but not really get to the top; or if he does get there, he won't understand that the top's no use unless you know which ridge to guard.[190]

Buller, with the dreaded memory of his own disastrous attack on Hlobane Mountain, two years prior to Majuba, was now about to sanction an attack on another infernal hill. Perhaps his recent disparaging remarks, alluding to Coke's would be 'Alpine excursions', were also a consequence of his memories. On the other hand, Warren, no doubt, reflected fondly on his accomplishment in 1878, when he defeated the Griqua rebels by dragging a cannon to the top of Gobatsi Heights. Were decisions now being influenced by the ghosts of the past and did Buller, exasperated by delays, concur with Warren because, having failed to take command himself, no alternative remained? It is interesting to note that 'Defender' maintained that Spion Kop was not an abnormally high hill. He later wrote: '. . . It is 1,500 ft. above the Tugela, about the height that the Rock Gun at Gibraltar is above the sea.' An incomprehensible comparison for most people but a further clue that Warren himself, who had carried out a detailed survey of Gibraltar, would later be the author of *Spionkop: A Vindication.* [191]

Warren had a further shock for Buller. Knowing that any advance along the Fairview Road would trigger a scramble of Boer riflemen into the crevices of Spion Kop's western slopes, where they would be out of sight of the naval guns on Mount Alice, and where they would be able to rain down a hail of lead on a foe below, he surprisingly proposed, after all the time he had dedicated to hauling the wagons across the river, they be sent back again. One of his objections to the Acton Homes Road had been, as he had seen it, its inability to accommodate his transport. Now he concluded that the Fairview Road, under fire, would be an equally hazardous passage. The answer, he believed, was to dispense with the wagons and for the men to carry five days' supply in their haversacks.[192] It was not an auspicious moment. He was advocating that, after a week of hardship and combat, the men hump all their kit, weapons and now their food and water, into what inevitably would be another bloody confrontation. René Bull, the war artist and correspondent of the *Black and White* magazine, wrote on 22 January:

On the Indian Frontier, bakeries followed the troops everywhere, and we always received our rations . . . One did not have to waste the best part of a day, as one does here, to secure a tin of bully beef or a pound and a quarter of hard ration biscuit . . . The big attack is expected this week; but I cannot understand the delay. We seem to be losing men in driblets . . . In the last three days we have lost about 200 killed and have very little bettered our position.[193]

However, the decision, reluctantly or not, had been made: Spion Kop was to be attacked. Buller sent a cable to that effect advising the Secretary of State. Conan Doyle later wrote: 'That evening there came a telegraph to London which left the Empire in a hush of anticipation.'

....

CHAPTER TWELVE

SPION KOP

Buller stipulated that the attack on Spion Kop must be made by 'tried troops': that is, men who had successfully been in action against the enemy. Eventually, Major-General Woodgate's Lancashire Brigade was selected for the task. Many of the men were reservists, having previously completed seven years' service and, if the grim determined faces that glare out of the photograph that was taken on their embarkation at Southampton are anything to go by, the Lancashire Fusiliers were as tough as they came. However, they did not meet the criterion of 'tried troops'.

Woodgate had been unwell and Warren had proposed that Major-General Coke command the assault. However, Coke was also not one hundred percent fit having broken a leg some while previously and being rather lame.[194] Buller concluded a poorly Woodgate was preferable to a hobbling Coke when it came to leading an attack up an unknown mountain in darkness. Furthermore, Buller and Woodgate were old comrades-in-arms having fought together throughout the Anglo-Zulu War: at the Battle of Kambula, while Buller had been attacking the Zulu right horn, Woodgate, then a captain, had led a bayonet charge, striding out, 'Sword aloft, marching as leisurely and unconcernedly as if he were pacing a piece of ground for cricket wickets'. [195]

Having arrived in South Africa only a month previously, the Lancashire Brigade had not taken part in any of the campaign's earlier battles. However, the Lancashire Fusiliers and South Lancs had, over the last few days, been in the forefront of Warren's experiment of 'meeting Mr. Boer face-to-face'.'

The assault force comprised: the 2nd Battalion Lancashire Fusiliers, commanded by Lieutenant-Colonel Charles Bloomfield; six companies of the Royal Lancaster Regiment, commanded by Lieutenant-Colonel Malby Crofton, (the next officer in seniority to Woodgate); several companies of the South Lancs; eight officers and 180 men of TMI commanded by Colonel Thornycroft; and half a company of the 17th Company Royal Engineers. In addition to each regiment or unit having its own Royal Army Medical Corps (RAMC) doctor and staff, the force was accompanied by the Natal Volunteer Medical Corps (NVMC), plus mules and their handlers carrying ammunition and tins of water. Originally instructed to assemble at 3.40pm on the 23 January at the bottom of a ridge known as Three Tree Hill, close to Warren's headquarters, it was realised that the force in that position would be visible to the enemy. Orders were amended changing the rendezvous point to a long ravine, about half a mile north of Trichard's Drift, where the force was brought together at about 7.30pm just at night fall. There they would be completely screened from the enemy; they would also be about a mile and a half from the bottom of Spion Kop's south-eastern spur, the intended route to the top.* Although the distance between the assembly ravine and the foot of the chosen spur was relatively short, it was over the roughest of terrain, full of dongas, rocks and boulders. It took the column, stumbling and cursing in the dark, a considerable time before the actual ascent began at 10.30pm. Strict orders were given: there was to be no talking, no lights, no smoking and no noise of any kind. Early in the day water, that would become as precious as ammunition, presented an unexpected problem. Although possessing the technology of the telegraph, the traction engine and batteries of guns that could throw 9-pound shells 3,000 yards into the enemy lines, Buller's army lacked a supply of simple watertight containers capable of conveying nine gallons of water 1,500 feet to the top of Spion Kop. The REs had made attempts to tie water in mackintosh sheets and lash the leaking bundles to the backs of mules. However, these attempts were futile as the contents emptied quicker than the sheets could be refilled. Therefore, they had, with only marginally more success, resorted to empty biscuit tins.[196]

---

*Note: much of the terrain that had formed the plain of the Tugela Valley in 1900, is now under water, a dam wall having been constructed in the 1960s just above Potgieter's Drift. This beautiful stretch of water now laps the foot of the Rangeworthy Hills, has engulfed Venter's Spruit and Venter's Laager and reaches the skirts of Spion Kop. The land surrounding the dam, once a battlefield, is now home to an Ezemvelo KwaZulu project supporting a large variety of wild animals.

Originally Woodgate had intended to lead the way but it became apparent that Thornycroft, assisted by his colonials with their local knowledge, was the best man for the job. The two native guides, who earlier had agreed to point out the path, had since disappeared into the night never to be seen again. An intermittent drizzle, obscuring the stars, began to fall as the climb commenced.

Amongst those who were making their way to the summit was Lieutenant Frederick Raphael of the 1st South Lancs. He had enjoyed the voyage out to South Africa immensely. He had shared a spacious cabin with one other officer, had appreciated the good food and had taken pleasure in watching the 'Tommies' sloshing and splashing in a big canvas contraption full of water that the sailors had rigged up for them. On arrival in Durban he and his regiment were soon in the grip of the realities of war having endured a cattle truck journey to Estcourt where the puff adders and scorpions would prove that the Boers were not the only enemy. Four days after disembarking in Durban, Raphael wrote home: 'I have to take my company out to form a picket in an outpost line this evening and remain out for twenty-four hours. It is rather jumpy work, especially with men who have never been on service before.' [197] They were hardly the 'tried troops' that Buller had stipulated.

As with most of the new arrivals, Raphael was soon struck down with 'sun fever', as he called it, his face and hands being covered in water blisters. Life had become very rough and although the regiment had tents, there was not even a box to sit on and everyone slept on the bare ground. A day or so later the first man in the regiment died of enteric fever. On 22 January, having met 'Mr. Boer face-to-face' Raphael managed to write home that he had not had his clothes or boots off for a week and that his company had 'fought splendidly' but 15 men had either been killed or wounded. Thus, having become 'tried troops' he and his men were about to assault Spion Kop.

Ahead of the South Lancs, there was an even later arrival: Second-Lieutenant Hugh McCorquodale, the 25-year-old scion of a wealthy family, an old Harrovian, an undergraduate of Trinity College, a polo player and a huntsman. He had appeared only that morning, 'looking for a job' as he had informed Churchill who knew him from school days. Such was the informality of TMI, he was enlisted on the spot.

Behind the South Lancs and Fusiliers came the stretcher bearers. George Howard, a colonial civilian who, to do his bit, had joined the NVMC, was now carrying a stretcher laden with picks and shovels and finding the climb to be a punishing experience. He had already seen action on the battlefield of Colenso and, during the fighting of the last few days, he had brought in wounded under fire.

Thornycroft, assisted by several of his officers, Lieutenants Farquhar, Gordon and Forbes and Privates Shaw and MacAdam, halted for a minute or two to get his bearings, then the column began to clamber upward. Earlier Thornycroft had made a limited reconnaissance noting from below various landmarks that would guide him in the ascent. Landmarks that, with luck, would be outlined against the night sky when the drizzle lifted. The first was a small group of native huts which were quiet, the inhabitants having either vacated or wisely remained silently inside. The dwellings had been reached at midnight, eight and a half hours since the men first assembled. The next objective was a small level upland where the column, which had become spread out, was able to close up; they were now close to their objective. So far the stealth that had accompanied the climb was commendable indeed. The only noise that had been made by the column's approach had been the grating of the men's hobnail boots. However, further back down the hill, the order for utter silence had not been followed with similar diligence. George Howard of the NVMC, remembered:

> . . . We started off but didn't know where we were going, but every now and then we had to stop to let the men pass us . . . We were told to keep strict silence . . . We got to the second landing [small plateau] and we, growling at each other and making a lot of noise with our billies [billy cans].[198]

Luckily a south-easterly wind helped to carry any sound away from the direction of the summit. In places, the men were forced to scramble up on hands and knees, passing their rifles up to those above. There was one unnerving incident when, 'Hound of the Baskervilles'-like, a large white dog suddenly appeared out of the darkness—either a regimental pet determined not to be left behind or an abandoned canine from the native huts. However, it sensed the need for silence and was quietly led away by one of Thornycroft's troopers. The second small plateau with a copse of trees, partly obscured by mist, was the next objective; the front of the column was now close to the top. Thornycroft and his men found themselves suddenly on a wide open slope leading to the summit. The Lancashire Fusiliers were quickly, and as silently as possible, formed into an extended line with 100 yards between each company. Thornycroft's Mounted Infantry were in front. Slowly the line, with bayonets fixed, moved forward just as the first glimmer of dawn, that would silhouette the enemy, began to break along the sky line. If there were enemy ahead, it seemed impossible that the crunching boots of a thousand men had not alerted them. Suddenly there was a guttural shout *'Wer kom daar?'* followed by a volley of Mauser fire, wounding three men of the Lancashire Fusiliers.[199] Every soldier, as ordered, flung himself to the ground as following volleys passed harmlessly overhead. Then, a pause and Woodgate bawled out the password: 'Waterloo' whereupon the extended line of infantry rose up with such a pent-up cry of vengeance, 'a fierce angry war-like shout' that a soldier of the Scottish Rifles, 1,500ft below, who heard it, remembered that it made his blood run cold.[200] A mad charge rushed forward. Twenty-four year old Lieutenant Awdry of the Fusiliers, a regimental athlete, was in the lead, outdistancing the fittest of those who followed, and was the first to engage.[201] A bayonet thrust and he was past; the lone grave of the burgher whom he killed, still marks the spot where the man fell.

The summit had been taken at a cost of a few men wounded but the entire force was now engulfed in a mist so thick that it was impossible to gauge their position. They were also unable to calculate the extent or the perimeter of the plateau on which they stood, or to judge the line of the enemy guns. However, all knew that the mist would soon rise and that it was imperative to entrench. It then became apparent that entrenching would be an impossible task as the surface of the plateau comprised rocks and stones with a little iron-hard soil in between. Nevertheless, the REs set about erecting trace lines that the trenches were intended to follow.

The picks and shovels were next to useless, but what rocks and soil that could be prised out of the ground, were piled up as a parapet along the trace line while attempts were made to scoop out a shallow ditch behind; at no place did ditch and parapet, from top to bottom, measure more than two feet six inches. Sandbags, which would have been of use, had been overlooked and were piled up at the bottom of the hill.[202]

Further back, Private Howard had been nearing the summit when the Boers fired their initial volley. He and his mate had dropped their stretcher and rushed for cover and, not knowing from which direction the firing had come, they hid amongst some boulders for half an hour. Then, keeping below the plateau, their thoughts turned to food and rummaging around in a little copse of trees, they found some branches and managed to get a fire going. Soon there were '. . . a crowd of fellows, over a fire, eating meat and vegetables and drinking coffee.' The troops on top had no such luxury; in fact, the only water they would have for the next 24 hours was that carried in their water bottles.

By 6.30am the REs, under the command of Major Massey, decided that no further improvements could be made to the scraped-out ditch. As the men were gathering together their picks and shovels as preparation to falling in, the Boers, despite the concealing mist, opened a brisk crackle of rifle fire in the direction of the *kop*, sending everyone diving for cover. After ten minutes the firing ceased and, for the time being, was not re-sumed. In the lull, the engineers made their way back down the hill where they set about attempting to widen the track into something like a pathway, which would hopefully give passage to artillery later in the day.[203] A spring was found half-way down whose water would do much to relieve the suf-fering of the wounded. However, not a drop would reach the firing line.[204]

At 7.30am, like a curtain being lifted from a stage, the mist cleared and, as it did so, the attackers became aware that their 'trenches' did not command the crest line of the plateau. They were atop the summit where they were completely exposed and, having failed to entrench the crest, the Boers, working through the dead ground between the crest and the summit, would be able to get within 150 yards of them without detection. Not only that, 300 yards east and outside the area taken by Woodgate's force, there was a small hill called Aloe Knoll that would shortly be the cause of much bloodshed as men fought for its possession, while 800 yards directly north, and at practically the same level as the plateau, was a feature known as Conical Hill where a warren of Boer rifle pits and trenches lay waiting. Green Hill, already occupied by the Boers, 1,500 yards north-west and 220 feet lower than the plateau, would provide an unobstructed view of the enemy for the burghers of the Boksburg Com-mando and a cannon shortly to be positioned there. Finally, 2,700 yards east on the reverse slopes of Twin Peaks, Boer artillery, out of sight of the British guns, would be able to pound with impunity the plateau with shell and shrapnel. However, for the moment the peril of the situation was not realised and Woodgate decided to report progress to Warren.

Buller had insisted that Colonel a'Court of his staff, should accom-pany the expedition and it was at about 7.45am that Woodgate ordered him back with a written message for Warren:

Spion Kop
24 January 1900

Dear Sir Charles,

We got up about 4 o'clock and rushed the position with three men wounded. There were some few Boers, who seemed surprised and bolted after firing a round or so, having one man killed. I believe there is another somewhere, but have not found him in the mist. The latter did us well, and I pushed on a bit quicker than I perhaps should otherwise have done, lest it should lift before we got here. We have entrenched the position, and are, I hope, secure; but fog is too thick to see, so I retain Thornycroft's men and Royal Engineers for a bit longer.

Thornycroft's men attacked in fine style. I had a noise made [the cheering] to let you know that we had got in.

Yours, and etc,

E Woodgate[205]

A rather jubilant a'Court bounded down the hill making, he believed, a record for the descent. At the bottom he commandeered a cavalry horse and within 30 minutes, at about 9.15am, had delivered Woodgate's cautious message. It was, however, plain to see from the columns of smoke erupting on the plateau, that things had changed dramatically since a'Court's departure.

When General Louis Botha heard the victorious cry of Woodgate's troops, and later learned from the Heidelberg Commando that Spion Kop was in enemy hands, he was momentarily in complete despair. He had never contemplated holding Spion Kop in strength with his own forces as the summit was dominated by the British naval guns on Mount Alice. But now that the British held the position, and if they did so with the addition of artillery on top, his line would be broken. The British had taken the *kop*, he must take it back. However, the rifle fire from the summit had also sounded the alarm to 39-year-old Commandant Henrik Prinsloo, a veteran of many native wars. He was already shaking together his Carolina Commando of 500 men in preparation to scale the north-eastern flank of Spion Kop, a route that would bring them to the crest and the verge of the British trench. General Schalk Burger, who commanded that side of the mountain was, as a member of the Transvaal Volksraad, more a politician than a soldier but would nevertheless have much to do with the outcome of the fighting to follow. Having seen the Carolinas on their way, Burger ordered 50 men of the Heidelberg Commando to Aloe Knoll where their rifle fire could enfilade the British trench. He then took

personal command of a Krupp cannon, newly situated on the gently slop-
ing ground below Twin Peaks, 2,700 yards from the plateau and perfectly
positioned to fire upon the British trenches.

At their bivouac, Deneys Reitz and his small band of comrades of the
Pretoria Commando, had enjoyed a less dramatic awakening. At daybreak, in the direction of the Rangeworthy Hills, the usual bombardment
had erupted. Unconcerned, the commando watched the misty drizzle and
dozed off to sleep until they were roused again by the crackle of rifle fire
above them. Rather than face the day, they brewed coffee and, resting
against their wagons hoped they were safe from the bullets that occasionally whined about. Then, at a furious pace, a messenger arrived: the British
had taken Spion Kop. There was a rush to saddle their horses and struggle
into their bandoliers. Then, all together, they galloped to Botha's headquarters at the bottom of Spion Kop. It looked like a horse market as there
were hundreds of tethered ponies waiting while their riders, the Boer
counter-attack, slowly made their way upwards.

On the plateau, at about 7.45am, shortly after a'Court had departed,
enemy artillery fire, with unerring accuracy, began sweeping the plateau,
an area no bigger than a modern supermarket car park, which was
crammed with 1,700 men. At first only two or three guns participated in
the cannonading but, as Botha gradually got his artillery into place,
moving his guns to where they could most effectively bombard the enemy,
the shellfire became more intense and the casualties more frequent and
horrific. Botha had been repositioning his guns from the first moment he
had heard that the British had taken the *kop*. Even the gun that had
guarded the Ladysmith road at Acton Homes had been inspanned and
driven four miles east to where it was within sight and easy range of Spion
Kop. It is interesting that both Boer and British accounts agree on the
number of guns that attacked the plateau during the early course of the
morning. There are only slight discrepancies relating to the positioning of
the various cannons. The map of the battle contained in the *Times History
of the Boer War in South Africa, 1899—1900*, Volume 3, shows four
Krupp 77mm cannons, each capable of firing a common or shrapnel shell
over a range of 6,600 yards, the shrapnel missile containing 103 cast iron
bullets; and two 37mm Maxim Nordenfeldt (Pom-Pom) belt-fed guns firing explosive rounds over a range of 3,000 yards—there were 25 rounds
in each belt and each gun limber carried 12 belts. The furthest positioning
from the plateau for any of these weapons was one of the Krupp guns at
3,500 yards and the closest, a Maxim Nordenfeldt at 1,500 yards. There

were, therefore, six guns in total. All were situated on the reverse sides of the hills facing the British gun positions at Three Tree Hill and the naval guns and howitzers on and below Mount Alice at Potgieter's Drift. Not only was British artillery retaliatory fire completely ineffective, it was extremely dangerous, as will be seen, to British troops fighting to hold the *kop*.

As the Boer shells began to burst across the plateau with shrapnel missiles exploding at little more than head height to discharge their terrible load of cast iron, and with common shell bursting on the rock-bound surface, sending fragments of stone, as deadly as shrapnel, hurtling in all directions, it was brought to Colonel Bloomfield's attention that enemy riflemen were fast approaching up the north eastern slopes. Crouching low, and leaving his officers and men lying huddled in groups as he passed, Bloomfield went to seek General Woodgate who, despite the lack of rank insignia, would be easy to recognise due to his distinctive gait. Woodgate, touring the summit, was soon found as he strode about recklessly encouraging the men. Together he and Bloomfield moved to the crest line where, a few hundred feet below, the Carolinas were making steady progress and, when they occasionally paused, subjecting the crest line to a steady onslaught of rifle fire. As the two British officers turned to leave, Woodgate was shot through the head above the right eye, a wound that after eight long weeks, would prove mortal.[206] He was carried to a dressing station, on an improvised stretcher made up of rifles and greatcoats, by men of the Lancashire Fusiliers. This little group, moving in the open, proved to be too tempting a target and before the dressing station was reached one man had been killed and another seriously wounded.[207]

It was now about 8.45am and one must decide whether a message, whose authenticity *The Times History* has questioned, was genuinely dictated by Woodgate. The message was received at Mount Alice at 10am, perhaps an hour after Woodgate was wounded, and read: 'Am exposed to terrible crossfire, especially near first dressing station; can hardly hold my own; water badly needed; help us. Woodgate.' Was it dictated or written by the general before he was wounded, or was it sent later by an officer not knowing of Woodgate's incapacity and thinking his name would add weight to a plea for help? Either way, the contents were a realistic description of the conditions on the summit. It is likely the message was delayed by the hazards of facing the journey to the signal station.

Before long it was found that there was insufficient room in the so-called trench. The Lancashire Fusiliers and Royal South Lancs occupied the right, or eastern end, just 250 yards from Aloe Knoll which by 8.30am was already occupied by the Heidelburgers. In the centre of the trench a number of TMI had taken up position as had Thornycroft himself; in places they were fewer than 100 yards from the edge of the crest line. Between them and the crest line was abundant dead ground through which their main adversaries, the Carolina Commando, could crawl even closer. The Royal Lancs and South Lancs occupied the western portion of the trench; here the crest line, at 150 yards, was not so close. In the intervening ground elements of TMI had positioned themselves behind rocks and boulders, finding what cover they could. The British position was now subjected to sweeping and continuous artillery fire and to close-range sniper fire from 600 of the finest fighting marksmen in the world.

The British signal station, the column's only contact with Warren's headquarters, except for foot-borne messages which could take up to four hours in one direction, was initially situated on the western slope of the spur that had given the column access to the plateau. The station was completely exposed, as was necessary if its heliograph and semaphore signals were to be seen at Warren's headquarters. It was so exposed that a signaller's life expectancy could be reckoned in minutes. Sensibly the station was relocated to the eastern, or reverse side of the spur. However, the disadvantage of this was that messages would first have to go to Buller's headquarters before being relayed to Warren. An officer who was present wrote: 'The heliograph, as the message was being sent, was struck by a shell and smashed, the signaller, however, gallantly continued, and finished it by means of flags.''

The dressing station, on the eastern side of the ridge, was also exposed to Boer artillery firing from the Rangeworthy Heights and to Boer riflemen on Green and Conical hills. By 8.30am George Howard had already been out with his stretcher bringing in the wounded. He and his mate had just managed to put up a red cross flag between two rocks when it was blown down by a shell. They were attempting to raise it again when it received a direct hit and the task was abandoned believing it had become a mark for Boer gunners.[208] The two stretcher bearers continued going from trench to trench doubling back with the wounded.

By 9am the burghers of the Carolina Commando had reached the crest line and by dragging themselves on their stomachs into the dead ground, were able to fire directly into the centre of the British trench. One section of TMI, who had occupied the boulder strewn ground to the west, attempted to retaliate and was wiped out to a man. One of the dead officers was the talented and wealthy young Hugh McCorquodale who had been with the regiment for fewer than 24 hours. Churchill had been alerted to his fate by being told: '. . . A smart, clean-looking young gentleman . . . had been found leaning forward on his rifle.' The shell that had killed McCorquodale also smashed his field glasses which bore his name.[209] Another section of TMI, also attempting a counter-attack, was severely mauled: Lieutenant Grenfell, who had been leading, was shot in the leg, then in the arm and before he could be given medical attention, was struck in the head and killed.

However, the Boers were not having it all their own way. After tethering their ponies, Reitz and his comrades began climbing to where they could already see the crest line in violent conflict. The way was strewn with dead and dying burghers; no fewer than eight of Reitz's friends were passed before the crest was reached and to step beyond the crest line would mean certain death: '. . . The effect of Lee Metford volleys at twenty yards must be experienced to be appreciated.' In the confusion, Reitz lost contact with the remainder of his commando and, believing it to be on Aloe Knoll, tried to reach it. Miraculously surviving the attempt, he had no heart to try again and so attached himself to the command of Rooi Daniel Opperman, the burgher who had been leading the commando along the Acton Homes Road earlier in the month when it had been ambushed by the colonials under Major Graham. Reitz and his new comrades were much demoralised by the huddled and dying forms all around them, and were unable to boost their morale at the sight of British casualties as those of the enemy dropped out of sight behind their breast work of boulders and rocks. However, the Boer artillery gave the commandos some respite when a brave young heliographer, by the name of Louis Bothma, established himself close below the crest line on the eastern slopes where he was able to relay to Botha's headquarters a continuous commentary on the accuracy of the Boer guns. In fact, so accurate was his information and the aim of the artillerymen that there is no record of any burgher being killed by friendly fire.

When General Woodgate was carried to the field hospital, Bloomfield went in search of Colonel Crofton, the officer next in seniority on the mountain, to advise him that he was now in command. Crofton immediately decided to signal Warren informing him of Woodgate's incapacity and to ask for reinforcements; it was a message that would rob him of his command. There was a standing instruction that all messages were to be given to signallers in writing but, such was the state of affairs on the

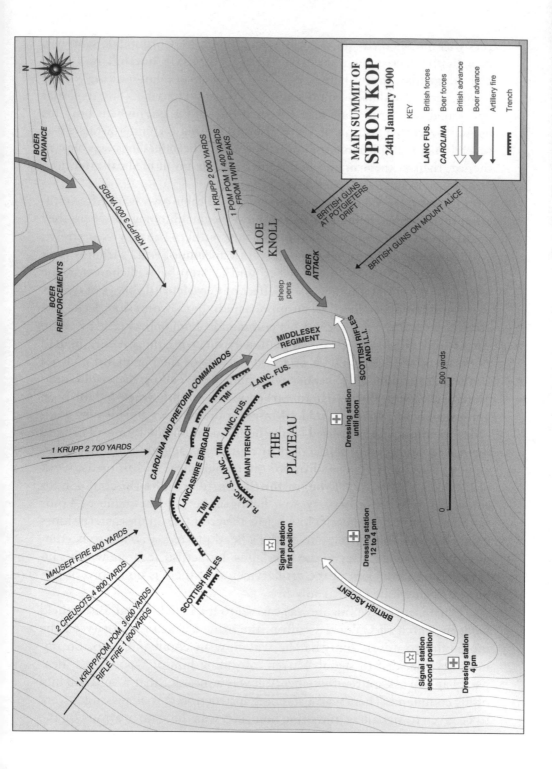

MAIN SUMMIT OF
SPION KOP
24th January 1900

KEY

LANC. FUS.   British forces
CAROLINA   Boer forces
             British advance
             Boer advance
             Artillery fire
             Trench

BOER
ADVANCE

BOER
REINFORCEMENTS

1 KRUPP 3 000 YARDS

1 KRUPP 2 000 YARDS
1 POM POM 1 400 YARDS
FROM TWIN PEAKS

ALOE
KNOLL

BRITISH GUNS
AT POTGIETERS
DRIFT

BOER
ATTACK

BRITISH GUNS ON MOUNT ALICE

sheep
pens

MIDDLESEX
REGIMENT

LANC. FUS.

CAROLINA AND PRETORIA COMMANDOS

TMI

LANC. FUS.

S. LANC. TMI

LANC. FUS.

LANCASHIRE BRIGADE

R. LANC.

MAIN TRENCH

SCOTTISH RIFLES
AND I.L.I.

1 KRUPP 2 700 YARDS

THE
PLATEAU

TMI

Dressing station
until noon

500 yards

0

MAUSER FIRE 800 YARDS

2 CREUSOTS 4 800 YARDS

1 KRUPP/POM POM 3 600 YARDS

RIFLE FIRE 1 600 YARDS

SCOTTISH RIFLES

Signal station
first position

Dressing station
12 to 4 pm

BRITISH ASCENT

Signal station
second position

Dressing station
4 pm

fire swept plateau that Crofton gave his signals officer, Lieutenant A. R. Martin, verbal instructions, later testifying that his message should have read: 'General Woodgate dead; reinforcements urgently required.' (At that time it was generally assumed Woodgate had been killed.) Martin, when questioned later, maintained that he had been instructed by Crofton to find some signallers and had been told: 'To get them at once and send a message to Sir Charles Warren and say "General Woodgate is dead", and ask for reinforcements at once.' Martin further testified that he found two signallers of the Lancashire Fusiliers and, with them, made his way to the signal station on the southern slopes where he found a Private Goodyear, another signaller, whom Martin instructed to heliograph Warren's head-quarters with the following message: 'General Woodgate is dead; send reinforcements at once.' Martin ended his testimony by stating that he did not write the message as he had no paper. The signal that was received by Buller and relayed to Warren, read: 'Reinforce at once or all lost. General dead.' A slightly more dramatic and urgent interpretation added, it would seem, by Private Goodyear.[210]

Subsequently, Crofton strongly protested that he had not been the author of the signal. However, as Buller, ensconced on his view site at Mount Alice, watched the turmoil on the plateau, which, with the aid of his powerful telescope, he could see quite clearly, the defeatist words of the bungled signal convinced him that Crofton was not the man to command on top. Furthermore, he could observe the huge form of Thornycroft, time and again, leading counter-attacks.

Warren, having received the alarming message initiated by Crofton at about 10am, and having already dispatched the ILI to reinforce the hill, ordered lame General Coke to proceed and: 'Take command of the troops.' Coke, accompanied by the Middlesex and Dorset Regiments, prepared to make the ascent; Warren cautioned: 'You must hold on to the last. No surrender.'[211] Thus, another 2,500 men were on the way up the mountain which would bring the total number of soldiers crammed on to the plateau, which was fast resembling a gigantic, fly-infested butcher's block, to 4,500.

Buller had made up his mind. He had concluded that Thornycroft was the man to be in command. He later testified that Crofton's signal:

> . . . did not give me confidence in its sender, and, at the moment,
> I could see our men on top had given way, and that efforts were
> being made to rally them. I telegraphed to Sir C. Warren: 'Unless

you put some really good hard fighting man in command on the top you will lose the hill. I suggest Thornycroft.'[212]

It was not exactly an order, but Warren complied. Thornycroft was immediately promoted to the temporary rank of brigadier-general, though it would be some time before he knew it. Buller had made the right choice. At about 10am, before any reinforcements had arrived, Lieutenant Sargeant of TMI saw a gap on the crest line unoccupied by the enemy and, with 20 men led a sortie to take possession at the very moment the enemy arrived. One of Thornycroft's troopers, throwing himself behind a rock paused, and then pushing his rifle forward at an angle, found it stopped by something soft and immediately pulled the trigger a split second before the Boer he killed had had time to kill him. At that moment the crest line was not completely in the hands of either side but was occupied by pockets of the combatants each within a biscuit's throw of the other. Then, Boer reinforcements making their way through dead ground made the position of Lieutenant Sargeant impossible to hold. Thornycroft, seeing this, gathered up all the men surrounding him, 20 of TMI and a similar number of Lancashire Fusiliers, and with Thornycroft in the lead they charged the crest. The bodies of three TMI officers, with dead or wounded troopers scattered around them, already lay in the intervening ground and such was the fury of the Boer fire that hardly a man survived the charge. Thornycroft, by a miracle, merely sprained a knee and, with the remnants of his men, hobbled back to the dubious shelter of the trenches.[213]

However, what was the plan? Warren had seen it as imperative that Spion Kop be taken in order to advance along the Fairview Road. Now, six hours after the objective had been secured, the witless British command could think no further than to cram more men into the hilltop cul-de-sac from which few would return uninjured. Rather than giving Warren the whip hand, the taking of Spion Kop had become a liability. Botha's repositioning of his artillery and riflemen meant that not only were the British being slaughtered on the plateau but, by the same deployment, Botha's forces now dominated the road by which Warren had hoped to proceed. However, on the other hand, the Spion Kop assault had severely dented the Boer line and morale. Reitz recalled that, apart from those who were first to climb the crest, the Carolinas, the Heidelburgers, the Pretoria Commando and various foreign elements: 'No reinforcements reached us throughout the day.' He further recalled:

. . . We had neither food nor water. Around us lay scores of dead and wounded men, a depressing sight, and by midday a feeling of discouragement had gained ground that was only kept in check by Commandant Opperman's forceful personality and vigorous language to any man who seemed to be wavering. Had it not been for him the majority would have gone far sooner than they did, for the belief spread that we were being left in the lurch. We could see large numbers of horsemen collecting in the laager on the plain below.[214]

However, it occurred neither to Buller nor Warren that they had unwittingly created what could be a master feint. With the Boer Creusot at Acton Homes having been relocated, there was no longer an artillery threat to a British advance in that direction, the direction that Buller all along had deviously inferred was his preferred route to Ladysmith. As we have read, Buller testified that: 'On the 19th [January] I ought to have assumed command myself . . . '[215] However, as we know, he did no such thing but he certainly should have done so early on the morning of the 24th. He would have had not only Dundonald's cavalry brigade and, excluding the Lancashire Brigade already on the hill, 13 battalions of infantry. He would also have had another 13,000 troops in Ladysmith, albeit starved and weary, to threaten Botha's rear. In addition, and almost forgotten, Barton's brigade on the south bank at Colenso, could be flung against Botha's overextended defences. However, Buller took no such action. It would be left to his soldiers to win the day as indeed they would, only to have victory snatched away by Buller himself; as an old Boer fighter remarked: 'We admit that the British soldiers are the best in the world and your regimental officers the bravest—We rely on your generals.' [216]

In the seemingly unlikely event that Warren had been contemplating some initiative against the enemy, he would have been deterred by Buller's message, delivered at 5am on the 22nd, to beware of a possible 'counter stroke'. Buller did not imply that such a possibility would be directed at Spion Kop, but merely commented that Warren's troops, unlike those of the enemy, were widely extended.

At 10am, General Lyttelton at Potgieter's Drift signalled Warren offering assistance wherever it would be most useful. Half an hour later Warren requested further support on the summit and Lyttelton ordered the Scottish Rifles and two squadrons of BMI to march the three and a half miles to the Tugela, wade the river, and then make the mile-long climb up the south-eastern face to the summit. The same private of the Scottish Rifles who earlier had heard the pent up cry of vengeance from the top of Spion Kop, later recorded that his battalion had spent a dismal night and had been:

> 'Stood to arms' at 4 a.m. but as the sun rose, the hills that had loomed through the rain and mist like great towering objects, now stood out quite clear and distinct and did not look as formidable as they had two hours earlier.[217]

He and his comrades had breakfasted on black coffee, biscuits and jam. They had also been told to set about cooking their dinners as an early move was anticipated. However, while in the middle of preparing the meal the order came to:

> fall in at once and never mind your dinners. You can get your dinners when you come back. No time for eating. Within five minutes 1,000 hungry, angry men were marching.[218]

Then Lyttelton, on his own initiative, ordered the KRR, under Colonel Robert Buchanan Riddell to also cross the Tugela and assault Twin Peaks where Boer artillery had, unmolested, been pounding the plateau since early morning. It was the only creative move, throughout the battle, made by a British general.[219]

Again at 10am there was a desperate appeal from the top for an attempt by British artillery to knock out some of the Boer guns. Although the naval detachment on Mount Alice, with the aid of a large telescope, could see Boer rifleman moving on Aloe Knoll, no artillery was visible as all the Boer guns were sited on the reverse slopes. Unaware that Aloe Knoll was no further than 250 yards from the British trench, the sailors opened fire. It took 30 minutes for a relayed signal from the top to have effect. At 11am, Buller and Lyttelton received a cryptic message: 'We occupy the whole of the summit and I fear you are shelling us seriously; cannot you turn your guns on the enemy guns?' [220] Under the circumstances, how polite. In reality, with the lack of maps and previous reconnaissance, none of the general officers had any idea of the topography of the mountain. From Warren's headquarters it was impossible to see Aloe Knoll and Twin Peaks. In fact, Aloe Knoll, 60 feet lower than the summit, but, nevertheless the pivot around which the battle was being fought, is not immediately visible from the top of Spion Kop. Also, as it was not occupied by British troops as soon as it was daylight, it is likely that its existence and significance were not known to Thornycroft and Crofton until it was taken by the enemy. Warren, in turn, requested the summit to give him directions to the enemy guns but the only answer he received was to the effect that the Boer fire was coming from all directions.

By noon, four hours after the fighting had started on what would be a sweltering mid-summer day, and 20 hours since the troops had first assembled, those of the Lancashire Brigade and TMI, who had not been obliterated or wounded, had been driven from the crest line. Most were demoralised and had become terrified by the remains of human forms, broken and torn apart by the tornado of shell fire, amongst which the survivors were forced to huddle. A man shot by a bullet, an acceptable death for a soldier, was one thing, but to be torn pieces, devoid of all dignity, as though shredded by a wild beast, was more than most could stand. There was already a trickle of men going back down the hill: some used the excuse of assisting a wounded comrade; others with dazed expressions merely wandered off. The main trench had now become the British front line. Officers were rallying and coaxing their men and, in the confusion, often those of other units who had become displaced. As the morning wore on, and the rocks that gave them cover became too hot to touch, the craving for water became frantic. However, there was no water to be had and Warren would later testify:

> Most elaborate arrangements were made for the water supply to the troops. It would have averaged one gallon per man for the troops originally sent up. Of course, a great deal of water was spilled from the [biscuit] boxes but they were the only receptacles we had.[221]

Major H. N. Sargent also testified to the Royal Commission:

> . . . I superintended generally the water supply myself, and made frequent enquiries as to whether the troops were getting sufficient quantity on top of the hill, and were told they were . . . [222]

Colonel A. W. Morris AAG 5th Division, concluded his testimony by stating:

Personally, I did not think the men were suffering very badly from the want of water. I considered that, under the circumstances, nothing could have been better than the very difficult arrangements made for the water supply; it was not plentiful, but sufficient for the purpose required.[223]

How different the story from the men in the fighting line. In reality little, if any, water got to the top. Mostly it was waylaid by the dressing stations and, no doubt, the mule handlers seeing the lines of maimed and broken men passing down the hill, deemed it safer to do likewise rather than risk making it to the plateau. Lieutenant Blake Knox of the RAMC, who was amongst the first to reach the top, wrote:

. . . a few tins [of water] had been sent up on mules; little however, reached the summit and some of the mules fell down the hill, and what was left was used for the wounded.[224]

Private S. T. Cornell of the ILI, recalled:

. . . I was suffering awfully from the want of water. I gave my water to a wounded man, and up to now, I had been all afternoon without water in a scorching sun.[225]

An NCO of the South Lancs wrote that on reaching a field hospital:

. . . It was here we got water, the first for 24 hours.[226]

And an officer of the Lancashire Brigade writing home stated:

. . . Our war correspondents couldn't exaggerate the terrible sufferings we've gone through this last week. Don't minimise the want of water. It was awful; I swear scores of our fellows were dying in agony through the want of it.[227]

And a final comment from Warren:

Everything was done that could be done, but the men were suffering from artificial thirst, due to their having just arrived [so much for 'tried troops'] in a very hot climate and having been exclusive fed on tinned meat.[228]

It was about noon when Thornycroft, sitting on the ground with his back against a rock, saw the first messenger bringing news of his promotion. However, Thornycroft's attention was focused elsewhere: Major Massey of the Royal Engineers had, but a moment before, been killed leading a charge of assorted troops, and young Lieutenant Raphael of the South Lancs, who had so enjoyed the voyage to Durban a month before, was also dead as were Captains Vertue and Birch of the South Lancs. A mutual friend of Raphael and Birch wrote that they had a regimental nickname of *Damon and Plythias* because they were so close. They had been killed almost at the same time trying to pull a wounded man into a trench. Soon, Lieutenant-Colonel McCarthy O'Leary of the South Lancs would be writing many letters beginning: 'It is with great sorrow and in heartfelt sympathy I write to announce to you the death of your dear son, killed in action on Spion Kop . . .' Colonel O'Leary survived the battle only to be killed the following month.

The messenger, hurrying with Warren's tidings across the fire-swept *kop*, '. . . The hail of shrapnel or the strings of Pom-Pom shells, flicking round the shoulder of the hill like the lash of a gigantic whip . . .',[229] got as far as Thornycroft and no further: 'Before he could utter a word he was killed instantly falling dead across Thornycroft's legs.' Hours later, amidst the confusion of battle, the news of Thornycroft's promotion finally reached him: Lieutenant Rose of TMI crept forward and shouted: 'Sir C Warren has heliographed that you are in command; you are a General.'[230] In the same breath he shouted that reinforcements were close at hand. Close, but yet to arrive, and the situation was critical. The far right of the main trench, occupied by the Lancashire Fusiliers, had not only been pounded relentlessly by artillery and enfiladed from Aloe Knoll by Mauser fire, which killed many a Fusilier with a single shot through the right temple, it had also been recently subjected to a shrapnel bombardment by the British guns on Mount Alice and there were no officers left to rally or lead. One man, unauthorised, waved a rag of surrender. No doubt some of his comrades were aghast but, as the enemy rifle fire began to slacken, there were others who also welcomed the feeling of relief from imminent death; and what had been the initiative of one man, now became a flood of capitulation. A mixed commando of Carolinas and Pretorians under Rooi Opperman and Field-Cornet Zeederberg, were quick to seize the moment, boldly walking towards the British trench yelling in English for the *Rooineks* to come forward. Young Cilliers of the Pretoria Commando, with levelled rifle, crouched over the parapet yelling into the trench: 'Who is your officer?'[231] However, there was no officer,

much less a senior officer whose presence was necessary to make the surrender valid. Nevertheless, the Boers had no intention of releasing their
prisoners and started herding them out of the trench at the very moment
a sergeant of TMI arrived on the scene. A Fusilier, anticipating his
prospects of old age were about to be curtailed, snatched the sergeant's
rifle yelling: 'You are a prisoner!' The sergeant, utterly confused, believed
it was the Boers who were surrendering, thinking that they had seen the
Middlesex Regiment who were now visible across the plateau. Then, suddenly realising what was taking place, the sergeant bolted. Minutes later,
whilst Opperman and his comrades were still disarming the Fusiliers,
Thornycroft, limping on a stick, all 18 stone of him bristling with fury,
burst upon the scene and, accosting the nearest Boer of apparent authority,
shouted: 'I'm Commandant here; take your men back to hell, Sir! There
is no surrender.' [232]

However, on their own initiative, the men had struck a deal. They had
surrendered and about 170 of them, now prisoners, were being disarmed
and passed back to the Boer crest line. That is, more or less, the description of the incident as reported in *The Times History of the South African
War*. However, Lieutenant Blake Knox, who was on Spion Kop at the time
wrote:

> About the same time [1.30pm] a nasty and regrettable incident
> was narrowly avoided by the gallantry and presence of mind of
> Colonel Thornycroft. About thirteen men of various regiments
> were on the point of surrendering; their rifles lay on the ground
> and they were advancing unarmed towards the enemy position.
> Thornycroft, whose stature made him everywhere conspicuous,
> rushed forth, limping on a stick. He pounced, like a hawk, on the
> Boer leader—a Transvaaler, by name De Koch, in whose words I
> shall continue the story of what happened (as De Koch afterwards
> described it to a British officer in the Biggarsberg): 'We had got
> up and we should have had the whole hill,' he said. 'The English
> were about to surrender, and we were all coming up when a great
> big, angry, red-faced soldier ran out of the trench on our right and
> shouted, "I'm the Commandant here; take your men back to H–,
> Sir! I allow no surrender."' 'The great big, angry, red-faced soldier'
> was Colonel Thornycroft, who, after delivering his ultimatum,
> hobbled back to the thirteen men and ordered them to follow him
> and, 'not to hesitate a second.[233]

Knox later described an incident that occurred half an hour later when the Boers were escorting 'some 170 of our men who in an advance position had been captured' and how British fire had slackened to let them pass; obviously Knox mistakenly took those who had surrendered for prisoners under escort.

A Regimental History of the Lancashire Fusiliers opined:

> It was about 1.30 o'clock when they [Boers] put into execution a ruse in which they excelled. A number of them walked towards the trench with their rifles slung, while those in front waved white handkerchiefs, and it was under cover of this audacious act that they got sufficient men into the trench to secure the defenders, who were without officers, and, it is stated, short of ammunition. It was the crisis in the fight: the moment when the best soldiers need the leading of their officers; and when we think of the fire to which they were exposed, that they held the most unprotected part of the position, the horrors of the trench, and the frenzy from want of water, who will be found to blame those who fell victims to a ruse put into execution with all the cunning and daring for which the Boer is remarkable?[234]

Thornycroft himself stated:

> The Boers closed in on the right and centre. Some men of mixed regiments at right end of trench got up and put up their hands; three or four Boers came out and signalled their comrades to advance. I was the only officer in the trench on the left, and I got up and shouted to the leader of the Boers that I was the commandant and that there was no surrender. In order not to get mixed up in any discussion, I called on all men to follow me, and retired to some rocks further back. The Boers opened a heavy fire on us. On reaching the rocks I saw a company of the Middlesex Regiment advancing, I collected them up to the rocks, and ordered all to advance again. This the men did and we reoccupied the trench and the crest line in front.[235]

Even Louis Botha formed an opinion for the Fusiliers surrender. Having questioned the prisoners he came to the conclusion it was the reported death of General Woodgate and the lack of water that caused the troops to surrender.

Now was the moment of destiny. The battle could swing either way. The Boers were in the British trench but the first section of the Middlesex, under the command of 48-year-old Lieutenant-Colonel Augustus Hill, were already on top and Thornycroft, knowing exactly where the ruptured holes in his line must be plugged, rushed forward to direct the Middlesex. Major Saville, leading a company with bayonets fixed, charged across the top towards the crest, encountering some abandoned sheep pens 100 yards from the burgher marksmen. In a flurry of indiscriminate rifle fire Saville was wounded, the charge floundered, and the Middlesex were driven back. However, more men were arriving at every moment and Thornycroft, reforming what was left of his regiment, led yet another sortie, forcing the Boers back once again across the summit, over the crest line and down the northern slopes. For an instant Thornycroft and his men, as they fired volley after volley into the retreating enemy, glimpsed the Boer camp in the valley below and, had they known in which direction to look, they would have seen, 25 miles away, the glitter of the tin roofs of Ladysmith. However, the Boer artillery, aided by their brave heliographer soon deprived Thornycroft and his band of their moment of triumph and, under a barrage of shrapnel and Pom-Pom shells, the *Rooineks* were driven back to the trench line. Within minutes the Boers were in command and, as their reinforcements reached the top, veldt cornets led their burghers across the plateau towards the trench where the Tommies, their morale wavering from the effects of the recent surrender, were abandoning their defences. This time it was Crofton and Bugler Russell who came to the rescue: Russell sounded *The Advance* as Crofton rallied the men.[236] Gradually a line was formed, to be joined moments later by a company of Middlesex under Captain Dyer. More of the regiment were arriving and elements of the ILI had reached the top, passing on the way members of their own regiment who, having been a few steps ahead, had already been wounded and were on their way down. The ILI were further from being 'tried troops' than any of the other soldiers on the summit. In fact, having little more than a week's recruit drill in Durban without arms or uniform, they were practically more civilian than militia.[237] A private of the regiment recalled:

> The first company of the ILI to reach the firing line got a severe cutting up but they advanced splendidly under heavy fire and gave the Fusiliers fresh heart . . . It was a very stiff climb on a hot day not to mention the bullets. We managed to get into a very tight

corner as we only controlled a portion of the hill while the Boers seemed to get a fire all round us—words cannot describe the situation . . . several times we made ready for a bayonet charge but it would have been the final act of madness to attempt one.[238]

It was now 2.30pm and both Boer and Briton had been fighting under a scorching sun, suffering agonies from the lack of water, for over six hours.

Coke and his staff had taken a full four hours to get within reach of the summit without quite venturing onto it. Coke, who had encountered numerous wounded and others wandering down, decided the top was too crowded and placed BMI and the Dorset Regiment, who despite the aid of artillery horses had been unable to get their Maxim gun little more than half way up the hill, in reserve. Both units took no further part in the battle.

At this time, in spite of the din and confusion that surrounded him, Thornycroft, during a few moments that it was not imperative that he personally command some facet of the battle, managed to write a lucid report to Warren:

> Spion Kop, 2.30pm.
> From Colonel Thornycroft to General Sir C Warren.
> Hung on until the last extremity with the old force. Some of the Middlesex are here now, and I have the Dorsets coming up, but the force is really inadequate to hold so large a perimeter. The enemy guns to the north-west sweep the whole of the top of the hill; they also have guns to the east. Cannot you bring artillery fire to bear on the north-west guns? What reinforcements can you send to hold the hill tonight? We are badly in need of water. There are many killed and wounded. If you wish to really make a certainty of the hill for the night, you must send more infantry, and attack the enemy guns.[239]

The report was given to Colonel Sandbatch of Buller's staff, who had arrived at that moment to judge the state of affairs, to take down to Warren. On the way, Sandbatch encountered Coke 200 feet below the summit where he and his staff had established a signal station. Thornycroft's message was given to Coke for perusal who, without having witnessed the carnage and conditions on top decided, with bewildering interference, to add a comforting post script that diminished the urgency of Thornycroft's appeal:

> I have seen the above [meaning Thornycroft, which was quite incorrect] and have ordered the Scottish Rifles and Kings Royal Rifles to reinforce. The Middlesex and Dorset Regiments and Imperial Light Infantry have also gone up . . . We appear to be holding our own at present.[240]

The confident tone of Coke's post script convinced Warren that '. . . so far there seem to be no anxiety', and nothing further was done.[241] In his later report Coke made no mention of having written the post script. However, it must be said that he had not been told of Thornycroft's temporary rank, which gave Thornycroft command of the summit, and believed Hill to be the senior officer. In the same web of confusion, Thornycroft was unaware that Coke had replaced Woodgate. Furthermore, on his way up, Colonel Cooke, leading the Scottish Rifles, would also believe that *he* was senior officer and should, therefore, be in command. Such was the intensity and confinement of the fighting that at times, the three officers concerned would be within a few yards of each other, each believing himself to be in overall command.

Had Warren, at 3pm, been aware of the true state of affairs, he would have had every reason to be very anxious. The merciless enemy shelling was still continuous, and Boer reinforcements had arrived who, from their rugged stronghold on Aloe Knoll, were attempting to enfilade the whole of the British rear. Major Scott-Moncrieff of the Middlesex Regiment had made a valiant attempt to cut off the enemy by edging along the steep southern crest. Had he been successful the balance of advantage would have tipped into British hands. However, the attack had been as forlorn as it had been gallant: Scott-Moncrieff was wounded five times before the knoll was reached and those of his men who remained uninjured sought shelter and endured a Mauser onslaught where they lay. The burghers were too close to success to stop now. Moving from cover to cover they drew ever nearer to the unprotected British rear where they would command the reverse slope behind the main trench. However, as the brave burghers' endeavours were all but awarded with success, the first of the Scottish Rifles arrived on the top and without hesitation charged across the plateau. Captain O'Gowan, leading the 2nd Company with swords (Light Infantry never used the term 'bayonets') fixed, took off to the right and, to the surprise of the infiltrating burghers, headed straight in their direction. Lieutenant Arthur Wood, the son of a famous British general Field Marshall Sir Evelyn Wood VC, described the climb and the battle to his father:

> The scene on the way up beggars description—men fallen out! Some for water, some to help the wounded, who blocked the narrow track. It was trying for the men going up. Every one of these holding forth as to the awful state of things on the hill. We pushed on to the top, and as each section of the companies climbed up almost man by man they were rushed on to the firing line. I managed to get hold of two and a half sections of my company. We went up the hill in single file with continual checks under fire. I got them in line and rushed them forward. We arrived at a trench vacated except by wounded, and a 'Pom-Pom' pitched about nine shells just beyond us. I gave them a breathe, then jumped out of the trench, and danced about and yelled at them. They came on grandly. Then I saw Major Twyford, who had come back for us. We crossed two more trenches vacated; in front of the men it was simply a gorgeous feeling! The fire was real hot, but we jumped the trenches and rushed on to the crest line of the hill, where we opened fire on a hill opposite [Aloe Knoll?] I found the crest line very thinly manned by a mixture of men of all regiments. After I had been firing for a bit I walked along the crest line and bucked the men up. When it grew dusk Twyford sent me back for orders. I wandered about till I found Thornycroft, and shortly afterwards my colonel.[242]

A private of the Scottish Rifles failed to experience the 'glorious feeling' that Lieutenant Wood had enjoyed:

> . . . and forward we went, men dropping at every step and almost the first to fall was our second in command, Major Strong. We were met by the most terrific fire force from the enemy, which at some places the distance between us did not exceed 100 yards and they were well backed up by the big guns, bursting shrapnel all over us, their pompoms [sic] raking the trenches from end to end. Truly we were having a fearful time of it, and in the midst of all this howling and shouting we were gradually getting the upper

hand of the Boer army, bit by bit it was being subdued; until we had time to look around and to allow our rifles to rest a little as they were, by this time, red hot and burning our hands. When we saw the effects of the Boers fire [artillery] it almost drove us mad. Men lying about in all shapes, legs, arms and heads blown off, in fact being blown to fragments. It was enough to turn the stoutest hearts but we had not much time to think of the wounded, or to attend them either, as the Boer fire was beginning to get severe again. We had gained a little advantage and were not going to lose it, so we turned all our attention to the mastering of the Boer fire and we succeeded after a time in completely silencing their rifle-men. We had accomplished our object, that is save the Lancashire Brigade from utter annihilation or surrender, which they would never have done, and we still had the hill and were able to hold it, but what a price we paid for it.[243]

At that moment, 3pm and one and a half miles to the east, the KRR who had been ordered to attack Twin Peaks three hours earlier, were making slow but steady headway. Having crossed the Tugela they had divested themselves of their rolled greatcoats, leaving them in good order and under guard on the river bank. Lieutenant-Colonel Buchannan Riddell had divided his regiment into two half battalions, he taking that of the right, that would be directed at the eastern peak, and Major Bewicke Copley, his second-in-command, aiming his half battalion at the slightly higher western turret.[244] The two units were then deployed 1,200 yards apart, each in well-spaced lines, one behind the other, with 500 yards between them, thus presenting a difficult target for the enemy riflemen above. The regiment had been practising such a deployment and were now reaping the reward.

It was a mile and a half from the river to the looming face of Twin Peaks which, now in shadow, took on the aspect of a forbidding perpendicular wall of bush and rock. Without haste, the riflemen advanced over the boulder-strewn terrain, reserving their stamina for the climb ahead. It was not until the leading companies got within 1,500 yards from the base of their objective that the first casualties were taken. However, as with Majuba, where the British had had to peer over the edge, silhouetting themselves against the skyline to find a target, the Boers were now forced to do likewise and as their heads appeared, some of the KRR having halted in anticipation and ready to take aim, fired volley after volley at the figures high above. Nevertheless, the closer the riflemen marched the hotter the enemy fire became, causing the attackers to double forward to the shelter of a deep donga from which alternative companies gave covering fire, allowing their comrades to double forward in batches to the safety of the ridge. Then the climb began, with the men making the ascent in little groups, scrambling, crawling and pushing one another up where necessary thus, passing up rifles to comrades who had managed to secure a seat on a ledge above, they slowly progressed. About two thirds of the way up, Buchannan Riddell's half battalion found a plateau, 200 yards wide, heavily entrenched by the enemy. As the riflemen attempted to cross it they suffered heavy losses, driving them for cover but, with the added fire power brought by the arrival of B Company, led by Major Kays, the burghers hurriedly withdrew and the intrepid climb of the Rifles continued. The sudden arrival of the retreating burghers on the peaks caused panic and consternation. Schalk Burger immediately sent a message to Botha, pleading that his enervated men would not hold firm against the enemy who were fast approaching the final stage of their climb. However, Botha, knowing those on Spion Kop, who had been fighting since daybreak, were barely holding their own, could only offer moral support. He dispatched his Chief of Staff, Commandant Edwards, with a written plea for Burger to stand firm and hold his ground:

> Let us fight and die together but, brother, please do not let us yield an inch to the English. I am confident and convinced that if we stand firm our Lord will give us victory.[245]

However, there was no response to this inspiring message as Burger and all but a few of the Carolinas, together with the Lydenburgers and the Krupp cannon, were in full flight to Ladysmith.[246] Finally, the KRR began to arrive on the top of the peaks and the entrenchments were cleared of the few burghers who had gallantly remained. Immediately, Buchannan Riddell began making arrangements to fortify the position; already mules carrying water and ammunition were on their way up by a gentler route and relief for the wounded had been implemented. Twin Peaks had been taken.[247] The Carolina Commando, in their headlong flight had started a panic-driven exodus in the Boer *laagers*. Deneys Reitz recalled:

> When we reached the [Carolinas] laager we found everything in a state of chaos. The wagons were being hurriedly packed, and

the entire Carolina Commando was making to retire.[248]

The Times History of the War in South Africa recorded:

Away galloped Burger's guns down the slope of the eastern peak
and the pom-pom from the slopes of the ridge, now exposed to
fire from above; down the hill and off the open ridge streamed
Burger's commandos and Botha's reinforcements.[249]

The King's Royal Rifle Corps stated:

. . . The majority of the Carolina Commando never stopped until
they had left Twin Peaks eight miles behind them . . . [250]

Although General Botha urged the impossibility of retreat, one objec-
tion he was unable to answer, and it chilled even those who agreed to
stand by him, was that Twin Peaks were in the hands of the British. The
KRR were elated by their success, not only because a British victory was
now assured, but also because they had redeemed the honour of the British
Army which 20 years earlier had been forfeited at the Battle of Majuba.

However, most probably known only to Buchannan Riddell and his
signals officer, he and his regiment had not only been bombarded all
afternoon by Boer missiles, but he personally had been bombarded by
missives from Buller. The first had arrived at around 3pm when the two
half-battalions had been under fire for over an hour and were already scaling their objective. Buchannan Riddell had been given no specific orders:
the following day Lyttelton wrote:

. . . I noticed that strong reinforcements were reaching Sir C.
Warren's right, which was unduly crowded with troops. It seemed
unnecessary to send more men there, and with a view to creating
a diversion, I directed Colonel Riddell to move his battalion
against Sugar Loaf Hill [Twin Peaks] and the hill between it and
the right of the main position. I had misgivings that there was too
wide an interval, and in instructing Colonel Riddell verbally I told
him to use extreme caution, sending out scouts and only extending
two companies, and having a half battalion in reserve. I told him
I could not give him definite instructions, and must leave a good
deal to his discretion.[251]

Buchannan Riddell had confidence in his regiment and in himself but, unknown to him, Buller, for reasons that still remain unclear, had been enraged at the sight of the KRR approaching Twin Peaks and had immediately interfered in Warren's battle by demanding, at about 2pm, their instant withdrawal. Lyttelton was also having second thoughts. Major Bayly of Lyttelton's staff who had accompanied the Scottish Rifles to Spion Kop had sent a message at 2.30:

> Very hot fire here, near flag, which is our observing station; only just holding our own. Bethune's and Scottish Rifles are now coming up. Do not think that King's Royal Rifles can get up on right; it is held by Boers. We are only holding up to your left on saddle. A heavy fire from Boers on our north-west, where they have a gun [Burger's gun on the slopes of Twin Peaks] which is causing damage. Cannot see left of our line or the Boers. Water badly wanted.[252]

The reference to the KRR unnerved Lyttelton and, with the pressure from Buller, he sent the following message by heliograph:

> . . . To Officer commanding King's Royal Rifles.
>   Retire steadily until further orders.

However, Buchannan Riddell was of sterner stuff and evoking the 'Nelson Touch', put the message in his pocket and continued to climb.[253] At 3.30pm a further heliographed message:

> Retire steadily till further orders. Please say how the last message was transmitted.

Buchannan Riddell also ignored it and an hour later, at close to 5pm, Lyttelton sent an instruction by mounted orderly who, having abandoned his horse at the foot of Twin Peaks and, unhindered by kit or rifle, would finally have overtaken Buchannan Riddell. Lyttelton's message read:

> Unless the enemy has retired, you will fall back, under cover of darkness, to the bridge [pontoon bridge] just made, which is near the ford you crossed at, and where a fire will be lit, after dark, to guide you. Keep this orderly if any use. Manners [a medical

officer] is at ford, with stretcher bearers, if you want any. Hope all is well.

Buchannan Riddell decided to make an evasive reply:

If I can recall the advance sections I will do so but it is difficult to communicate, and the hill is fearfully steep. I have two or three wounded to help down.

Finally, when General Burger and the Carolina Commando were in full retreat at about 6pm, Buchannan Riddell flagged his final defiant signal:

We are on top of the hill. Unless I get orders to retire I shall stay here.

Instantly Lyttelton flagged back:

Retire when dark. [254]

However, Buchannan Riddell at the time was surveying his prize and in doing so peered over the northern crest of Twin Peaks in order to witness the commandos, like panic-driven ants, scattering in all directions, and in so doing was shot through the head and killed. It was still early in the war and the British were yet to learn that even a target as meagre as had been offered to the few burghers still lurking amongst the boulders below, beckoned instant death. A further signal from Lyttelton followed, again delivered by a mounted orderly. It was sent at 6pm:

I am sending you a signal lamp. The General Officer-Commanding [Buller] considers you could not hold the Sugar Loaf unsupported, and having no troops to support you with, he orders a retirement across the footbridge below ford, and bivouac on Naval Gun Plateau. Please report when you get in. I have rum, tea, and wood ready for you. [255]

Command of the KRR had now devolved on Benwick Copley who could not refuse such a direct order and, with much bitterness and bewilderment, the regiment began to descend, 'often on the seat of our britches',

being forced in the gathering darkness to leave behind a number of
wounded. The first message ordering the KRR retirement was found in
Buchannan Riddell's pocket the following morning.

Most likely the capture of Twin Peaks was not accomplished with the
ease that the official reports would have us believe, especially so as the
sacrifice of 90 casualties was squandered by the withdrawal of the regiment at its moment of victory. René Bull, the war artist and correspondent, wrote in rage at the naval guns shelling the climb of the KRR: 'The
shrapnel bursting high was falling on our own men and this continued for
an **hour and a half.**' (Bull's emphasis).[256]

Why had Buller, after such a heroic achievement that offered the key
to Ladysmith, insisted in stifled anger that the KRR abandoned Twin
Peaks? He offered the illogical excuse that if the KRR had been annihilated
it would have 'imperilled' the whole operation. However, at the same
moment, six other regiments were being obliterated on the top of Spion
Kop without, it would seem, endangering the outcome of the battle. What
was going on in Buller's devious mind? Was he still haunted by the ghosts
of battles past and his dread of mountains? Or was it that the 3rd Battalion of the Kings Royal Rifles was his regiment and he being its Colonel-
Commandant, did not want it seen that he had sent it to oblivion? Then,
having ordered its withdrawal, was he too stubborn to reverse his decision? Or, as suggested by the *Times History*, had he already decided that
Spion Kop was a lost battle and that, having shown Warren to be a loser,
would, (as in fact he did) take over full command of the army himself on
the morrow?

However, what had been the reaction of Warren and Coke, the
generals who were in actual command of the battle at the moment Twin
Peaks were taken? It is most likely that they were unaware the event had
taken place. At 6.50pm, after the KRR had started to withdraw, Warren
cabled to Lyttelton: 'The assistance you are giving most valuable. We shall
try to remain in status quo tomorrow . . .' Coke, the following day,
revealed his incompetence and lack of tactical appreciation, by stating in
his official report:

> . . . General Lyttelton had accordingly despatched the Scottish
> Rifles as an actual reinforcement, and a battalion of the Kings
> Royal Rifles against the hill to the north-west of Spion Kop. It was
> on the furthest slope of this hill that one of the Vickers-Maxim
> guns was placed. (This battalion worked its way some distance up

the hill, but its action did not materially affect the situation).[257]

By 4.30pm on Spion Kop itself the British still hung on to the main trench; some of the Scottish Rifles were sheltering amongst the boulders before Aloe Knoll, while remnants of the original attackers and later reinforcements found refuge where they could. The Boers were equally shattered by thirst and by their numerous casualties, many of whom, unlike those of the British, could have been kin: fathers, sons and brothers. For the moment, the actual fighting had become stalemate. However, Botha, determined to give the enemy no respite, continued to rake the plateau with his guns. At 5.50pm, just as the KRR started to abandon Twin Peaks, Coke now badly shaken, wrote a despatch to Warren:

> The original troops are still in position, have suffered severely, and the dead and wounded are still in the trenches. The shellfire is, and has been, very severe. If I hold on to the position all night, is there any guarantee that our artillery can silence the enemy's guns? Otherwise today's experience will be repeated, and the men will not stand another complete day's shelling. I have Bethune's Mounted Infantry and the Dorset Regiment intact to cover a retirement. If I remain I will endeavour to utilise these units to carry food and water up to the firing line. The situation is extremely critical. If I charge and take the koppie in front, [Conical Hill?] the advance is several hundred yards in the face of the entrenched enemy in strength, and my position as regards the q.f. guns is much worse. Please give orders, and should you wish me to cover retirement from Connaught's Hill.[258]

Within the message lay a strong inference that Spion Kop should be abandoned but Coke had no intention of saying so outright. He showed the message to Hill, whom he still believed to be the officer next in order of seniority on the plateau. However, Hill did not like the defeatist sound of 'retirement' so Coke changed it to 'withdraw' with which Hill was satisfied.

Meanwhile Thornycroft, apart for the verbal message regarding his promotion, had received no communication since he had joined the column 14 hours earlier. Nor had he met Coke or been informed that Coke had replaced Woodgate. With twilight fast approaching, Thornycroft knew that a decision would have to be made and if he could not find a general to speak to, he would at least confer with some of the regimental officers. Since early afternoon, whenever the opportunity had presented itself, Thornycroft had attempted to contact Hill but no one seemed to know where he might be found. At about this time Thornycroft, in conferring with Crofton, was assured that he had indeed been promoted to brigadier-general and thus, with the absence of an officer of higher rank, he was in command of Spion Kop. The news gave Thornycroft the confidence he required in order to decide, like Coke, that Spion Kop must be abandoned. However, prior to implementing a withdrawal, he decided to send one final despatch before conferring with his senior officers. At 6.30pm he wrote to Warren:

> The troops which marched up here last night are quite done up. They have had no water, and ammunition is running short. I consider that even with the reinforcements which have arrived it is impossible to permanently hold this place so long as the enemy's guns can play on the hill. They have three long range guns, three of shorter range, and several Maxim-Nordenfeldts, which have swept the whole of the plateau since 8am. I have not been able to ascertain the casualties, but they have been very heavy, especially in the regiments which came up last night. I request instructions as to what course I am to adopt. The enemy are now (6.30) firing heavily from both flanks (rifle, shell, and Nordenfeldt), while a heavy rifle fire is being kept up on the front. It is all I can do to hold my own. If my casualties go on at the present rate I shall barely hold out the night. A large number of stretcher bearers should be sent up, and also all the water possible. The situation is critical.[259]

Thornycroft, in discussion with Cooke of the Scottish Rifles, decided to follow the latter's suggestion that he, Cooke, go and find Coke whom he believed to be located some distance down the hill. There followed much confusion regarding what actually happened and who had met whom and who was present. Thornycroft, it seems, wrote a note for Cooke to present to Coke should he happen to find him. The message read:

> I have been in command here for the afternoon. Will you please come and discuss the situation? It is impossible to hold the hill unless the Boer artillery is first silenced.

Cooke later maintained that he first found Hill and then Coke, to whom he gave the note, being told at the same time that Hill was in command. However, Coke later denied that he had been given the message or had seen the officer who had supposedly delivered it. Only Hill recalled meeting Cooke, but not until Coke had left. The note was certainly written but it is doubtful that it reached its destination. Yet another baffling incident amongst many.[260]

Earlier, Churchill, enjoying the dual roles of Lieutenant in the SALH and war correspondent of the *Morning Post*—roles that gave him access to positions and people more difficult to reach for the ordinary correspondent—decided that the action on top of the plateau was worthy of a description for his readers. At about 4pm he and a fellow officer, Captain Brooke, began the climb, first through the ambulance village that had grown at the bottom of the hill and then through a steady stream of wounded and those who could take no more and had, in bewilderment, merely walked or crawled away. Churchill counted the number of shells as they exploded on the plateau above and, apart from the thud-thud of the Pom-Poms, he made the tally seven a minute.[261] The two officers found the summit a 'bloody reeking shambles'[262] and too hot a place for sight-seeing. They determined to hurry down at once and give a first-hand account of the conditions to Warren. During the course of the day, Warren had moved the wagon he used as a headquarters as it had attracted enemy artillery fire. Churchill's report, straight from the top, was the first Warren had received since 3.40pm.[263] Later messages from Coke and Thornycroft were yet to arrive. Warren was impressed and greatly alarmed at what Churchill and Brooke had to say. Later Churchill wrote: '. . . infantry could not, perhaps would not, endure another day.'[264]

There was nobody more aware of this fact than Thornycroft. Conceivably there was a whiff of mutiny on the *kop*. Much earlier in the day, as they were preparing to scale Twin Peaks, the KRR had encountered men coming off the *kop* and making their way to camp who, at that early hour, said the summit was being evacuated.

It is baffling that Warren, who would have had a number of staff officers and orderlies, should instruct Churchill, no more than an 'honorary' colonial cavalry lieutenant, to go back up the hill in order to ascertain Thornycroft's views. Not to give Thornycroft orders it will be noted, but merely to obtain his view which, with Churchill making the return trip in the dark, would take at least four hours to accomplish. Nevertheless, Churchill set out once more and struggled upwards through the thickening jam of descending men.

In the meantime Thornycroft, having eventually found Hill and convinced him that he was not the superior officer present, had conferred with Crofton and Cooke—Colonel Bloomfield had not been seen for some time, no one being aware that he had been wounded and taken prisoner. It was agreed that, as there was no evidence of any plan or purpose nor any possibility of silencing the Boer guns on the morrow, the order "No surrender' would be defied inasmuch as Spion Kop would be evacuated. Thus, at 6.30pm, there came about an unprecedented paradox—two gallant and dedicated British officers, both fighting the same battle and both disobeying orders to achieve completely opposing objectives: Buchannan Riddell flouting orders to retire and Thornycroft spurning instructions to stand firm.

Churchill wrote two versions of his finding Thornycroft on the mountain: they differ considerably in detail but were in essence the same. By the time Churchill had tracked down Thornycroft amongst the mayhem of the summit, Thornycroft had already given the order to evacuate and despite Churchill's rather timid 'Had I better not go and tell Sit Charles Warren before you retire from the hill? I am sure he meant you to hold on',[265] Thornycroft replied in no uncertain terms: '. . . I ordered a general retirement an hour ago . . . Better six good battalions safely off the hill tonight than a bloody mop-up in the morning.' [266] Thornycroft in his report written a day or so later on 26 January, stated:

> In forming my decision as to retirement I was influenced by the following:
>
> The superiority of the Boer artillery, inasmuch as their guns were placed in such positions as to prevent our artillery fire being brought to bear on them.
>
> By my not knowing what steps were being taken to supply me in the morning with guns, other than the mounted battery which, in my opinion, could not have lived under the long-range of the Boer artillery.
>
> By the total absence of water and provisions.
>
> By the difficulty of entrenching on the hill, to make a trench in any way cover from artillery fire with the few spades at my disposal, the ground being so full of rocks.
>
> Finally, I did not see how the hill could be held unless the Boer artillery was silenced and this was impossible.[267]

In the darkness Thornycroft gave orders for all the troops to come in. They were then formed up and sent down the hill, later followed by Churchill and Thornycroft. Due to the lack of stretcher bearers, many of the wounded had to remain behind; those who were lucky enough to reach the dressing station, a short way below the summit, would have found it to be more of a military thoroughfare than a first aid post as all the retreating troops were forced to march through it. Men stumbling, cursing and some dragging mules behind them were, by dint of much shouting, kept clear of the long lines of stretchers lying on the ground. Lieutenant Knox of the RAMC had dressed that morning in nothing more than his thin khaki drill uniform and, now that a heavy dew was falling, he and his patients were feeling bitterly cold. He found an old canvas bag which he slipped over his head and with his belt secured it around his waist. Likewise, Private Howard and his stretcher bearer mate had had a busy day. On one occasion they had gone out under fire to bring in their severely wounded commanding officer:

> As we were running across the open they put a Pom-Pom and a Maxim on us. They made a big dust but never touched us . . . We took him [their CO] down to the dressing station and there I saw a sight that well-nigh sickened me! There were three or four poor fellows lying on stretchers with both legs shattered—flesh, bone, putties and trousers all hashed up together.[268]

Later in the day Howard, leading some reinforcements up the hill, lost the track and took a tumble, almost going over the edge. He injured his ankle and in the darkness made his way off the hill on his hands and knees.[269]

Just after 9pm, when Churchill had been approaching the plateau, Coke, whom Churchill must have passed near the signal station, received a message from Warren ordering him down to headquarters. Coke demurred, not relishing the descent with his lame leg, and signalled back for permission to report at first light. Receiving no response, Coke eventually stumbled off erroneously believing, as he knew nothing of Thornycroft's promotion, that he was leaving Hill in command. The utter confusion that was taking place is exemplified by the troops being formed up on the plateau at 8.15pm, in preparation to retire, while Coke, at 9.40pm, was still at the signal station not knowing that by then many units had already passed and gone down. Finally, Coke started on his way leaving Major Phillips, his staff officer, at the signal station in his stead. Phillips, presumably, decided there was nothing that required his attention and so found a quiet corner and went to sleep.[270] Most of the British forces that had been on Spion Kop had now left apart for some stragglers and the two regiments that had been held in reserve, the Dorsets and BMI. The latter two units had not been involved in the fighting and initially refused to leave but eventually they too retired, BMI reaching the southern plain where their horses were still tethered, just as dawn was breaking.

During their descent, Thornycroft and Churchill encountered Lieutenant-Colonel Sim of the Royal Engineers who was supervising various tasks that his regiment had been ordered to undertake: to carry 2,000 sandbags to the top (an average of fewer than one bag per man); to construct slides on some of the boulders over which the naval guns could be hauled upwards by hand, and to construct a zigzag pathway for the mountain gun. However, by 2.30am, after Spion Kop had been abandoned, the men of the mountain gun detachment, having marched all day from Chieveley, had only reached Trichard's Drift where Buller ordered them to rest until morning.[271] The commandant of the Royal Artillery had deemed it impossible to get Maxim machine guns and the 15-pounders up the slopes but believed the naval guns could be hauled to the summit. This feat was never realised, as Thornycroft ordered Sim and his men to retire. However, before doing so, Sim handed Thornycroft a letter from Buller which urged him to hold the hill. It also contained a detailed sketch of how best to construct a trench: it showed, despite two of Buller's staff officers having seen the rock-hard conditions of the plateau, a trench about four feet deep with a cave-like shelter to the rear that would take, as had the Boer trenches on Twin Peaks, dynamite to excavate. Thornycroft read the letter, told Sim it had arrived too late and ordered him and his men off the hill.

Meanwhile, still on the upper slopes, aroused by the sound of marching feet, Major Phillips awoke with a start and rushed forward in alarm: he was told the hill had been abandoned and that Thornycroft had already gone. Finding that he was facing little more than the rear guard and stragglers from other units, Phillips ordered an immediate halt and, with little success, attempted to confer with any officers who would listen to him. He then scribbled a memorandum which, no doubt, he hoped would both halt the withdrawal and salvage his reputation for sleeping on duty:

This withdrawal is absolutely without the authority of either Major-General Coke or Sir Charles Warren. The former was called away by the latter a little before 10am. When General Coke left the front about 6pm and the men were holding their own, he left the situation as such, and reported that he could hold on. Some-one, without authority, have given orders to withdraw, and has incurred a grave responsibility. Were the General here, he would order an instant reoccupation of the heights.[272]

Obviously in the anxiety and confusion, Phillips made errors in his written timings.

Having listened to Phillip's memorandum, a group of officers agreed to halt their men if Phillips could produce proof of his authority. This he attempted to do by signalling Warren's headquarters, but the lamps had run out of oil. Nevertheless, the officers agreed to wait while more oil was found and finally, at 2.30am, Phillips sent off a message announcing an unauthorised retirement had taken place but that the slopes were still in British possession. All waited in anguished anticipation for a reply but astonishingly, there was none. Phillips, it would seem, was not the only person who slept on duty and at 4am the retirement continued.

As the weary and shell-shocked survivors reached the lower slopes, all they longed for was water and uninterrupted sleep. A private of the ILI recalled:

What a shaking of hands as the different stragglers came in. It was an awful experience for a volunteer regiment . . . to go through in their first engagement. The roll was called about 11 o'clock. The colonel himself came along the lines but he could hardly speak, he seemed to feel the whole thing so much.[273]

A History of the Lancashire Fusiliers recalls that the men spoke and acted as if they were in a remorse state of drunkenness and, although unwounded, were suffering from nervous prostration and were in agonies of pain.[274]

Coke finally arrived at Warren's headquarters at 2am. He had not been informed that Warren's wagon had been moved and consequently spent an extra two hours stumbling around in the dark, looking for it. At that moment Coke still believed the summit to be secure and that Colonel Hill was in command. A short time later Thornycroft and Churchill arrived with their shattering news. According to Churchill, Warren had gone back to bed and was found to be asleep.

> I put my hand on his shoulder and woke him up. 'Colonel Thorny-croft is here, Sir'. He took it all very calmly. He was a charming old gentleman. I was genuinely sorry for him. I was also sorry for the army.[275]

Thornycroft's message, which he had written at 6.30pm and in which he had emphasised how perilous the situation was, also arrived at about 2am. It had taken eight hours to reach its destination.

However, the *kop* was not completely devoid of British soldiers going about their duty. Lieutenant Knox of the RAMC, with a number of men, was still attending to the wounded. Just before dawn he mustered all the medics he could find and climbed to the plateau. '. . . Not a living soul, either Britain or Boer, was moving. A deathlike silence reigned.' They actually found some completely unwounded men, in a state of utter exhaustion, lying intermingled with the dead. As he set about evacuating the wounded he was suddenly halted by a harsh cry of 'Hands up!' For a moment Knox could not comprehend, then he suddenly realised he and his men were prisoners.[276]

General Botha, despite the wholesale desertion of Twin Peaks and later Spion Kop by Boer forces, was nevertheless, convinced that if the commandos stood firm, the British would themselves abandon the hill. At midnight, it was confirmed that horsemen and wagons were everywhere preparing to move or had indeed already gone. Deneys Reitz recalled:

> When we reached the bottom most of the horses were gone, the men who had retired having taken their mounts and ridden away, but our own animals and those belonging to the dead or wounded, were still standing without food or water where they had been left at daybreak . . . We fully believed that the morning would see them [the British] streaming through the breach to the relief of Lady-smith, and the rolling up of all our Tugela line.[277]

As Reitz, still in the company of Commandant Opperman, pondered amongst other equally uncertain men, a number of whom were already astride their horses, a man rode into their midst shouting at them to halt.[278] Reitz discovered it was General Botha who then addressed them from the saddle with such force and eloquence that the burghers halted and led their horses back to the foot of Spion Kop. Botha's unshakable belief that the British would abandon the hill was based on information from British prisoners and his own intuition: Woodgate had been killed; there had been no water on the summit; the soldiers had been utterly demoralised by Boer artillery and the British had failed to attack else-where. Botha spent the remainder of the night riding from one commando to the next, beseeching the burghers to have faith, while Reitz and his comrades, huddled at the foot of the hill, soaked by the falling dew, waited with apprehension.[279]

With the coming of dawn the skyline of Spion Kop was revealed: two figures suddenly appeared waving their hats. They were Boers and, as Botha had predicted, the British had gone. There was now a scramble to occupy the prize that all except Botha had believed to have been lost. However, the Boers, in their moment of triumph, were sickened at the price the enemy had paid for his futile endeavour. As Botha and General Tobias Smuts viewed the '. . . scores of dead faces upturned with staring eyes in the sun as if upbraiding high heaven for permitting such murderous work amongst men belonging to God-fearing nations' Smuts wished he had the power to transport some of the headless bodies and shattered limbs to the bedrooms of Joseph Chamberlain, the Secretary of State for the Colonies and his henchman, in Cape Town, Sir Alfred Milner, so that on waking, the two chief authors of the war should see some of the results of their policy.[280] When Deneys Reitz reached the plateau he too was stunned by the abomination he confronted: 'There cannot have been many battlefields where there was such an accumulation of horrors within so small a compass.'[281]

Warren had sent Woodgate and Coke, both slightly lame, to the top of Spion Kop but, despite the message received from Thornycroft at 4.30pm: 'The enemy guns sweep the whole top of the hill . . . What rein-forcements can you send to hold the hill tonight?' , and despite the sight of the plateau engulfed in fire and smoke for most of the day and the ever increasing number of casualties, Warren, who had boasted he could walk 'thirty miles with the best', made no attempt to see for himself the state of affairs on the summit. He who only a month earlier had written: '. . . he, [Buller] 'could not see his way to relieve Ladysmith. My business was to tell him it could be done and that I could do it' now, at 2am, sent a message requesting Buller's assistance.

Buller arrived at about 5am to be told by Warren that, in his opinion, the Boers were in retreat. However, it was not until 8am that Colonel Burn Murdoch was ordered to take his regiment of Dragoons to reconnoitre Spion Kop and ascertain whether or not the Boers were in possession. The colonel replied that it was impossible work for cavalry and proposed to reconnoitre on foot. Taking two troops, Burn Murdoch galloped to the foot of Spion Kop where the force remained while he and another officer climbed on foot, encountering walking wounded and stretcher bearers all the way. They continued climbing until warned there were Boers just ahead and in going a little further, they could clearly see the enemy. Having returned to the bottom of the hill, the dragoons galloped back to Warren's headquarters where there was a discussion for half an hour.[282] However, Buller had already come to a conclusion: he would assume full command and take his army back over the Tugela to try again elsewhere.

Having reoccupied the *kop* without a shot being fired, Botha sent forward a flag of truce in order that the wounded on both sides could be attended and the dead buried. Whilst the latter gruesome task was put in hand, the British, assured by the truce, made haste to evacuate its massive army of men and equipment beyond the reach of the Boer guns which might be brought to bear upon them as soon as the truce expired. However, attempting to intern so many British dead in such unaccommodating ground, and in so short a time, proved to be an almost impossible task. An obvious solution was to utilise the trenches. Early on the morning of the 25th, three army chaplains climbed to the plateau and the work began. However, it was never properly completed despite burgher assistance. The delay offered the local natives an opportunity to loot, which they duly exploited.[283] Botha objected to the dilatory way in which the British burials were being conducted and complained:

> I had granted an armistice of twenty-four hours to General Warren for the purpose of attending to the wounded and of burying the dead, but it looked by the delay which occurred as if he were more anxious to march his big force back across the Tugela than to attend to the duties for which the armistice had been agreed to by me.[284]

Nevertheless, Botha was able once again to cable President Kruger with the news of another seemingly miraculous, Boer victory: 'Battle over and by the grace of God a magnificent victory for us.'

Had the British attacks on Bastion Hill, Tabanyama, the Rangeworthy

Heights and Spion Kop, been carried out with half the efficiency that was shown during the evacuation, the outcome of the battle may well have been different. By the 26th the whole army, guns, wagons, pontoon bridges and equipment were over on the south bank of the Tugela. Botha, his men battle-weary after a week's non-stop fighting, wanted only rest. The Battle of Spion Kop had been lost and won and Buller was no nearer to Ladysmith. Churchill, like most junior officers and other ranks, still held him in awe despite disrespectful nicknames used behind his back: 'Reverse Buller', and 'The Ferryman of the Tugela'. Churchill exemplified, perhaps naively, the confidence which the troops still had in Buller, despite the bitterness that many felt at the useless sacrifices that had been made. Churchill wrote:

> He arrived on the field calm, cheerful, inscrutable as ever, rode hither and thither with a weary staff and a huge notebook, gripped the whole business in his strong hands, and so shook it into shape that we crossed the river in safety, comfort, and good order, with most remarkable mechanical precision, and without the loss of a single man or a pound of stores.[285]

Churchill's sweeping statement omitted to take into account, amongst other things, no doubt, the greatcoats of the Scottish Rifles. Two days after the battle the soldier diarist wrote '. . . we were surprised by the rumbling of wagons coming from our rear and we found out it was our great coats and mess tins, a good many great coats were deficient . . .'[286]

What a pity for Buller's army that he had not gripped the operation in his strong hands days earlier. During the hours of the 25th, Botha made no attempt to follow up his victory and the British walked away unmolested.

Two weeks later, on 13 February, Field-Marshall Lord Roberts wrote to the Secretary of State for War giving a summary of the irregularities and failures of the Spion Kop campaign and those who had fought in it.[287] In brief, Roberts' censure could be considered benign as no disciplinary action against any of those responsible was recommended. Buller was criticised for not taking command of the battle himself:

> . . . His non-interference can hardly be accepted as adequate . . . No personal considerations should have deterred the officer in chief command . . . from insisting on it [the battle] being con-

ducted in the manner in which, in his opinion, would lead to the attainment of the object in view, with the least possible loss on our side.

Of Warren, Roberts wrote:

It is to be regretted that Sir Charles Warren did not himself visit Spion Kop during the afternoon or evening, knowing as he did that the state of affairs there was very critical, and that the loss of the position would involve the failure of the operations . . . and I think that Sir Redvers Buller is justified in remarking that 'There was a want of organisation and system which acted most un-favourably on the defence'.

Roberts further concluded that the defeat was in some measure due to the commanding position of the enemy '. . . probably also to errors of judgement and want of administrative capacity on the part of Sir Charles Warren'. Coke merely got a passing mention, neither commendable nor derogatory. Thornycroft came in for the most severe censure:

. . . I regret I am unable to concur with Sir Redvers Buller in think-ing that Lieutenant-Colonel Thornycroft exercised a wise discre-tion in ordering the troops to retire . . . I am of the opinion that Lieutenant-Colonel Thornycroft's assumption of responsibility and authority was wholly inexcusable.

Buller and Thornycroft jointly featured in Roberts' final summing up:

but whatever faults Sir Charles Warren may have committed, the failure must also be ascribed to the disinclination of the officer in supreme command to assert his authority and see that what he thought best was done, and also to the unwarranted and needless assumption of responsibility by a subordinate officer.

The only officer who received unreserved praise was he who had slept on duty. 'Captain Phillips, the brigade major of the 10th Brigade, on the occasion in question, is deserving of high commendation."
To what can the British defeat of the Spion Kop operation be ascribed? Certainly the discord between Buller and Warren and in particular Buller's

strident demand for the return of the KRR in their moment of victory; over confidence; the lack of reconnaissance; the dearth of maps; the want of efficient water containers; the archaic method of passing information. All in all, it was a battle fought with 20th-century weapons but with medieval communications. Most of all, it was the lack of purpose and resolve on the parts of Buller and Warren. René Bull, in writing his despatch of 25 January opined the disaster was due to a series of blunders—of criminal blunders—for which someone is accountable.[288]

The Spion Kop operation, from 17 to 24 January, had cost the British in casualties, as estimated by the American military attaché, Captain Slocum: 364 killed or died of wounds; 1,056 wounded; and 318 captured or missing. The total was 1,738 all told. The British, however, claimed their total losses to be only 1,204 including 300 prisoners, while the Boers put the British dead alone at between 1,200 and 1,500. Boer casualties are even more difficult to ascertain. General Botha declared them to be 50 killed and 120 wounded, of whom no fewer than 50 or 60 per cent were Carolina Commandos.

A campaign medal for British troops who had served in the war was approved and named 'Queen's South Africa Medal'; on the obverse side was the crowned and veiled head of Queen Victoria while on the reverse side Britannia, with a flag in her left hand, held a laurel wreath towards a group of advancing soldiers. In total 177,000 medals were struck and 24 battle bars, or honours, were approved for various battles including Talana, Elandslaagte, the Defence of Ladysmith and the Relief of Ladysmith but, through no failing of the men who fought, the battle of Spion Kop was deemed unworthy of a battle honour.

. . . .

CHAPTER THIRTEEN

LADYSMITH RELIEVED

With the battle over and the guns silent, the hopes of those besieged in Ladysmith were dashed once again. It was a particular disappointment as on the 24th the outlying picquets of the town had watched the enemy's preparations for whole sale flight: '. . . The Boers can be seen driving away cattle so I guess they are finding things a bit too warm and are clearing out with as much stock as possible while they can.'[289]

Six miles north-east of Potgieter's Drift on the northern side of the Tugela, in the direction of the besieged town, there is a ridge of hills called Vaal Krantz that is visible from both Spion Kop and Mount Alice. One wonders whether or not, during the days Warren unsuccessfully attacked the Rangeworthy Heights, Buller had pondered upon this enticingly alternative route with the open planes beyond the hills clear to see. It is also possible that due to the absence of maps, and the rain obscuring the scene on the day Buller arrived at Potgieter's Drift, he was unaware of this seemingly straightforward way to Ladysmith. Perhaps, having this alternative in mind, may also explain the alacrity with which he abandoned Spion Kop on the morning of the 25th.

Within three days of the withdrawal from Spion Kop, Buller set in motion the construction of a 20-mile long rough road to a dominating hill called Swartkop. After immense physical effort on the part of his weary troops, he had installed artillery on its crest. Including the guns on Mount Alice, which were still within striking distance of Boer targets, and the newly arrived reinforcements, the British could array 61 artillery pieces against an estimated 10 Boer guns.

This time there was to be no head-on blunder against the enemy. A feint towards Brakfontein just two miles east of Twin Peaks Bridge, was to be launched across the Tugela while the real attack waited for the deception to be accomplished. At 6am on 5 February battle commenced. A pontoon bridge, under cover of British artillery, was thrown across the river a mile downstream from Potgieter's Drift and four British regiments stormed across. They had been ordered, when 1,500 yards from the Boer defences, to throw themselves on the ground while a massive bombardment was hurled overhead. The Boers on the other hand, having been ordered to hold their fire until the enemy were within 500 yards, received the British barrage without firing a shot. The bombardment continued for almost two hours then, the feint having been accomplished, the British troops withdrew with hardly a casualty.[290]

Around midmorning, the main offensive began with another massive bombardment, this time directed at Vaal Krantz itself, while engineers under severe fire, set about throwing a second pontoon across the Tugela. British guns, increased in number to over 70, began to pound Vaal Krantz while the Light Infantry Brigade, having crossed the pontoon and finding themselves under heavy fire, advanced along the river bed, the steep banks of the Tugela giving splendid cover.[291] Eventually, leaving the protection of the river, the infantry in skirmishing order marched across the intervening plane and, with swords fixed, began to ascend Vaal Krantz. The southern summit was taken and the defenders withdrew having suffered, like the British, heavy casualties.

By late afternoon, the whole of the southern portion of the ridge was in British hands. However, Boer reinforcements from Colenso and Ladysmith had arrived and the burgher guns had been repositioned so as to enfilade the British lines. The following morning, 6 February, was occupied with an exchange of artillery fire between the combatants while the northern end of the ridge remained in Boer hands. Buller estimated that a frontal assault would result in excess of 2,000 casualties and demurred from the responsibility. Instead, he cabled Lord Roberts asking if he should proceed. Roberts replied that the honour of the British Empire was at stake and Buller should resume the attack. However, Lyttelton, whose Light Brigade held the ridge, reported that it was not only inadvisable but that the nature of boulder-strewn ridge made the establishment of artillery, the main purpose of the attack, completely impractical. At nightfall, Lyttelton reported that his brigade had been '. . . shot at day and night from nearly all sides by an invisible foe, against whom our fire was perfectly innocuous.' [292]

The following day, the 7th, the guns on both sides continued to bombard each other. However, while the Boer guns searched and found concentrations of enemy troops the British tried in vain to silence the Boer artillery. By late afternoon Buller had decided that further endeavour at Vaal Krantz was not a proposition and had made up his mind to try again elsewhere.

Like the withdrawal from Spion Kop, the evacuation of Vaal Krantz was immensely successful, the Boers being completely unaware that the deed had taken place until the following morning when there was not a British gun or soldier left on the north bank of the Tugela.

Two days later, Buller's army was back at Chieveley from where, almost two months earlier, it had launched its first attack in its endeavour to relieve Ladysmith. British casualties incurred during the assault on Vaal Krantz were 369 killed or wounded; Boer estimated casualties were 87.

In Ladysmith Stevens, the war correspondent, noted the distant sight of returning Boer wagons and livestock, which a few days earlier had been making haste towards the Free State. Rumours and counter-rumours were rife; the municipal cemetery was running out of space; everyone was bordering on starvation; and the blunders of the relieving army were too difficult to comprehend or condone.[293]

Buller had exhausted all possible ways to Ladysmith except one: the route via Hlangwane, the ridge dominating Colenso. Choosing this route would mean outflanking the western end of the enemy line. It will be remembered, that this was the way originally favoured by Warren who had maintained that the Boers, when fighting in the open, had the advantage of possessing long-range vision. By forcing the burghers to fight at close quarters, in the ambit of deep railway cuttings, the Tugela gorge, re-entrances, salients, scrub and boulders, Warren believed the Boers would be robbed of their advantage.

On 17 February, Buller, now in command of his army en masse, ordered Dundonald and his Colonial Cavalry Brigade to turn the enemy left flank situated to the west on a distant hill named Cingolo.[294]

Pushing, and at times cutting, their way through thick undergrowth, the cavalry took the Boer pickets by surprise and by evening, with infantry support, Cingolo had been captured. After heavy fighting on the following day, further dominating hills were taken, forcing the Boers westwards towards the railway cutting and the Tugela gorge. On the 18th, Barton's

Brigade that for two months had been more or less inactive facing Hlang-wane, now attacked the hill encountering little opposition. With Colenso at last dominated by the British on Hlangwane, the town was abandoned and the Boers retired across the river into a vastness of scrub-covered hills and ravines.[295]

Buller's final objective was Pieter's Hill, the northern extremity of the enemy defences, beyond which lay the open plane and Ladysmith. His intention was to cross the Tugela below Pieter's Hill and encircle the enemy. Instead, having been persuaded that the route to Pieter's Hill was too heavily defended, he ordered the crossing of the river above Colenso and advanced into the Boer labyrinth. There followed two days of inten-sive close-quarter fighting, the command of which Buller handed over to Warren despite having said a month earlier that he would never employ Warren again in an independent command.[296] On the 22nd the Lancashire Brigade, which had suffered so many casualties on Spion Kop, were in the forefront of the engagement and were again subjected, with little protec-tion, to intense artillery fire. The hills amongst which the fighting was tak-ing place, soon took by dint of association, regimental and other army names: Hart's Hill; Naval Gun; Inniskilling; Wynne; Railway; and Pom-Pom.

Despite the growing number of casualties, the infantry made steady progress. However, during the night of 22nd/23rd, the Middelburg, Hei-delberg, Krugersdorp, and Standerton Commandos counter-attacked and retook lost ground only to be counter-attacked in return by the KRR. The next day, in confused fighting, the battle continued with Hart and his Irish Brigade, always to the fore, leading the attack on yet another hill, named Hart's Hill[297]. The approach was so confined that the advance was initially made in single-file ending at a stream, spanned by a narrow bridge, which had been carefully noted by the waiting enemy. The crossing became known as 'Pom-Pom Bridge' and as the Irish crossed it seemed as though every second man fell dead or wounded. At last, having found the safety of dead ground below the hill they were to storm, the Irish enjoyed a short respite before the hazardous ascent. They made the top only to find another crest line beyond. The British guns ceased firing for fear of hitting their own men, allowing the Boers to take unmolested aim at the Irish-men.[298] Despite the arrival of the Rifle Brigade the Boers held firm. The following day a truce was called for a few hours in order to bury the dead. Then the battle resumed with undiminished ferocity. Buller decided to bring the whole of his army into the area between Hart's and Wynne's

Hills with the railway line snaking in its cutting to the west and the Tugela, deep in its gorge a mile away, descending to the north. Warren now prevailed on Buller to attack Pieter's Hill, urging that if the attack were successful it could be used as a springboard and base to finally surround the Boer defenders.

The following day, 27 February, the choking yellow fumes of lyddite infused the burgher trenches on Pieter's Hill and a bayonet attack by Barton's Fusiliers soon followed.[299] With Warren commanding, bitter fighting continued all day until finally at evening time the hill was taken. The feat was cheered not only for what the troops had accomplished but also for the news that far away to the west, General Cronje had surrendered to Lord Roberts. The day was especially memorable as it was the anniversary of Majuba. Warren's plan had worked and with more relentless fighting, often hand-to-hand, the remaining hills were taken and Ladysmith lay open to welcome he who would claim the honour of being first into town; and there were many who would assert to having been the foremost, Churchill amongst them. He described the moment:

> The evening was deliciously cool. My horse was strong and fresh
> ... Beyond the next ridge lay Ladysmith, the centre of the world's
> attention—the excitement of the moment was increased by the
> exhilaration of the gallop.[300]

The Battle of Tugela Heights, as the combined battles fought between 14 and 27 February became known, was a victory achieved at great cost—greater even than Spion Kop. There were 2,300 British casualties killed, wounded and missing and this is believed to be a conservative estimate. Boer casualties are even more difficult to ascertain.

To those besieged the departure of the enemy was abrupt and unexpected. Suddenly two great convoys of wagons were on the move, one towards the Free State and the other north to the Transvaal. 'Pursuit! Pursuit!' the garrison cried but, alas, the horses that could have carried the Dragoons and the Lancers in vengeful chase had all been eaten. Instead, the Ladysmith guns were sighted on the departing wagons. However, the wily Boers knew the range and much to their delight and mockery the shells fell short.[301] Then Buller's cavalry arrived, thousands of horsemen fit and eager to pursue the vulnerable foe. Buller, inscrutable as ever, to the vexation and fury of his officers, held his horsemen in and the burghers passed into the distance unmolested.[302] Perhaps it was a gesture of gratitude in return for the unimpeded evacuation that Botha had granted the day after Spion Kop?

Nevertheless, the Boer's escape could not diminish the defenders' joy. The soldiers and civilians cheered themselves hoarse despite many stumbling about, in danger of falling in their weakened state. After 114 days they were free.

The first troops into the town were the Imperial Light Horse and the Natal Carabineers, the best of friendly rivals. It had seemed as though there would be a race to claim the honour, but it was agreed the two regiments would ride in side-by-side, shoulder-to-shoulder and share the accolade. As they rode down the main street Donald MacDonald recalled how men, unashamed of their emotions, cheered and laughed for joy, many with tears streaming down their cheeks. James Bayley, still writing regularly to his fiancé, penned a letter on 27 February mentioning that it was once again believed that Buller was but a few days away, adding sarcastically: 'He sent a message yesterday to say he hoped to be here in a few days—we hope so too'. The very next morning at last true to his prediction, Buller arrived and dour, unemotional, Bayley scrawled in an excited hand: 'Hurrah, Hurrah! What cheering and shouting. The relief of Ladysmith is accomplished!' However, what bad luck. The previous night one of the last shells to descend on Ladysmith demolished Bayley's furniture store '. . . and all sorts of furniture was smashed up, lamps and glass show cases smashed to smithereens'. Bayley promised his fiancé that he would save her a fragment of the shell. Like a true Briton he concluded: 'I should not wish to get clear of any of my experiences since leaving home and I trust I shall be more of a true man for all of them.'

Then Sir George White, shaken and pale, rode amongst the joyful throng. With a voice trembling with emotion he declared

> I thank you men from the bottom of my heart, for all the help and support you have given me . . . It grieved me to have cut your rations, but I promise you I will not do it again. I thank God we kept the flag flying.[303]

He then called for three cheers for the Queen.

EPILOGUE

The siege was over as was that of Kimberley; the siege of Mafeking would take a further two and a half months to lift. Buller continued to command the Natal campaign to a successful conclusion. In May Lord Roberts captured Johannesburg and a week later Pretoria. By October both the Orange Free State and the Transvaal had been annexed and proclaimed British colonies. Lord Kitchener had succeeded Lord Roberts as Commander-in-Chief in South Africa, Roberts and Buller had returned to England as heroes with Warren having preceded them by several months. The careers of Winston Churchill and Mohandas Gandhi are legendary and one is compelled to ponder how the history of the world would have differed had either one been struck down on Spion Kop. Thorneycroft, despite Roberts' disparaging remarks, continued with his army career, retiring in 1912 with the rank of colonel. Many men of the Lancashire brigade who had suffered so severely on Spion Kop were Liverpudlians. In 1906 the Liverpool Football Club built a new stadium at Anfield and named it Spion Kop in honour of the local men who had fallen in battle six years earlier. However, it is not only Liverpool that has a Spion Kop stand. Many football clubs throughout the world have followed suit and where there is a steep embankment it often becomes known as 'Spion Kop' or 'The Kop.'

By the end of May 1900 Britain believed the war had been won but it had not reckoned with the indomitable guerilla army that would call itself 'The Bitter Enders'. In September a Boer Council of War held at Hectorspruit near the border of Portuguese East Africa, present day Mozambique, decided that only well-armed and equally well-mounted men who would not be an encumbrance to their comrades, would be considered for the new phase of the war The Bitter Enders planned to wage.[304] Of those assembled, over 3,000 failed to qualify, being mainly elderly burghers, foreign volunteers, Cape rebels, deserters or men who until recently had just been hiding in the bush. This motley army, led by General Francois Pienaar, crossed into Mocambique where they surrendered to the Portuguese. In accordance with international law, they were interned and warned they would be imprisoned or shot if they attempted to return to South Africa. However, the British were unhappy with such a large Boer presence on its border and the Portuguese, to avoid any confrontation with Britain, decided to ship the majority of the internees to Europe, out of harm's way.[305]

Two thousand elite burghers remained and, under the command of generals Louis Botha and Ben Viljoen, they moved north, split into will-o-the-wisp units, and collaborated with thousands of other burghers who had also decided not to give up the fight. In the vastness of the Orange Free State General Christiaan de Wet still commanded 9,000 well-mounted men while Botha was set to range the eastern Transvaal and General de la Rey to cause havoc in the west, beyond Pretoria. The Cape was not immune to the depredations of the raiders either. General Christiaan Smuts, a Cambridge graduate and lately the Transvaal State Attorney, led a raid to within sight of Table Mountain. These units struck at enemy columns, isolated garrisons, cut telegraph wires, destroyed bridges, and attacked the vulnerable railway lines. To inflict these vital blows, they became accomplished in the art of demolition and even invented a contraption that could be planted under the line with the full confidence that when they were safely miles away it would explode a charge of dynamite. An old Martini Henry rifle would be procured and the butt sawn off behind the breech. The trigger guard would also be removed and a cartridge without a bullet, but accompanied by a stick of dynamite, would be laid in the cut-off breech. Next, a shallow cavity was dug under the railway line and packed with explosives. Finally, the primed breech was placed on top of the charge with the trigger uppermost just touching the rail, then, as the train with its engine leading, reached the trap, its weight would slump the line, exploding the charge as effectively as if a finger had pulled the trigger.[306] Kitchener himself was a victim of a Boer derailment, narrowly escaping with his life.

In order to defeat these depredations, Kitchener rallied a huge army of 200,000 men consisting of both mounted troops and infantry. He divided the most hard-hit parts of the country into a series of imaginary squares in which the cavalry would hunt down the commandos in what became known as sweeps or drives, attempting to push the foe into the waiting arms of other cavalry within the square. Although vastly outnumbered, the Boers invariably evaded this net.

The main task of the infantry was to guard the railway and bridges. To do so effectively Kitchener deemed it, irrespective of cost, necessary to construct several thousand small forts or blockhouses as they became known, each manned by eight or more men, depending on size, and usually equipped with a machine gun. The prefabricated blockhouse, designed by the Royal Engineers, proved at £1,000 each to be the most economical.[307] As they were usually roofed with corrugated iron, during summer the buildings must have been agonizing for the occupants. It was necessary to provision each blockhouse by the railways whereas the commandos required no such monumental organization in order to keep themselves in the field. Every Boer farm and home became a place of succor and supply with the wives, the elderly and the young not only provisioning the commandos but passing on information regarding the enemy. If Kitchener was to beat the Bitter Enders, draconian measures would be required. He decided to uproot thousands of families, burn their farms, destroy their crops and create a waste land. Those who had once been the inhabitants were taken off and concentrated into camps—concentration camps, a term Nazi Germany would make infamous 40 years later.

Throughout South Africa more than 60 of these concentration camps were established in which over 22,000 people died, mostly of malnutrition or enteric fever.[308] Similarly, to an extent, more British troops died of dysentery and pneumonia then were killed by the Boers. In clearing the land it is estimated that 116,000 blacks, mainly those who had been employed by Boer farmers, were also moved into camps where the British took advantage of this vast pool of labour, not only for manual work for which they were paid, but also for growing, under protection of the blockhouses, vegetables for the consumption of the British Army.[309]

When the existence of the concentration camps became known, Britain was censored not only by most of the world, but was condemned by many in Britain itself. In July 1900 David Lloyd George, a future prime minister declared:

A war of annexation against a proud people must be war of exter -

mination, and that is unfortunately what, it seems, we are now committing ourselves to—burning homesteads and turning women and children out of their homes.[310]

Women's movements in particular, such as the Women's Liberal Federation and the women's branch of the South African Conciliation Committee, were extremely vocal. Also, it was members of these organizations, such as Miss Emily Hobhouse, who travelled to South Africa and exposed the conditions prevailing in the camps.

Despite everything, it was the Battle of Spion Kop that had revealed to the Boers that Britain, irrespective of her casualties and the cost, was also determined to pursue the war to the bitter end. Thus it became apparent to many Bitter Enders that no matter how fiercely they continued with the struggle they could never win. To continue would not only mean ruination of the country but, perhaps, civil war or the extinction of the Boer race.

Gradually, more and more Boers gave in and defected to the enemy— some, in fact, being formed into colonial regiments, scornfully called 'The Hands Uppers' by the Boers, and used to hunt down their former comrades.[311] Towards the beginning of 1902, with Boer resistance having collapsed throughout the country except for scattered pockets of waning defiance, the terms of peace, with Kitchener presiding, were deliberated and finally agreed on 31 May at Vereeneging, an industrial Transvaal town. Botha, Smuts, and Rooi Opperman, who will be remembered for his part in the Battle of Spion Kop, were foremost among the Boer delegates. However, Commandant Henrik Prinsloo of the Carolina Commando, perhaps the most courageous and tenacious of the Boer leaders to fight on Spion Kop, was not so lucky. On 7 November 1900, while leading an attack, he fell into a British ambush and was killed within sight of his family. Twenty six years later, General Horace Smith-Dorrien, who had led the ambush, erected a memorial in Prinsloo's honour at the spot where he and his comrades had been killed.[312]

Britain, literally having conquered the republics of the Transvaal, the Orange Free State and having crushed any Boer resistance in its own Cape Colony, now set about attempting to restore the country to its former prosperity. Three million pounds was paid in compensation, reconstruction and in claims made by its Boer citizens. Britain also built 2,500 miles of new railway line to the agricultural hinterland. Five years later the unification of the four colonies, Natal included, was considered. It was decided that each would become a province with its own parliament within the Union of South Africa, headed by a governor general representing the British King Edward VII.[313] General Botha was elected its first prime minister. One item high on the agenda was the question of franchise for the black, coloured and Indian populations. Britain, evading responsibility, left each individual province to decide for itself. Needless to say, consent for the black, coloured and Indian population to vote was withheld.[314] Thus South Africa was set on the rocky road to the distant 1994 elections after which the citizens of the new Republic of South Africa became neither black, white or coloured, but people of The Rainbow Nation.

Author's Note

The little town of Ladysmith, which had cost so many lives, had been built on soil belonging to neither Boer nor Briton; it had been the home of black people, though in 1900 it is unlikely that the white contestants gave this fact even the briefest consideration.

However, over a century later things in Ladysmith were different. On a busy Saturday morning, during the week of the 110th anniversary of the lifting of the siege, I happened to be driving along Murchison Street, the main road through town. The little house with its tin roof that had been General White's headquarters was still there, as were the two hotels with their colonial names, *The Royal* and *The Crown*. On the opposite side of the road, the town hall with its clock tower, once shattered by Boer gunfire, stood back from the pavement, guarded by several cannons used during the siege. Ladysmith was, in fact, much the same except the site of the old cricket ground now sported a shopping centre while mile-long Murchison Street teemed with thousands of shoppers but, ironically in view of the white blood that had been spilt for the possession of Ladysmith, there was not a white face to be seen.

BIBLIOGRAPHY

PUBLISHED SOURCES

Aikenhead, C., *Ladysmith's 20 VCs*, Private Publication (No date of publication)

Amery, L. S., *Times History of the War in South Africa 1899–1900*, London, 1905

Arthur, M., *Symbol of Courage*, London, 2005

Barker, A., *Battles and Battlefields of the Anglo-Boer War*, London, 1999

Bolsmann, E., *Winston Churchill*, Alberton, 2008

Bourquin, S. B. and Torlage, G., *The Battle of Colenso*, Randburg, 1999

Byron, F., *The Great Boer War*, London, 1977

Chisholm, R., *Ladysmith*, Braamfontein, 1979

Churchill, W. S., *London to Ladysmith*, London, 1900

Churchill, W. S., *My Early Life*, London, 1930

Churchill, Winston, *The Boer War*, London, 2002

Coetzer, O., *The Road to Infamy*, South Africa, 1996

Davitt, M., *The Boer Fight for Freedom*, South Africa, 1902

De Wet, C. R., *Three Years War*, London, 1903

'Defender' (Pseud.), *A Vindication*, London, 1902

Dixon, N., *On the Psychology of Military Incompetence*, Cape, 1976

Doyle, A. C., *The Great Boer War*, Galago Edition, 1999. First published London, 1900

Farwell, B., *The Great Boer War*, London, 1976

Gibson, G. F., *The Story of the Imperial Light Horse*, South Africa, 1937

Gilbert, M., *Churchill, A Photographic Portrait*, Middlesex, 1974

Gillings, K., *The Battle of Thukela Heights*, Randburg, 1999

Gon, P., *The Road to Isandlwana*, London, 1979

Greenwall, Ryno, *Artists and Illustrators of the Anglo-Boer War*, Vlaeberg, 1992

Haldane, A., *How We Escaped From Pretoria*, Edinburgh, 1901

Hall, D., *Colenso*, South Africa, 1994

Hall, D., *The Hall Handbook of the Anglo Boer War*, Pietermaritzburg, 1999.

Hardy, E. G., *Mr Thomas Atkins*, London, 1900

Hare, S., *The King's Royal Rifle Corps Chronicle*, London, 1929

Hare, S., *The King's Royal Rifle Corps*, London, 1929

Jenkins, R., *Churchill: A Biography*, London, 2001

Knox, E. Blake, *Buller's Campaign with the Natal Field Force*, London, 1902

Krause, L., *The War Memoirs of Commandant Ludwig Krause*, Cape Town, 1995

Lee, E., *To the Bitter End*, Harmondsworth, 1985

Lehmann, J. H., *All Sir Garnet*, London, 1964

Lehmann, J. H., *The First Boer War*, London, 1972

Lock, R. and Quantrill, P., ed., *Dennison, Zulu Frontiersman*, London, 2008

Lock, R. and Quantrill, P., *Zulu Vanquished*, London, 2005

Lock, R. and Quantrill, P., *Zulu Victory*, London, 2002

Lock, R., *Blood on the Painted Mountain*, London, 1995

MacDonald, D., *How We Kept the Flag Flying*, London, 1902

McFadden, P., *The Battle of Elandslaagte*, Randburg, 1999

Packenham, T., *The Boer War*, Futura Edition, 1982

Parsons, N., *A New History of Southern Africa*, London, 1982

Pearse, H. H. S., *Four Months Besieged*, London, 1900

Pemberton, W. B., *The Battles of the Boer War*, London, 1964

Powell, G., *Buller: A Scapegoat?*, London, 1994

Reitz, D., *Commando*, London, 1929

Rumbelow, D., *Jack The Ripper*, London, 1975

Slocum, S., *Boer War Operations in South Africa*, Melville, 1987

Smyth, B., *A History of the Lancashire Fusiliers*, Lancashire Fusiliers Museum, 2007

Stalker, J., *The Natal Carbineers*, Durban, 1912
Symonds, J., *Buller's Campaign*, London, 1963
Thomasson, W. H., *With the Irregulars*. London, 1881
Tylden, G., *The Armed Forces of South Africa*, Johannesburg, 1954
Uys, I., *South African Military Who's Who*, Germiston, 1992
Venter, C., *The Great Trek*, Cape Town, 1985
Watt, S., *The Battle of Vaalkrans*, Randburg, 1999
Williams, W. W., *The Life of General Sir Charles Warren*, Oxford, 1941
Wilson, H. W., *With the Flag to Pretoria*, London, 1900
Wood, E., *Winnowed Memories*, London, 1917

UNPUBLISHED SOURCES AND PRIVATE INFORMATION
Diary of Private S. T. Cornell, Imperial Light Infantry (courtesy of
    Major P. Naish)
Privately Published in Afrikaans by O.J.O. Ferreira, *Viva ons Boers*,
    Pretoria, 1994
Royal Archives Windsor, Ref. RA Vic/ADD EI/8629
The Battle of Talana, Brochure, Talana Museum, Dundee, South Africa
The Spion Kop Despatches, London, 1902
Unpublished diary of J. R. Bayley covering the period of the Siege
    of Ladysmith
Unpublished diary of unknown private soldier of the Scottish Rifles
Unpublished letter of 'Charlie', Private of the Imperial Light Infantry,
    October, 1900 (courtesy of Major P. Naish)
Unpublished letter of an officer, 1st Royal Dragoons (courtesy of
    Nicki von der Hyde)
Unpublished letter of Private G. Howard, Natal Medical Corps, July,
    1901 (courtesy of Major P. Naish)
Unpublished letter, descendant of Mr Mitchell-Innes
Unpublished letters of Lieutenant Frederick Raphael, Lancashire Brigade

NEWSPAPERS, JOURNALS AND PERIODICALS
Barnard, C. J., *The South African Military History Society Journal*,
    Volume No. 1, March, 2007
The Illustrated London News, April, 1881
Black and White magazine, January and February Issues, 1900
The South African Military History Society Journal, December, 2006
Tichmann, P., *Soldiers of the Queen*, Issue 87, December, 1996

ENDNOTES

[1]Reitz, D., *Commando*, p 26, London, 1929
[2]Ibid
[3]Davitt, M., *The Boer Fight for Freedom*, p 124, London, 1902
[4]Wilson, H. W., *With the Flag to Pretoria*, p 23, London, 1900
[5]Talana Museum, South Africa, Brochure *Battle of Talana*
[6]Parsons N., *A New History of South Africa*, London, 1982
[7]Lock, R. and Quantrill, P., ed., *Zulu Frontiersman*, p 3, London, 2008
[8]Cape Government proclamation dated 2 December, 1841, signed by the Governor, Sir Charles Napier
[9]Lock, R. and Quantrill, P., ed., *Zulu Frontiersman*, p 17, London, 2008
[10]Lock, R. and Quantrill, P., *Zulu Victory*, p 64, London, 2002
[11]Lehmann, J., *The First Boer War*, London, 1972
[12]Ibid
[13]Wolseley, G., South African Journal 1879–80, Cape Town, 1973
[14]Lehmann, J., *The First Boer War*, p 12, London, 1972
[15]Royal Archives, Windsor, Ref Royal Artillery VIC/Add E1/8629
[16]Lehmann, J., *The First Boer War*, p 97, London, 1972
[17]Ibid, p 116
[18]*Illustrated London News*, April, 1881
[19]Ibid
[20]Talana Museum, South Africa, Brochure, *Battle of Talana*
[21]Reitz, D., *Commando*, p 27, London, 1929
[22]Talana Museum, South Africa, Brochure, *Battle of Talana*
[23]Reitz, D., *Commmando*, London, 1929
[24]McFadden, P., *The Battle of Elandslaagte*, p 3, Randburg, 1999
[25]Ibid, p 3
[26]Unpublished letter. Descendant of Mr Mitchell-Innes
[27]McFadden, P., *The Battle of Elandslaagte*, p 22, Randburg, 1999

[28]Schiel, A., *Twenty Three Years of Storm and Sunshine in South Africa*
[29]Steevens, G. W., *From Cape Town to Ladysmith*, Edinburgh, 1900
[30]Lee, E., *To The Bitter End*, p 84, Harmondsworth, 1985
[31]McFadden, P., *The Battle of Elandslaagte*, P 19, Rand Buller, 1999
[32]Wilcox, W., *The Fifth (Royal Irish) Lancers in South Africa, 1899–1902*, p 218, York, 1981
[33]Macdonald, D., *How We Kept the Flag Flying*, p 8, London, 1900
[34]Davitt, M., *The Boer Fight for Freedom*, p 139, London, 1902
[35]Unpublished letter. Officer of the Kings Royal Rifles, KRR Museum, Winchester
[36]Reitz, D., *Commando*, p 36, London, 1929
[37]Byron, F., *The Great Boer War*, p 81, London, 1977
[38]De Wet, C. R., *Three Years War*, p 23–24, London, 1903
[39]Reitz, D., *Commando*, p 40, London, 1929
[40]Churchill, W., *My Early Life*, p 189, London, 1930
[41]Haldane, A., *How We Escaped From Pretoria*, Edinburgh, 1901
[42]Churchill, W., *London to Ladysmith*, p 81, London, 1900
[43]Ibid, p 82
[44]Ibid, p 95
[45]Dixon, N, *On the Psychology of Military Incompetence*, p 62, Cape, 1976
[46]Bolsmann, E., *Winston Churchill*, p 68, Alberton, South Africa, 2008
[47]Unknown Soldier of the Imperial Yeomanry: paper presented to the South African Military History Society
[48]Powell, G., *Buller: A Scapegoat?*, p 137, London, 1994
[49]Lock, R. and Quantrill, P., *Zulu Vanquished*, p 82, London, 2005
[50]*South African Military History Society Journal*, December, 2006
[51]Ibid
[52]Thomasson, W. H., *With The Irregulars*, p 14, London, 1881
[53]Lock, R and Quantrill, P., *Zulu Vanquished*, p 104, London, 2005
[54]Ransford, O., *The Battle of Spionkop*, London, 1969
[55]Macdonald, D., *How We Kept the Flag Flying*, London, 1900
[56]Macdonald, D., *How We Kept the Flag Flying*, p 39, London, 1900
[57]Stalker, J., *The Natal Carbineers*, p 136, Durban, 1912
[58]Davitt, M., *The Boer Fight for Freedom*, p 274, London, 1902
[59]Hall, D., *Colenso*, p 26, South Africa, 1994
[60]Davitt, M., *The Boer Fight for Freedom*, p 258, London, 1902
[61]Krause, L., *The War Memoirs of Commandant Ludwig Krause*, p 33, Cape Town, 1995
[62]Ibid, p 37
[63]Churchill, W., *The Boer War*, London, 2002
[64]Pakenham, T., *The Boer War*, p 229, London, 1979
[65]Spiers, E., *Letters from Ladysmith*, p 55, United Kingdom, 2010
[66]*Black and White* magazine, February, 1900
[67]Wilson, H., *With the Flag to Pretoria*, p 95, London, 1900
[68]Coetzer, O., *The Road to Infamy*, p 85, South Africa, 1996
[69]Krause, L., *The War Memoirs of Commandant Ludwig Krause*, p 37, Cape Town, 1995
[70]Ibid, p 37

[71]Lieutenants Melville and Coghill received the posthumous award of the Victoria Cross after saving the Regimental Colour. They were killed by pursuing Zulus near to Rorke's Drift approximately sixty miles from Colenso.
[72]Hall, D., *Colenso*, p 88, South Africa, 1994
[73]Ibid, p 90
[74]Arthur, M., *Symbol of Courage*, p 164, London, 2005
[75]Hall, D., *Colenso*, p 89, South Africa, 1994
[76]Ibid, p 91
[77]Chisholm, R., *Ladysmith*, p 150, Johannesburg, 1979
[78]Farwell, B., *Eminent Victorian Soldiers*, p 271, Middlesex, 1980
[79]Davitt, M., *The Boer Fight for Freedom*, p 271, London, 1902
[80]Farwell, B., *The Great Boer War*, p 137, London, 1976
[81]Davitt, M., *The Boer Fight for Freedom*, p 274, London, 1902
[82]Chisholm, R., *Ladysmith*, p 149, Johannesburg, 1979
[83]Ibid
[84]Coetzer, O., *The Road to Infamy*, p 84, South Africa, 1996
[85]Ibid, p 87
[86]Ibid, p 87
[87]Slocum, S., *Boer War Operations in South Africa*, p 15, Melville, South Africa, 1987
[88]Coetzer, O., *The Road to Infamy*, p 78, South Africa, 1996
[89]Ibid, p 79
[90]Ibid, p 79
[91]Stalker, J., *The Natal Carbineers*, p 158, Durban, 1912
[92]Macdonald, D., *How We Kept the Flag Flying*, p 122, London, 1900
[93]Gibson, G. F., *The Story of the Imperial Light Horse*, p 79, South Africa, 1937
[94]Macdonald, D., *How We Kept the Flag Flying*, p 123, London, 1900
[95]Ibid, p 119
[96]Coetzer, O., *The Road to Infamy*, p 24, South Africa, 1996
[97]Ibid, p 133
[98]Churchill, W., *My Early Life*, p 74, London, 1930
[99]Churchill, W., *The Boer War*, p 49, London, 2002
[100]Churchill, W., *My Early Life*, p 351, London, 1930
[101]Gilbert, M., *Churchill, A Photographic Portrait*, p 34, Middlesex, 1974
[102]Williams, W. W., *The Life of General Sir Charles Warren*, p 250, Oxford, 1941
[103]Ibid, p 251
[104]Lehmann, J. H., *All Sir Garnet*, p 387, London, 1964
[105]Coetzer, O., *The Road to Infamy*, p 82, South Africa, 1996
[106]Powell, G., *Buller: A Scapegoat?*, p 7, London, 1994
[107]'*Defender*', (pseudo), *Sir Charles Warren and Spion Kop, A Vindication*, p 18, London, 1902
[108]Powell, G., *Buller: A Scapegoat?*, p 15, London, 1994
[109]Ibid
[110]Gon, P., *The Road to Isandlwana*, p 87, London, 1979
[111]Lock, R. and Quantrill, P., *Zulu Vanquished*, p 128, London, 2005
[112]Ibid, p 125
[113]PRO, Ref. T/16653
[114]Ibid

[115]Rumbelow, D., *Jack the Ripper*, p 32, London, 1975
[116]Powell, G., *Buller a Scapegoat?* p 81, London, 1994
[117]Ibid, p 101
[118]Ibid, p 52
[119]Gon, P., *The Road to Isandlwana*, p 174, London, 1979
[120]Coetzer, O., *The Road to Infamy*, p 114, South Africa, 1996
[121]Ibid, p 115
[122]Hardy, E. J., *Mr. Thomas Atkins*, p 336, London, 1900
[123]Ibid
[124]Coetzer, O., *The Road to Infamy*, p 116, South Africa, 1996
[125]Ibid, p 116
[126]Ibid, p 114
[127]Davitt, M., *The Boer Fight for Freedom*, p 292, London, 1902
[128]Bayley, J. R., *Unpublished Diary*, p 22
[129]Macdonald, D., *How We Kept the Flag Flying*, p 147, London, 1900
[130]Reitz, D., *Commando*, p 67, London, 1929
[131]Kestell, J. D., *Through Shot and Flame*
[132]Gibson, G. F., *The Story of the Imperial Light Horse*, p 85, South Africa, 1937
[133]Ibid, p 84
[134]Ibid, p 110
[135]Ibid, p 99
[136]Ibid, p 107
[137]Ibid
[138]Ibid, p 88
[139]Macdonald, D., *How we Kept the Flag Flying*, p 156, London, 1900
[140]Pearse, H. H. S., *Four Months Besieged*, p 139, London, 1900
[141]Chisholm, R., *Ladysmith*, p 172, Johannesburg, 1979
[142]Kestell, J.D., *Through Shot and Flame*
[143]Churchill, W., *The Boer War*, p 106, London, 2002
[144]Coetzer, O., *The Road to Infamy*, p 118, South Africa, 1996
[145]Ibid
[146]Ibid
[147]'Defender', (pseudo), *Sir Charles Warren and Spion Kop, A Vindication*,
p 18, London, 1902
[148]Ibid
[149]Uys, Ian, *South African Military History Who's Who*, p 128, Germiston, 1992
[150]Coetzer, O., *The Road to Infamy*, p 122, South Africa, 1996
[151]Wilson, H. W., *With the Flag to Pretoria*, p 238, London, 1900
[152]Churchill, W., *My Early Life*, p 304, London, 1930
[153]Barnard, C. J., *South African Military History Society Journal*, Johannesburg, 2007
[154]Ibid
[155]Reitz, D., *Commando*, p 72, London, 1929
[156]Churchill, W., *London to Ladysmith*, p 237, London, 1930
[157]Churchill, W., *The Boer War*, p 120, London, 2002
[158]Ibid
[159]Coetzer, O., *The Road to Infamy*, p 125, South Africa, 1996
[160]Churchill, W., *The Boer War*, p 120, London, 2002

[161]'*Defender*', (pseudo), *Sir Charles Warren and Spion Kop, A Vindication*, p 18, London, 1902
[162]Churchill, W., *The Boer War*, p 125, London, 2002
[163]Ibid, p 126
[164]Coetzer, O., *The Road to Infamy*, p 125, South Africa, 1996
[165]Macdonald, D., *How We Kept the Flag Flying*, p 174, London, 1900
[166]Ibid, p 172
[167]Pearse, H. H. S., *Four Months Besieged*, p 225, London, 1900
[168]Macdonald, D., *How We Kept the Flag Flying*, p 226, London, 1900
[169]Bayley, J. R., *Unpublished Diary*, p 30
[170]Ibid
[171]Ibid
[172]Churchill, W., *London to Ladysmith*, p 276, London, 1902
[173]Ibid, p 291
[174]Amery, L. S., *Times History of the War in South Africa*, Map no. 19b
[175]Symonds, J., *Buller's Campaign*, p 200, London, 1963
[176]Ibid, p 201
[177]'*Defender*', (pseudo), *Sir Charles Warren and Spion Kop, A Vindication*, p 18, London, 1902
[178]Lock, R. and Quantrill, P., *Zulu Vanquished*, p 211, London, 2005
[179]*The Spion Kop Despatches*, p 17, London, 1902
[180]Ibid, p 15
[181]Coetzer, O., *The Road to Infamy*, p 131, South Africa, 1996
[182]Churchill, W., *The Boer War*, p 148, London, 2002
[183]Ibid, p 146
[184]*The Spion Kop Despatches*, p 19, London, 1902
[185]Ibid, p 41
[186]Ibid, p 16
[187]Ibid, p 16
[188]Ibid, p 16
[189]Ibid, p 23
[190]Bull, R., *Black and White* magazine, February 1900, London, 1900
[191]*The Spion Kop Despatches*, p 13, London, 1902
[192]*The Spion Kop Despatches*, Appendix M, London, 1902
[193]Bull, R., *Black and White* magazine, January, 1900
[194]*The Spion Kop Despatches*, p 23, London, 1902
[195]Lock, R., *Blood on the Painted Mountain*, p 196, London, 1995
[196]Knox E. Blake, *Buller's Campaign with the Natal Field Force*, p 81, London, 1902
[197]Unpublished Letter, Officer of the Royal South Lakes Regiment
[198]Unpublished Letter, Private Howard, Natal Medical Corps
[199]Smyth, B., Pamphlet, p 4 of 18, Lancashire Fusiliers Museum
[200]Unpublished Letter, Private of the Scottish Rifles
[201]Smyth, B., Pamphlet, p 4 of 18, Lancashire Fusiliers Museum
[202]*The Spion Kop Despatches*, p 26, London, 1902
[203]Ibid, p 32
[204]Ibid, p 32
[205]Ibid, p 26

206Uys, Ian, *South African Military History Who's Who*, p 274, Germiston, 1992
207Smyth, B., Pamphlet, p 7 of 18, Lancashire Fusiliers Museum
208Unpublished Letter, Private Howard, Natal Medical Corps
209Churchill, W. S., *London to Ladysmith*, p 38, London, 1900
210*The Spion Kop Despatches*, p 38, London, 1902
211Ibid, Appendix M, London, 1902
212Ibid, p 23
213Amery, L. S., *Times History of the War in South Africa*, p 265, London, 1905
214Reitz, D., *Commando*, p 78, London, 1929
215*The Spion Kop Despatches*, p 17, London, 1902
216Pearse, H. H. S., *Four Months Besieged*, p 148, London, 1900
217Unpublished Letter, Private of the Scottish Rifles
218Ibid
219*The Spion Kop Despatches*, p 41, London, 1902
220Amery, L. S., *Times History of the War in South Africa*, p 261, London, 1905
221*The Spion Kop Despatches*, Appendix M, London, 1902
222Ibid
223Ibid, p 34
224Knox, E. Blake, *Buller's Campaign with the Natal Field Force*, London, 1902
225Unpublished letter, Private Connell of The Imperial Light Infantry
226Smyth, B., Pamphlet, Lancashire Fusiliers Museum
227Unpublished letter. Unknown Officer of Lancashire Fusiliers
228*The Spion Kop Despatches*, p 35, London, 1902
229Amery, L. S., *Times History of the War in South Africa*, p 266, London, 1905
230Ibid, p 266
231Ibid, p 268
232Ibid, p 269
233Knox, E. Blake, *Buller's Campaign with the Natal Field Force*, p 16, London, 1902
234Smyth, B., Pamphlet, p 11–18. Lancashire Fusiliers Museum
235*The Spion Kop Despatches*, p 28, London, 1902
236Amery, L. S., *Times History of the War in South Africa*, p 270, London, 1905
237Unpublished Letter, Private Cornell of the Imperial Light Infantry
238Ibid
239Amery, L. S., *Times History of the War in South Africa*, p 271, London, 1905
240Ibid, p 272
241*The Spion Kop Despatches*, Appendix M, London, 1902
242Wood, E., *Winnowed Memories*, p 298, London, 1917
243Unpublished diary of unknown private soldier of the Scottish Rifles
244Hare, S., *The King's Royal Rifle Corps Chronicle*, p 133, Winchester, 1902
245Barnard, C. J., *South African Military History Society Journal*, Volume 2, No 1, March 2007
246Ibid
247Hare, S., *The King's Royal Rifle Corps*, p 230, London, 1929
248Reitz, D., *Commando*, p 81, London, 1929
249Amory, L.S., *Times History of the War in South Africa*, p 277, London, 1905
250Hare, S., *The King's Royal Rifle Corps*, p 229, London, 1929
251*The Spion Kop Despatches*, p 45, London, 1902

[252]Ibid, p 45

[253]Amery, L. S., *Times History of the War in South Africa*, p 277, London, 1905

[254]*The Spion Kop Despatches*, London, 1902

[255]Ibid

[256]Bull, R., *Black and White* magazine, February 1900, London, 1900

[257]*The Spion Kop Despatches*, p 29, London, 1902

[258]Amery, L. S., *Times History of the War in South Africa*, p 279, London, 1905

[259]Ibid, p 282

[260]Ibid, p 281

[261]Churchill, W. S., *London to Ladysmith*, p 306, London, 1900

[262]Ibid, p 307

[263]*The Spion Kop Despatches*, Appendix M, London, 1902

[264]Churchill, W. S., *London to Ladysmith*, p 309, London, 1900

[265]Churchill, W. S., *My Early Life*, p 309, London, 1930

[266]Amery, L. S., *Times History of the War in South Africa*, p 289, London, 1905

[267]*The Spion Kop Despatches*, p 29, London, 1902

[268]Unpublished letter, Private Howard, Natal Medical Corps

[269]Ibid

[270]*The Spion Kop Despatches*, p 30, London, 1902

[271]Amery, L. S., *Times History of the War in South Africa*, p 283, London, 1905

[272]*The Spion Kop Despatches*, p 32, London, 1902

[273]Unpublished Letter, Private Cornell of the Imperial Light Infantry

[274]Smyth, B., Pamphlet, p 14 of 18, Lancashire Fusiliers Museum

[275]Churchill, W S., *My Early Life*, p 310, London, 1930

[276]Knox E. Blake, *Buller's Campaign with the Natal Field Force*, p 89, London, 1902

[277]Reitz, D., *Commando*, p 81, London, 1929

[278]Ibid, p 81

[279]Ibid, p 82

[280]Davitt, M., *The Boer Fight for Freedom*, p 325, London, 1902

[281]Reitz, D., *Commando*, p 83, London, 1929

[282]Unpublished Letter, Officer of the Royal Dragoons

[283]Davitt, M., *The Boer Fight for Freedom*, p 352, London, 1902

[284]Ibid, p 352

[285]Churchill, W. S., *London to Ladysmith*, p 342, London, 1900

[286]Unpublished diary of unknown private soldier of the Scottish Rifles

[287]*The Spion Kop Despatches*, p 3, London, 1902

[288]Bull, R., *Black and White* magazine, February 1900, London, 1900

[289]Bayley, J. R., Unpublished diary

[290]Wilson, H., *With the Flag to Pretoria*, p 311, London, 1900

[291]Watt, S., *The Battle of Vaal Krantz*, p 17, Randburg, 1999

[292]Ibid, p 26

[293]Macdonald, D., *How We Kept the Flag Flying*, p 259, London, 1900

[294]Churchill, W. S., *London to Ladysmith*, p 387, London, 1900

[295]Gillings, K., *The Battle of the Thukela Heights*, p 20, Randburg, 1999

[296]Barker, A., *Battles and Battlefields of the Anglo-Boer War, 1899–1902*, p 113, Milton Keynes, 1999

[297]Gillings, K., *The Battle of the Thukela Heights*, p 28, Randburg, 1999

[298]Barker, A., *Battles and Battlefields of the Anglo-Boer War, 1899–1902*, p 117, Milton Keynes, 1999
[299]Ibid, p 121
[300]Churchill, W. S., *The Boer War*, p 209, London, 2002
[301]Macdonald, D., *How We Kept the Flag Flying*, p 259, London, 1900
[302]Churchill, W. S., *The Boer War*, p 212, London, 2002
[303]Macdonald, D., *How We Kept the Flag Flying*, p 226, London, 1900
[304]Ferreira, OJO, *Viva ons Boers*, Pretoria, 1994
[305]Ibid
[306]Lee, E., *To the Bitter End*, P126, London, 1985
[307]Ibid, p 157
[308]Hall D., *The Hall Handbook of the Anglo-Boer War*, p 220, Pietermaritzburg, 1998
[309]Ibid, p 222
[310]Lee, E., *To the Bitter End*, p 131, London 1985
[311]Ibid, p 121
[312]Uys, I., *South African Military Whose Who*, Germiston, 1992
[313]Parsons, N., *A New History of South Africa*, p 227, London, 1982
[314]Ibid, p 227

INDEX

a'Court, Colonel 170, 171
Acton Homes 138, 154, 159, 160, 172
Acton Homes Road 152, 154, 155, 156, 162, 175
Africa, Britain acquires vast tracts of land in 27
Africa, West Coast, expedition to 99–100
Afrikaans language 16
Albrecht, Tpr Herman, VC 124
Alexandria 104, 105
Aloe Knoll 170, 171, 174, 180–181, 183, 188
amaHlubi tribe 57
amaNgwane tribe 57
amaXhosa tribe 100, 101
American visitor to Colenso battlefield 76–77
Anderson, Dr 150
Anglo-Egyptian War (1882) 104–106
Anglo-Zulu War (1879) 165
Anstruther, Col Philip 21–22
Aqaba 105, 106
Arabi Pasha 105
'Ashanti Ring' 99
Ashanti tribe 99, 100
Atkins, J. B. 135
Ava, Lord 149
Awdry, Lieutenant 169

Balfour, Arthur 79
balloons, observation 133, 159
baPedi tribe 20
Baptie, Major 74, 75, 76
Barker, Archdeacon 59
Barton, Maj-Gen Geoffrey 60, 63, 64, 68, 70, 72

Bastion Hill 138, 152, 157–158, 159, 205–206
Bayley, James 87–88, 127–128, 149–150, 214
Bayly, Major 193
Bechuanaland 27
Bechuanaland Mounted Police 27
Bedouin, the 104-106
Bethune, Maj Sir Edward 137
Billings, Trooper 75, 76
Birch, Captain 183
'Bitter Enders, The' 215, 216, 217, 218
Blaauwkrantz River 57
Black and White magazine 162–163
black people moved into camps 217
'Black Week' 77, 89
Blomfontein 18
Blood River, Battle of (1838) 17
Bloomfield, Lt-Col Charles 166, 173, 175, 199
Bodicea, HMS, sailors 22–23
Boer Army
    artillery at Spion Kop 170, 172–173, 175, 180, 186, 199
    at Battle of Colenso 69, 70, 71, 73, 74, 76, 77
    at Battle of Elandslaagte 35, 36–37, 40, 42
    at Battle of Laings Nek 23
    at Battle of Majuba 24–25
    at Battle of Talana Hill 15–16, 29, 30–31
    besieges Kimberley and Mafeking 13
Bethal Commando 62

Boksburg Commando 62, 170
Bronkhorstspruit engagement 21–22
Carolina Commando 62, 171, 173, 174, 178, 183, 191–192, 194, 208
demolition charges 216
Dundee occupied by 31–32
Ermelo Commando 62, 64
gathers at Sandspruit 14–15
German Corps 33, 36
Heidelberg Commando 44, 62, 64, 122, 123, 171, 174, 178, 212
Heilbron Commando 43
at Hlangwane Hill 63, 64, 65, 67, 68, 72
Johannesburg Commando 33
Kock's commandos capture Elandslaagte 31, 32–33
Kroonstad Commando 43
'Kruger's Own' commandos 30–31
Krugersdorp Commando 44, 62, 64, 212
Ladysmith assault 119–125, 126–128, 129
Ladysmith assault losses 129
Ladysmith besiegers 117, 118, 210, 211, 212, 213
Lyndenberg Commando 191
Middelburg Commando 62, 64, 212
mobility 53
Natal, northern, marches into 15
Natal, numbers in 145
and Natal Field Force advance 152–153, 158, 159–160, 162

233

Natal infiltrated beyond
    Estcourt 51
Orange Free State Commando
    62, 64
Pretoria Commando 139, 172,
    175, 178, 183
recriminations after failure of
    Platrand assault 148
recruits 115
rout after surrender at
    Elandslaagte 37–40
at Spion Kop 169, 170, 171–
    172, 174, 175, 178–179,
    183–184, 185, 186, 187,
    188–190, 196, 197, 203–
    204, 205
Standerton Commando 62,
    118, 212
Transvaal *Staatsartillerie* 30,
    34, 42, 59, 84, 86
at Tugela River 62
Utrecht Commando 62, 118
Vrede Commando 62
Vryheid Commando 62, 64,
    118
Wakkerstroom Commando 44,
    47, 48, 49, 62, 63, 65, 68,
    118
Zoutpansberg Commando 62,
    64
Boer Council of War 215–216
Boer Fight for Freedom, The 161
Boer rebellion (1815) 16
'Boer War, First' (1880–81) 22–25
Boers
    attitude towards foreign
        miners (*uitlanders*) 26–27
    British attitude to 20–21, 56
    British peace negotiations with
        24, 25–26, 27
    defect to British 218
    establish Republic of Natalia 17
    eyesight of 117
    history of 16, 17
    inspired to regain
        independence 19–20
    lives of 18
    meet at *Paardekraal* farm to
        form army 21
    placed in concentration camps
        217, 218
    settlers, British act of injustice
        against 16–17
    Tranvsaal restored to 26
    ultimatum to British 15
Boomplats, Battle of (1848)
    17–18, 31
Border Mounted Rifles (BMR)
    60, 81, 148
Botha, Gen Louis 62, 80,
    159–160, 216
    and advance into Natal 51
    and Hlangwane position 63
    and Battle of Colenso 70–71
    in wretched state 138–139

at Spion Kop 171, 172, 178,
    185, 191, 192, 196
convinced British would
    abandon Spion Kop
    203–204, 214
and burial of British dead 205
rests after battle 206
and Boer casualties at Spion
    Kop 208
and peace agreement 218
as first prime minister 219
Bothma, Louis 175
Bowen, Captain 124
Bridle Drift 64, 67
Briel, Commandant 63, 65, 67
Brigade Operations 158
Britain acquires vast tracts of land
    in Africa 27
British acts of injustice against
    Boer settlers 16–17
British annex Transvaal 19, 20
British Army *see also* Natal Field
    Force; Spion Kop, Battle of
    accused of looting after
        Elandslaagte 39
    Army Corps arrives in Cape
        Town 53–54
    attack launched from
        Ladysmith 42–43
    attack Zulus 19, 20
    at Battle of Elandslaagte and
        rout of Boers after
        surrender 35–37
    at Battle of Hlangwane 71–72
    at Battle of Majuba 24, 25
    at Battle of Talana Hill 15–16,
        29–30, 31
Barton's Brigade *see* British
    Army: Infantry Brigade, 6th
Bethune's Mounted Infantry
    (BMI) 60, 102, 137, 179–
    180, 187, 193, 196, 201
Black Watch 100
blockhouses, prefabricated 217
Boer defectors' regiments 218
Boers, first attack by 15–16
Border Regiment, 1st 61, 157
Colenso, advance on 60, 63,
    64, 65, 67–68
Colonial Cavalry Brigade 211
Connaught Rangers, 1st 61
convoys 53
Devonshire Regiment 35–36, 37
Devonshire Regiment, 2nd 61,
    126, 127, 148
Division, 5th 94, 116, 117, 140
Dorset Regiment, 2nd Bn 114,
    177, 187, 188, 196, 201
Dragoon Guards, 5th 35, 38,
    39, 81
Dublin Fusiliers 29, 46, 48, 157
Dundee, withdrawal from 31,
    32
Durham Light Infantry, 1st 61
East Surrey Regiment, 2nd 61

Elandslaagte, attempts to relieve
    34
Gloucestershire Regiment 43
Gordon Highlanders 24, 25, 35,
    36, 37, 119, 120, 122, 123
Grenadier Guards 109
Hussars, 13th 60, 151, 152
Hussars, 18th 30, 31, 81
Imperial Light Horse (ILH) 35,
    36, 37, 59, 81, 119, 120,
    121, 124, 148, 152, 214
Imperial Light Infantry (ILI)
    177, 186–187, 188
Imperial Light Infantry private
    202
Imperial Yeomanry 54–55
Indian Stretcher Bearer Corps
    29
infantry battalion equipment 52
Infantry Brigade, 2nd (Hild-
    yard's) 61, 64, 67–68, 70–71
Infantry Brigade, 4th (Lyttel-
    ton's) 61, 64, 68, 70, 140
Infantry Brigade, 5th
    (Irish/Hart's) 61, 64, 67,
    68–69, 70, 72, 78–79, 212
Infantry Brigade, 6th (Bar-
    ton's) 60–61, 64, 68, 70,
    179, 211–212, 213
Infantry Division, 2nd 53–54
Irish (5th) Brigade (Hart's) 61,
    64, 67, 68–69, 70, 72,
    78–79, 212
Irish Fusiliers 29
King's Royal Rifles 29
King's Royal Rifles, 3rd 61,
    119, 122, 124, 159, 180,
    188, 190–191, 192–195,
    198, 207–208, 212
King's Royal Rifles, 3rd,
    private 38
Lancashire Brigade 157, 165,
    170, 181, 190, 212, 215
Lancashire Brigade officer 182
Lancashire Fusiliers, 2nd Bn
    114, 165, 166, 168–169,
    173–174, 177, 178, 183,
    185, 202
Lancers, 5th 34, 35, 38, 40, 81
Lancers, 5th, officer 38–39
Lancers, 18th 38
Lancers, 21st 45
last time colours carried into
    battle 23
Life Guards 109
Light Infantry Brigade 210–211
Manchester Regiment 35, 37,
    119, 122, 127
maps, lack of 141, 180
Middlesex Regiment, 2nd Bn
    114, 177, 185, 186, 188
Mounted Brigade 60, 61, 63–
    64, 65, 67, 71–72
Natal, lack of knowledge of 58
oath taken 115

Pontoon Troop 142–143, 144
recruits 115
Regiment of Foot, 1/24th 101
Regiment of Foot, 58th ('Steel-
backs') 23, 24
Regiment of Foot, 94th 21, 22
reinforcements arrive at
Modderspruit 34–35
reinforcements arrive to quell
Transvaal rebellion 23–24
retreat after Battle of Nichol-
son's Nek 43–44
Rifle Brigade, 1st 61, 82, 86–87
Rifles, 60th 95, 96, 98, 152
rout of Boers after surrender at
Elandslaagte 37, 38–40
Royal Army Medical Corps
166, 200, 203
Royal Artillery commandant
201
Royal Dragoons, 1st 60, 151,
152
Royal Dublin Fusiliers, 2nd 61,
69, 70
Royal Engineers 60, 133, 201,
217
Royal Engineers, 17th Com-
pany 166, 169, 170, 171
Royal Field Artillery (RFA) 15,
35, 42–43, 81
Royal Field Artillery, 7th
Battery 67
Royal Field Artillery, 14th
Battery 61, 64, 70, 71,
72–73, 74
Royal Field Artillery, 53rd
Battery 125
Royal Field Artillery, 58th
Battery 122
Royal Field Artillery, 68th
Battery 61, 64, 70, 71, 72–
73, 74
Royal Field Artillery, 72nd
Battery 61
Royal Inniskilling Fusiliers, 1st
61, 68
Royal Irish Fusiliers 43
Royal Irish Fusiliers, 2nd
60–61
Royal Lancaster Regiment,
2nd Bn 114, 166, 173–174
Royal Scots Fusiliers, 2nd 61
Royal Welch Fusiliers, 1st 60
Royal West Surrey Regiment,
2nd 61
Scottish Rifles, 2nd 61, 159,
169, 179–180, 188–189,
193, 195, 196, 206
Scottish Rifles private 189–190
service with 114–115
Somerset Regiment, 2nd Bn 114
South Lancashire Regiment,
1st Bn 114, 165, 166,
173–174, 183
South Lancs NCO 182

South Natal Field Force 60–62,
73–74
stationed in northern Natal 14
Thornycroft's Mounted
Infantry (TMI) 60, 137,
152, 154, 166, 167, 168,
169, 171, 174–175, 177,
178, 181
West Africa Regiment 114
West India Regiment 100
West Yorkshire Regiment, 2nd
61
York and Lancaster Regiment
114
British attitude to Boers 20–21,
56
British Intelligence Office 145
British occupy Cape 16
British peace negotiations with
Boers 24, 25–26, 27
British response to Boer rebellion
in Transvaal 22–24
British South Africa Company 27
British South Africa Police 27
Brockie, Sergeant Major 91
Bronkhorstspruit ('The
Watercress Stream')
engagement (1880) 21–22
Brooke, Captain 198
Bull, René 162–163, 195, 208
Buller, Lady Audrey 104, 110
Buller, James 100
Buller, Lt-Gen Sir Redvers
ancestry 95
education 95
breaks up Army Corps 54
and command of Frontier
Light Horse 54
in Zululand 155
attends to administrative
demands of army 55–56
fights in Sudan 63
diversity of career 95–96,
97 98, 99, 100, 101, 102,
103–104, 105, 106, 107,
109–110–111
in China 96
in India 96
in Canada 97–98
with Wolseley's expedition to
West Coast of Africa 99, 100
in 9th Frontier War 101, 102,
103
and promotion to lieutenant-
colonel 103–104
awarded Victoria Cross 103,
104
marries Lady Audrey Howard
104
appointed Administrator of
Natal 40, 104, 111
in Egypt 105, 106, 107
and relief of Khartoum 107
as Special Commissioner for
Ireland 109–110

as Adjutant-General at War
Office 110–111
voyage to and arrival in Cape
Town 13, 44
supports Wood 25
and armoured train 47
priority to relieve Ladysmith 52
whereabouts kept secret 52
and death of Piet Uys 56
takes over command in Natal
56–57
rejects then decides on idea of
frontal attack 58
advances on Colenso 60, 63,
65, 68
and Battle of Colenso 67, 68,
70, 71, 73, 75, 77–78
and attempted retrieval of guns
73, 75, 77
orders forces to retire at
Colenso 75
and commissions from ranks
75–76
held responsible for defeats
77–78
advocates surrender of
Ladysmith 78, 79
receives knighthood 105
and Warren's role in the Cape
113–114
after Battle of Colenso 116
plans next move on Ladysmith
with Warren 117
plans to take initiative 131–133
fails to disclose adverse report
to Warren 134
abandons responsibilities as
overall commander 134,
154, 179
at Potgieter's Drift 140, 141
censures General Coke 141
gives Warren his orders
142–143, 151–152
addresses troops at Springfield
143
wrangling with Warren
155–156
unable to see what was
happening 160
visits Warren 160, 161
criticises Warren's performance
160–161
desperate to achieve action
161, 162
decides to attack Spion Kop
162, 163, 165
message from Woodgate on
Spion Kop 170–171
signal from Colonel Crofton
on Spion Kop 175, 177–178
suggests promoting
Thornycroft 177–178
warns of possible
'counter-stroke' 179
enraged at KRR approaching

Twin Peaks 193, 195, 207–208
message urging Thornycroft to hold hill 201
after Spion Kop battle 204–205, 206
criticised by Lord Roberts 206–207
lack of awareness of straightforward way to Ladysmith 209
orders construction of road to Swartkop 209
and relief of Ladysmith 81–82, 210, 211, 212–213, 214
commands Natal campaign to successful conclusion 215
returns to England 215
at Royal Commission 78–79
Bullock, Colonel 74, 76
Burger, Gen Schalk 171–172, 191, 194
Burgers, Thomas 19, 20
Bushmen 57
Butler, Lt-Gen Sir William 56
Byng, Lt-Col the Hon Julian 137

Cambridge, HRH the Duke of 104
Canada, punitive expedition to (1870) 97–98
cannon see guns
Cape Colony, Europeans settle in 16
Cape Frontier 16–17
Cape Town 52
Carleton, Col Frank 43
Carlisle, Lieutenant 140
Carnarvon, Lord 19
Carnegie, Capt the Hon R. F. 122, 123
Carrington, Lt Frederick 101
Chamberlain, Joseph 204
Charrington, Lieutenant, RN 104, 105
Chelmsford, Lord (formerly Lt-Gen the Hon. Frederick Thesiger) 21, 100, 101, 102
Chieveley 80, 115, 128–129, 211
railway station 46
China, Second Opium War 96
Churchill, Winston Spencer
and Col Hamilton's disfigured hand 35
contemplates military career 89–90
travels to Cape as war correspondent 45
alcohol brought to Cape 52–53
on armoured train 46, 47, 48, 49, 50, 90, 92
captured 50, 89, 90, 106
as prisoner of war 90–91
escapes 89, 91–92
and Buller's arrival at

Potgieter's Drift 140
and advance on Ladysmith 129, 144, 153, 158, 159, 160
and plans for relief of Ladysmith 152
visits Dublin Fusiliers 'Officers Mess' 157
and Hugh McCorquodale 167, 175
at Spion Kop 198–199, 200, 201, 202–203
holds Buller in awe 206
and relief of Ladysmith 213
returns to contest Oldham 92
lecture tour 92
later career 215
leadership in World War II 92
Cilliers (Pretoria Commando) 183
Cingolo hill 211
Clery, Lt-Gen Cornelius Francis 61–62, 73, 79, 154, 160
Coetzer, Owen 134
Coke, Maj-Gen Sir John Talbot 114, 141, 154, 161, 162, 165, 177, 187–188, 204
and taking of Twin Peaks 195–196
despatch to Warren 196
Thornycroft's message to 197–198
ordered down to HQ 200–201, 202
Colenso 44, 46, 58, 64, 70, 71, 179, 212
advance on 60, 63, 64, 65
railway bridge 57
Colenso, Battle of (1899) 67, 68–75, 76, 77, 78–79, 80
map 66
attempted retrieval of guns 72–74, 75
aftermath 76–77
losses 80
Colley, Maj-Gen Sir George Pomeroy 22–24, 25, 99–100, 161
Conan Doyle, Arthur 163
concentration camps 217, 218
Congreve, Capt Walter 74
Conical Hill 170, 174
Cooke, Colonel 188, 197, 198, 199
Copley, Maj Bewicke/Benwick 190, 194
Cornell, Pte S. T. 182
Coster, Dr 33
Crofton, Lt-Col Malby 166, 175, 177, 186, 197, 199
Cronje, General 64, 213
Curran, Colonel 122

Daily Mail 37, 137
Dartnell, Colonel 119
Davies, Surgeon-Major W. 125
Davitt, Michael 161

De Aar railway junction 114
de Jager, Zaccharias 123
De Koch (Transvaaler) 184
de la Rey, Gen Adolf 106, 216
de la Rey family 106
de Mentz, Field-Cornet 153
de Villiers, Cmdt Jakob 123, 124, 126, 127
de Wet, Christiaan 43, 216
'Defender' 134–135, 144, 154, 155, 160, 162
demolition charges, Boer 216
Dervishes 63, 80, 107
Diamond Field Horse (DFH) 101–102
diamonds, discovery of 98
Dingane, King, Zulu impis of 57
Doornkloof Road 152
Downes (Devon country mansion) 96, 100, 104, 111
Drakensberg Mountains 57–58, 136, 139
Dundee, Natal 14, 15, 29, 31–32, 40
Dundonald, Col The Earl of 60, 61, 63–64, 65, 67, 71–72, 136, 137, 138, 139, 140, 144, 152, 153, 154, 155–156, 159, 179, 211
Dunne, Bugler 69
Dunnotar Castle, RMS 13, 40, 45, 52
Durban (formerly Port Natal) 17, 23, 54
smoking concert 137
Durban Light Infantry 46, 47, 49
Dutch settle in the Cape 16
Dyer, Captain 186

Edmonds, Trooper 119
Edwards, Colonel 120, 123–124
Edwards, Commandant 191
Egypt 104–107
Egyptian Army 105
Elandslaagte 32–33, 34
railway station 31, 32–33, 34, 91
Travellers' Rest Hotel 33
Elandslaagte, Battle of (1899) 35–37
map 41
British rout of Boers after surrender 37–40
Elgin, Lord 96
Emmett, Field-Cornet Joseph 77
English as official language in Cape 16
Erasmus, Cmdt Daniel 15, 60
Erasmus, Gen S. P. 29
Estcourt 45–46, 51, 117, 167

Fairview Road 152, 155, 156, 158, 160, 162, 178
Farquhar, Lieutenant 168
football stadiums, 'Spion Kop /

The Kop' in 215
Forbes, Lieutenant 168
Fort Garry, Canada 97, 98
Fort Wylie 68, 70
Fourie, General 64
Fourie's Spruit 148
French, Maj-Gen John 33, 34, 44
Frere 89, 91, 129, 133, 144–145
    British camp 56–57
    railway station 46, 47, 50, 56
Frere, Sir Bartle 19, 98–99
Frontier Light Horse (FLH) 54,
    101, 102–103
Frontier War, 9th (1878) 100–103

Galthorp (Englishman at
    Elandslaagte) 33
Gandhi, Mohandas 215
Gatacre (British officer) 63
Gcaleka clan 100
George V, King 74
Gibraltar 95, 96, 162
Gibson, G. F. 121
Gill, Captain, RE 104, 105
Gobatsi Heights 102, 111, 162
gold, discovery and production of
    26
gold miners, foreign (*uitlanders*)
    26–27
Goodyear, Private 177
Gordon, Maj-Gen Charles 33, 60,
    80, 107
Gordon, Lieutenant 168
Goshonland 106
Gough, Captain 87
Graham, Maj-Gen Sir Gerald
    106, 107
Graham, Major 152, 175
Graphic, The 148–149
Green Hill 138, 170, 174
Grenfell, Lieutenant 175
Griqua people 101, 102, 162
Griqua Town 101
Griqualand West 98, 99
Grootehoek hill 138
Grylls, Lieutenant 75
guns *see also* rifles
    cannon, 7-pounder 46, 48
    cannon, Krupp 172
    Creusot 155mm ('Long Tom')
        42, 44, 60, 84, 117, 125
    Maxim-Nordenfelt 72, 172, 197
    naval 64–65, 71, 73–74, 77,
        173, 195
Hadendowa tribesmen 108
Haggard, H. Rider 19
Haig, Maj Douglas 33–34, 44
    father 33–34
Haldane, Capt Aylmer 46–47, 48,
    49, 50, 91
Hall, Major 33
Hamer, De Wit 33
Hamilton, Col Ian 35, 36,
    125–126
'Hands Uppers, The' 218

Harris, Mr (mine general
    manager) 34
Hart, Maj-Gen Arthur Fitzroy 54,
    61, 67, 68, 70, 72, 78–79, 154,
    157, 212
Hart's Hill 212
Hectorspruit 215–216
Hely-Hutchison, Sir Walter 14,
    115
Hicks Pasha 106
Hildyard, Maj-Gen Henry 54, 61,
    64, 67–68, 70–71, 79, 154,
    158–159
Hill, Lt-Col Augustus 186, 196,
    198
*History of the Lancashire
    Fusiliers, A* 202
Hlangwane Hill 63, 64, 65, 117,
    211, 212
Hlangwane Hill, Battle of (1899)
    68, 71–72, 137
Hlobane Mountain, Battle of
    (1879) 56, 103, 162
Hobhouse, Emily 218
How the Poor Live 108
Howard, Lady Audrey (later Lady
    Buller) 104, 110
Howard, Pte George 167–168,
    169–170, 174, 200
Hunt-Grubbe, Lieutenant 122
Hunter, Maj-Gen Sir Archibald
    59–60, 141

Impati Hill 15
'India Ring' 99
Ingogo, Battle of (1881) 23
Inniskilling hill 212
Ireland 109–110
Isandlwana, Battle of (1879) 101,
    102

Jack the Ripper 109
Jameson, Dr Leander Starr 27
Jameson Raid (1895) 27, 34
Johannesburg 215
Johannesburg Police Commando
    43, 62, 64, 77
Jones, Lt Digby, VC 119, 124
Joubert, J. A. 64
Joubert, Cmdt-Gen Piet 14, 20,
    57
    ultimatum to British 15
    at Battle of Majuba 24
    and gold 26
    surrenders after Jameson Raid
        27
    calls on Free State burghers for
        support 42, 43
    and Battle of Nicholson's Nek
        44
    with advance into Natal 51
    and siege of Ladysmith 59,
        118, 119
    death after council of war
        51–52

Joubert, Mrs 14, 24

Kambula, Battle of (1879) 103,
    165
Kays, Major 191
Kestell, Chaplain John 120–122,
    125, 126–127
Khartoum, relief of 107
Kimberley 101
    discovery of diamonds in 98
    relief of 54, 56
    siege of (1899) 13, 52, 215
King's Royal Rifle Corps, The 192
Kipling, Rudyard 107
Kitchener, Lord Horatio Herbert
    80, 215, 216–217, 218
Knight, Corporal 75
Knox, Lt Blake 182, 184, 185,
    200, 203
Kock, Gen Johannes 31, 33, 34,
    37, 39, 40, 42
Kofi, King of the Ashanti 100
Kraaipan 46–47
Kràuse, Ludwig 72–73
Kreigsraad (War Council) 118
Krog, Dietzsch 72
Kroonstad council of war 51
Kruger, President Paul 15, 17, 20,
    24, 26–27, 63, 106, 118, 139
Kumasi 99, 100

Ladysmith 31, 32, 33, 40, 42, 58,
    139
    British assault on Gun Hill
        59–60
    British force retreats to 44
    Murchison Street 219
    Platrand (Caesar's
        Camp/Wagon Hill) feature
        118, 119, 120–122,
        125–127, 147
    Platrand cemetery 147–148
    Royal Hotel 84, 219
    strike force at 81–82, 83
    today 219
Ladysmith, Siege of (1899–1900)
    52, 58–59, 81–88, 209
    map 85
    Buller advocates surrender 78,
        79
    food stocks 83, 149
    bombardment 84, 86
    raid on Boers 86–87
    Town Guard 88
    Buller and Warren plan next
        move 117
    sightseers 117
    Boer besiegers 117, 118, 210,
        211, 212, 213
    Kruger requires assault 118
    Christmas 118–119
    assault 119–129
    assault losses 129
    plans for relief of 142–143,
        151–152

after Battle of the Platrand
    147–148
disease 148, 149–150
horses 149
rations 149
conditions 149, 211
sound of relief column reaches
    150
relief of 209–214
Boers depart 213–214
Laing, Sgt J. W. 123
Laings Nek 23, 24
Laings Nek, Battle of (1881) 23
Lampton, Capt the Hon Hed-
    worth, RN 134–135
Lansdowne, Lord 58, 78, 79, 80
Lanyon, Maj Sir Owen 20, 21,
    22, 101
Lehmann, Joseph 94
Little Tugela River 136, 137
Liverpool Football Club 215
Lloyd George, David 217–218
London, Trafalgar Square
    108–109
London Gazette 103
London in 1880s 108
Long, Col Charles 61, 63, 64, 70,
    71, 72, 73, 74
Lyttelton, Maj-Gen Neville 54,
    61, 64, 68, 70, 132, 154, 159,
    179–180, 192, 193–194
and relief of Ladysmith
    210–211

MacAdam, Private 168
Macdonald, Donald 39, 82, 83, 84,
    120, 124–125, 147, 148, 214
Mafeking 106
Mafeking, Siege of (1899) 13, 52,
    215
'Mahdi, The', and his forces
    106–107
Majuba, Battle of (1881) 23,
    24–25, 35, 104, 161, 190, 192
Majuba (Hill of Doves) mountain
    23, 24
Malan, Lieutenant 60
Manchester Guardian 135
marksmanship 121
Martin, Lt A. R. 176
Massey, Major 170, 183
Mathias, Captain 121
Maude, William 148–149
McCorquodale, 2nd Lt Hugh
    167, 174–175
Medal, Queen's South Africa 208
Melbourne Argus 82, 83, 84
Metcalfe, Colonel 86
Methuen, Lord 54–55, 56, 113
Méti people 97
Meyer, Cmdt Lukas 15, 29
Milner, Sir Alfred 27, 56, 115,
    204
Mitchell, Mr (Ladysmith resident)
    150

Mitchell-Innes, Mr (mine
    director) 34
Modder River, Battle of (1899) 58
Modderspruit 34
Mohawk 115
Moller, Colonel 31
Morning Post 45, 198
Morris, Col A. W. 181–182
Mount Alice 139, 140, 159, 171,
    173, 180, 209
    Observation Rock 140, 141,
    142
Mozambique 216
Murdoch, Col Burn 205

Napier, Sir Charles 17
Natal 57–58
    Boers advance into 51
    Dutch claim on 17
    northern 15
    northern, imperial troops
    stationed in 14
Natal Carbineers 59–60, 81,
    83–84, 152, 214
Natal Field Artillery (NFA) 34
Natal Field Force see also Spion
    Kop, Battle of
    Cavalry Division 136, 139,
    140, 144, 151
    Mounted Division 137–138,
    179
    conditions experienced 135,
    136
    advance 138, 143–144,
    151–155, 157–158, 159,
    160–161, 162–163
    Composite Regiment 152–153,
    155–156
    and relief of Ladysmith
    209–212
Natal Guides 86
Natal Mounted Police 19, 46
Natal Mounted Rifles (NMR)
    34–35, 60, 119, 122
Natal Volunteer Medical Corps
    (NVMC) 166, 167–168
Natalia, Republic of 17
Naval Gun Hill 212
Newcastle, Natal 22, 24
Nicholson's Nek, Battle of (1899)
    43–44
Ntombi Hospital Camp 148
Nurse, Corporal 73, 74

O'Gowan, Captain 188–189
O'Leary, Lt-Col McCarthy 183
Omdurman, Battle of (1897) 63,
    158
Opium War, Second (1856–60) 96
Opperman, 'Rooi' Daniel 153,
    175, 179, 183, 184, 203, 218
Orange Free State 18, 215, 216
Orange Free State Boers 148
Orange River Sovereignty 18
ox wagons 52, 53, 135, 136

Palestine 96–97
Palestine Exploration Fund, The
    96–97
Palmer, Professor 104, 105
Pardekraal farm 21
Park, Colonel 126
peace terms agreed 218
Penn Symons, Maj-Gen Sir
    William 14, 15, 16, 29, 31
Pepworth Hill 42
Phillips, Captain 207
Phillips, Major 201–202
Phoenix Park 110
Pienaar, Gen Francois 32, 33, 216
Pieter's Hill 212, 213
Pietermaritzburg 115
Platrand, Battle of the (1900)
    119–125, 126–128, 129
Pohlmann, Lieutenant 77
police, British 27
Police, Metropolitan 108, 109
Pom-Pom Hill 212
Port Natal see Durban
Potgieter's Drift 58, 132, 138,
    139–141, 154, 159, 173, 179
    ferry 139, 140
Powerful, HMS, guns from 134
Pretoria 19, 22, 26, 215
    railway station 91
    State Model School 91
Pretorius, Gen Andries 17–18
Prinsloo, Cmdt Henrik 171, 218
provisions 136

Railway Hill 212
Rangeworthy (Tabanyama)
    Heights 138, 151, 152, 155,
    159, 174, 205–206, 209
Raphael, Lt Frederick 167, 183
Ravenhill, Pte George 74
Regimental History of the
    Lancashire Fusiliers, A 185
Reil, Lee 97
Reitz, Deneys 30, 31, 42, 43, 52,
    119, 120, 139
    brother and father 139
    at Spion Kop 172, 175, 178–
    179, 191–192, 203–204
Rhodes, Cecil 27, 52
Rhodesia 27
Riddell, Lt-Col Robert Buchanan
    180, 190, 191, 192–194, 195,
    199
rifles
    Lee Enfield 87
    Lee Metford 87, 175
    Martini-Henry 87
    Mauser 59, 87
Ripper, Jack the 109
Road to Infamy, The 134
Roberts, Field Marshal Lord, VC
    25, 26, 79–80, 94, 115, 131,
    206–207, 210, 215, 213
Roberts, Lt the Honourable
    Freddy 74, 80

Romilly, Commodore, RN 25
Rooi Koppies (Red Hills) 68, 70
Rorke's Drift, Battle of (1879) 102
Rose, Lieutenant 183
Rosslyn, Earl of 137
Rowlands, Col Hugh, VC 19, 20
Royal Commission into conduct of war (1902) 78–79, 81, 82, 94–95, 181–182
Royal Navy 17, 96
Naval Brigade 22–23, 58, 64, 119, 124, 134, 180
Royston, Colonel 122
Russell, Bugler 186

St John Ambulance Brigade 93, 116
Sandbatch, Colonel 187
Sandspruit 14–15
Sargeant, Lieutenant 178
Sargent, Maj H. N. 181
Saville, Major 186
Schiel, Col Adolf 33, 34, 35, 36–37
Schofield, Capt Henry 73–74
Schreiber, Lieutenant 75
Scott, Capt Percy, RN 64
Scott-Moncrieff, Major 188
Shaka, King 57
Shaw, Private 168
Shepstone, Sir Theophilus 19, 20
Shoeburyness, School of Gunnery 98
Sim, Lieutenant-Colonel 201
Sims, George 108
Singapore 110
Sir Charles Warren and Spion Kop: A Vindication 134–135, 162 *see also* 'Defender'
Sivewright, Sir James 161
slave trade 99
Slocum, Captain, US Army 80, 208
Smith, Gen Sir Harry 17–18, 44
wife of 44
Smith-Dorrien, Gen Horace 218
Smuts, Gen Christiaan 216, 219
Smuts, Gen Tobias 204
South Africa, Republic of 219
South Africa, Union of 218–219
South African Conciliation Committee, women's branch 218
South African Light Horse (SALH) 60, 137, 140, 151, 152, 157, 158
Spion Kop, Battle of (1900)
map 176
British assault force 166
ascent of 166, 167–169
water supply problems 166, 170, 181–182, 185, 187, 204
Boer forces on 169, 170, 171–172, 174, 175, 178–179, 183–184, 185,

186, 187, 188–190, 196, 197, 203–204, 205
British forces on 169–171, 172, 173–175, 177, 178, 179–180, 181–190, 196–202, 203
Boers engaged and summit taken 169, 171, 172, 178
British attempts to dig in 169, 170
Boer counter-attacks 172, 173, 174, 175, 185, 186
British signal station 174, 177
British dressing station 174, 200
British reinforcements ascend 177, 179–180, 188
British driven from crest line 181
British confusion over surrender 183–185
British attempts to retake summit 186–187, 188–190
Boer reinforcements arrive 188
British confusion over commanders 188, 197–198, 200
British officers flouting orders 193–194, 199
stalemate 196
British forces ordered to retire 199–200, 201–203, 205–206
aftermath 204, 205–206
British dead buried on 205
reasons for British defeat 207–208
casualties 208
Spion Kop Hill 138, 139–140, 141, 155, 160, 161, 162
attack proposed 162, 163, 165
Springfield *see* Winterton
Stark, Dr 125
Steevens, G. W. 37, 148
Stellaland 106
Stevens (war correspondent) 211
Steyn, President 27
Stormberg, Battle of (1899) 58
Strong, Major 189
Suakin 106, 108
Sudan 106–107
Suez Canal 104, 106
Surprise Ridge 86
Swartkop hill 209
Swaziland Police Commando 62, 64

Tabanyama (Rangeworthy) Heights 138, 151, 152, 155, 159, 174, 205–206, 209
Taku Forts 96
Talana Hill, Battle of (1899) 15–16, 29–31
Tamai, Battle of (1884) 107
Tatham, Maj G. F. 83–84
Tel-El-Kebir, Battle of (1882) 105
Terrible, HMS, sailors from 58, 64

Thesiger, Lt-Gen the Honourable Frederick (later Lord Chelmsford) 21, 100, 101, 102
Thornycroft, Col Alexander 137, 166, 167, 168, 171, 174, 177, 178, 183, 186, 188, 196–197
promoted to brigadier-general 178, 183, 188, 197
prevents surrender 184, 185
report to Warren 187–188
message to Warren 197, 203, 204
message to Coke 197–198
confers with Crofton and Cooke 199
gives order to retire 199–200
Buller's message urges him to hold hill 201
descends Spion Kop 201, 202–203
criticised by Lord Roberts 207
later career 215
Three Tree Hill 173
Times History of the Boer War in South Africa, 1899–1900, Vol. 3: 172, 173, 184, 192, 195
traction engines, steam 133, 135
train, armoured (*Hairy Mary*) 45–50, 90, 92, 106
driver 49
Transvaal (South African Republic)
established 18
inability to subdue tribes 18–19
annexed by British 19, 20, 215
rebellion in 21–24
gold production 26
restored to Boers 26
Jameson Raid on 27
Transvaalers 148
treks 17, 18
Trichard's Drift 142, 144, 151, 152, 155, 201
Tugela defence line 138, 139, 140, 159–160, 161
Tugela Heights, Battle of (1900) 211–213
Tugela River 51, 57, 58, 62–63, 64, 67, 68, 69, 70, 76, 117, 129, 138, 139, 144, 145, 151, 210, 213
Tugela Valley 166
Twin Peaks 170, 172, 180, 190–192, 193–195
Twyford, Major 189

uitlanders (foreign gold miners) 26–27
Ulundi, Battle of (1879) 103
Uys, Piet 56

Vaal Krantz hills 209, 210, 211
Vaal River 18
Valentine Baker Pasha, Col 106

Van Rensburg, Commandant 64, 68
Venter's Laager 145, 154, 155, 156
Venter's Spruit 154, 159
Vereeneging 218
Vertue, Captain 183
Victoria, Queen 69, 79, 103, 109
Victoria Crosses awarded 74, 75, 103, 124
Viljoen, Gen Ben 216
Villebois-Mareuil, Col Georges de Comte 118

Wagon Drift 151
wagons, ox 52, 53, 135, 136
Walker, Lieutenant 120
War Commission 141
War Office 54, 93, 103–104, 114
Warner, Corporal 75
Warren, Sir Charles
  father 95
  education 95
  diversity of career 95–97, 98–99, 101, 102, 104–106, 107, 108, 109, 110
  in Palestine 96–97
  posted to Africa for first time 98–99
  in 9th Frontier War 101, 102
  at Military School of Engineering 104
  mission to Egypt 104–106
  appointed Special Commissioner in Africa 106
  as Governor of the Red Sea Littoral 108
  as Chief Commissioner of Metropolitan Police 108, 109
  commands troops in Singapore 110
  hopes of securing a command against the Boers 93–94, 111
  appointed to command 5th Division 94, 95
  appointed C-in-C in South Africa 94
  receives knighthood 106
  returns to Africa 113–114
  arrives in Natal to command 5th Division 115–116
  plans next move on Ladysmith with Buller 117
  arrives at Frere HQ 129
  disapproves of Buller's plan 132, 133
  attitude to the war and Boer people 133–134
  Buller fails to disclose adverse report to 134
  and A Vindication 134, 135, 162
  at Potgieter's Drift 140–141

  and Springfield defences 141
  orders received from Buller 142–143, 151–152
  makes himself known to his men 144–145
  forestalls cavalry from possibility of liberating Ladysmith 153–155, 159, 160
  wrangling with Buller 155–156
  decides to take Fairview Road 156, 161
  'special arrangements' (absurd theories) 156–157, 160
  orders general advance on Ladysmith 157
  places cavalry under command of Hildyard 158–159
  Buller criticises performance 160–161
  and Gobatsi Heights 162
  proposes to send wagons back 162
  send reinforcements to Spion Kop 177
  promotes Thornycroft 178, 183
  and artillery support at Spion Kop 180, 181, 183
  and Spion Kop water supply 181, 182
  Thornycroft sends report to 187–188
  and taking of Twin Peaks 195
  Coke's despatch to 196
  Thornycroft's message to 197, 203, 204
  receives report from Churchill and sends him to Thornycroft 198–199
  Churchill wakes 203
  after Spion Kop battle 204–205
  criticised by Lord Roberts 207
  and route for relief of Ladysmith 211
  and relief of Ladysmith 212, 213
  returns to England 215
Wauchope (British officer) 63
Wessels, Gert 123
White, Lt-Gen Sir George, VC 14, 31, 33, 40, 84
  launches attack from Ladysmith 42
  and Ladysmith strike force 81, 82, 83, 88
  demoralised at Ladysmith 118
  and Buller's plan 132–133
  strategy of tying up Boer Army at Ladysmith 138
  and relief of Ladysmith 214
Willemse (officer of Kruger's guard) 120
Willow Grange farm engagement 51, 61, 62
Wilson, H. W. 69

Windrum, Sgt A. J. 68
Winterton (formerly Springfield) 132, 140, 141, 143
  bridge over Little Tugela River 136, 138, 139
With the Flag to Pretoria 69
Wolseley, Lt-Gen Sir Garnet 20–21, 22, 80, 93, 94–95, 97, 98, 99, 100, 105, 107
'Wolseley Ring' 99
Women's Liberal Federation 218
Wood, Lt Arthur 189
Wood, Brig-Gen Sir Evelyn, VC 23–24, 25, 99–100, 101, 102, 103, 104
Woodgate, Major-General Sir Edward 114, 154, 165, 167, 169, 170–171, 204
  mortally wounded on Spion Kop 173, 175, 177, 185
Woolwich, Royal Military Academy 95
wounds, lance thrust 38
Wynne Hill 212

Yule, Brig-Gen James 29, 31, 32, 33, 40, 63

Zeederberg, Field-Cornet 183
Zulu Army 102, 103
Zulu War (1879) 102–103
Zululand 102–103, 155
Zulus 14, 19, 20